Philosophical Writing

T0355776

Philosophical Writing

An Introduction

FIFTH EDITION

A. P. Martinich

WILEY Blackwell

For general information on our other products and services or for technical support, please contact our Customer Care Department within the United States at (800) 762-2974, outside the United States at (317) 572-3993 or fax (317) 572-4002.

Wiley also publishes its books in a variety of electronic formats. Some content that appears in print may not be available in electronic formats. For more information about Wiley products, visit our web site at www.wiley.com.

Library of Congress Cataloging-in-Publication Data Applied for
Paperback ISBN: 9781394193394

Cover Design: Wiley
Cover Image: © The M.C. Escher Company

Set in 10/12.5pt Plantin Std Light by Straive, Pondicherry, India

For my grandchildren
with their bright eyes and fresh thoughts

Contents

Note to the Fifth Edition

I read and revised the text of the fourth edition. Clarity and brevity were my rules of thumb. Two chapters 10 and 11, have been added for the fifth edition. Some of the ideas in these two chapters were developed in my course, "Interpretation and Meaning." The main ideas occur in different form in "Interpretation and Hobbes's Political Philosophy," *Pacific Philosophical Quarterly* (2001), 82: 309–31, and "Four Senses of 'Meaning' in the History of Ideas," *Journal of the Philosophy of History* (2009), 3: 225–45.

I want to thank my editor Will Croft and managing editor Pascal Raj François; other staff at Wiley to whom I am grateful are Sarah Milton, Aswini Murugadass and Sivasri Chandrasekaran. Several others helped me. Jo Ann Carson read chapters 10 and 11, Jeff Leon read chapter 10; Ryan Born proofread chapters 10 and 11; and Leslie Martinich helped in many ways.

Much of the revision of this edition occurred in Einstein Bros. Bagels, on the Drag near the University of Texas at Austin. The hardworking, helpful, and darn nice staff have my gratitude. Their manager Andrew, who rightly cares as much for his staff, as he does his customers, has my special gratitude.

Note to the Fourth Edition

This edition contains several new sections, such as one on how to read a philosophical essay, one on quantification and modality, and one on rhetoric in philosophical writing. It also includes new and more examples. Another feature of this edition is a website that complements the material in the book. The website contains four kinds of material: (1) some additional explanation of some topics treated in the book; (2) some additional examples of topics discussed in the book; (3) some additional exercises, which I think of as being primarily for the benefit of the student; and (4) a few additional topics that were not essential to the purpose of the book but will still be helpful to many students. The website can be found at www.wiley.com/go/Martinich.

I thank Leslie Martinich, who helped enormously with editing, as always; Neil Sinhababu, who updated the appendix on using internet sources; and J. P. Andrew, who commented on the section on quantification. My editor at Wiley-Blackwell, Deirdre Ilkson, has been helpful and supportive on this and other projects; and Sarah Dancy and Allison Kostka have ably shepherded this edition through the publication process.

Note to the
Third Edition

This edition contains a number of changes. In general, I have tried to improve the sample essays and other examples, correct errors of fact, and make the prose more straightforward. Some of the most important changes are several new appendices, such as the one about the use of the internet by Neil Sinhababu. I thank Jo Ann Carson and Charles Hornbeck for several suggestions and, as usual, I thank my wife Leslie for her versatile help.

Note to the
Second Edition

Writing to a friend, Pascal apologized for the length of his letter: "If I had had more time, this letter would have been shorter." In revising the sections that appeared in the first edition of this book, I often found ways to make them shorter, and, I think, better. But I also had ideas about how I could add other topics to the book in order to make it better. Primarily these are sections on definition, contraries and contradictories, distinctions, and a glossary of terms that may be helpful in your philosophical writing.

In preparing the second edition, I have happily acquired debts to some of my current and former students who commented on the text: Stephen Brown, Sarah Cunningham, Nathan Jennings, and Lisa Maddry. My wife Leslie, as usual, read the entire manuscript. Also, I thank my very helpful editor Steve Smith.

Finally, a large part of my thinking and reading about philosophy has been done in Miami Subs and Grill on the Drag. I thank the owners, Michael and Lisa Mermelstein, for their hospitality.

About the Companion Website

This book is accompanied by a companion website.

www.wiley.com/go/Martinich5e

The website contains four kinds of material:
(1) Some additional explanation of some topics treated in the book.
(2) Some additional examples of topics discussed in the book.
(3) Some additional exercises, primarily for the benefit of the student.
(4) A few additional topics that were not essential to the purpose of the book but will still be helpful to many students.

Introduction

Those who know that they are profound strive for clarity. Those who would like to seem profound strive for obscurity.
Friedrich Nietzsche, The Gay Science

Philosophical essays may have many different structures. For experienced writers, the choice of a structure is often neither difficult nor even conscious. The essay seems to write itself. For inexperienced writers, the choice is often tortured or seemingly impossible. I offer this book to the latter group of people, of which I was a member for more than three decades. And rather than survey many possible structures, I have concentrated on what I think is the simplest, most straightforward structure that a philosophical essay might have. My purpose is to help students write something valuable so that they might begin to develop their own styles. The project is similar to teaching art students to draw the human hand. The first goal is accuracy, not elegance.

Elegance is probably not learned but is the product of a kind of genius, and genius begins where rules leave off. The topic of this book is something that can be learned: how to write clear, concise, and precise philosophical prose. Elegance is desirable, but so is simplicity. And that is what I aim for.

Avrum Stroll (1921–2013) once said, "Half of good philosophy is good grammar." Like any good aphorism, it is difficult to explain. Before I try to describe part of what it means, let me forestall a possible misunderstanding. Although good philosophical writing is grammatical, there is virtually nothing about grammar in this book in the sense in which your eighth-grade teacher, Mrs. Grundy, discussed it. Virtually all students know the rules of grammar, and yet these rules are often flagrantly violated in their philosophical prose. Why does this happen?

One reason is that philosophers often try to assign things to their proper categories, and those philosophically contrived categories are not clear, or at least they are initially hard to understand. Philosophers have sometimes

Philosophical Writing: An Introduction, Fifth Edition. A. P. Martinich.
© 2025 John Wiley & Sons, Inc. Published 2025 by John Wiley & Sons, Inc.
Companion website: www.wiley.com/go/Martinich5e

divided reality into the things that are mental and the things that are material. Sometimes they have divided reality into things that are substances (things that exist on their own) and things that are accidents (things that are properties or depend upon other things for their existence). There is even a grammatical correlation between these categories. Nouns correlate with substances (*man* with man), and adjectives correlate with accidents (*rectangular* with rectangular). When philosophers argue that things that seem to belong to one category really belong to another, grammar is strained. Most theists maintain that *God is just*. But some (theistic) philosophers have maintained that this cannot be true. The reason is that if *God is just*, then God has the property of being just, and if God has a property, then he is not absolutely simple and might therefore be corruptible. So, these philosophers have said that *God is (identical with) the just* or that *God is (identical with) justice*, even though these latter claims stretch the grammatical limits of most natural languages.

Sometimes the attempt to say something new and correct about the limits of reality causes the grammar to break down completely, as when Martin Heidegger says, "Nothing nothings." The noun *nothing* cannot be a verb, so the pseudo-verb *nothings* is unintelligible. Further, Heidegger seems to be construing the word *nothing* as a noun, as if *nothing* named something, when obviously it cannot. (Of course, Heidegger would disagree with my grammatical remarks, and that is just one more reason why philosophy is difficult: It is hard to get philosophers to agree even about grammar.)

Thomas Hobbes was one of the first to discuss the propensity of philosophers to mistakenly combine words that belong to one category with words that belong to a different and incompatible category. This is known as a category mistake. Roughly, a category mistake is the logical equivalent of mixing apples and oranges. The sentence "Colorless green ideas sleep furiously" involves several category mistakes. Colorless things cannot be green or any other color; ideas cannot sleep or be awake; and nothing can sleep furiously. Objects belonging to one of these categories don't fit with objects that belong to some of the others. One of his examples is "The intellect understands." According to Hobbes, *the intellect* is the name of an accident or property of bodies, which is one category, while *understands*, even though it is grammatically a verb, is the name of a body (humans), which is another category. And thus he holds that the sentence "The intellect understands" is literally absurd. What Hobbes thinks is literally true is the sentence "Man understands by his intelligence." In a related way, John Locke thought it was a serious mistake to say "The will wills (or chooses)." What is true is "A human being wills (or chooses)."

It is quite possible for someone to disagree with Hobbes about whether the sentence "The intellect understands" makes sense or not, and to criticize the philosophico-grammatical view that underlies his grammatical judgment. Philosophers often disagree about what is absurd and what is not. Consider the sentence "Beliefs are brain states." Does this sentence express a category mistake or a brilliant insight into the nature of the mental? Philosophers disagree. So it is not always easy to say whether some philosophical thesis constitutes a great philosophical insight or a laughable grammatical blunder. Thus, added to the inherent difficulty of philosophy is the difficulty of philosophical writing, which often groans under the burden placed on syntax and semantics.

Another reason that students often write patently ungrammatical sentences is that the philosophy they have read seems ungrammatical to them. It seems that way because the thought being expressed is radically unfamiliar. Since philosophers often invent categories or concepts that are unfamiliar to students or revise familiar categories, there is no place for the category in the student's initial system of thoughts, and it is hard to adjust one's concepts to make room for the new or revised category. Often the category will be initially situated in an inappropriate place, or the wrong things will be placed in it. In a word, the category is strange. As a consequence, when students come to explain, criticize, or even endorse propositions using that category, they may produce incoherent and ungrammatical sentences. Their writing, though muddled, is an accurate representation of their understanding. This is nothing to be ashamed of; it's nothing to be proud of either. It's just part of the process of learning to think philosophically.

If you find yourself writing a sentence or paragraph that is grammatically out of control, then your thought is probably out of control. Consequently, you can use your own prose as a measure of the degree to which you understand the issue you are writing about and as an index to the parts of your essay that need more consideration. (I owe the ideas in this paragraph to Charles Young.)

This explanation of why half of good philosophy is good grammar inspires a partial criterion: Good philosophical writing is grammatical. If a person can write a series of consistently grammatical sentences about some philosophical subject, then that person probably has a coherent idea of what she is discussing.

Another related criterion of good philosophical writing is precision. Contrary to the conventional wisdom prevalent among students, vague and verbose language is not a sign of profundity and astuteness but of confusion. Teachers of philosophy who are dedicated to the above criteria in effect issue a challenge to students: Write grammatically, clearly, and precisely. Since language is the expression of thought, clear language is the expression of clear thought. Writing style should facilitate the comprehension of philosophy. Style should enhance clarity.

If half of good philosophy is good grammar, then the other half is good thinking. Good thinking takes many forms. The form that we will concentrate on is often called *analysis*. The word *analysis* has many meanings in philosophy, one of which is a method of reasoning (discussed in chapter 5). Another meaning refers to a method or school of philosophy that reigned largely unchallenged for most of the last century. Many people think that this method is passé in our postanalytic era. I do not take a stand on that issue. I use "analysis" in a very broad sense that includes both analytic (in a narrower sense) and postanalytic philosophy. The goal of analytic philosophy, as it is understood here, is the truth, presented in a clear, orderly, well-structured way. I take a strong stand in favor of clarity, order, and structure. The goal of analysis, in its broad sense, is to make philosophy less difficult than it otherwise would be. This is just a corollary of a more general principle: Anyone can make a subject difficult; it takes an accomplished thinker to make a subject simple.

Philosophical writing has taken many forms, including dialogue (Plato, Berkeley, and Hume), drama (Camus, Marcel, and Sartre), poetry (Lucretius), and fiction (Camus, George Eliot, and Sartre). I will discuss only the essay form. There are three reasons for this decision. First, it is the form in which you are most likely to be asked to write. Second, it is the easiest form to write in. Third, it is currently the standard form for professional philosophers. Although the dialogue form is attractive to many students, it is an extremely difficult one to execute well. It tempts one to cuteness, needless metaphor, and imprecision.

It is often advisable to preview a book. That advice holds here. Skim the entire book before reading it more carefully. Depending on your philosophical background, some parts will be more informative than others. Chapter 1 discusses the concepts of author and audience as they apply to a student's philosophical prose. Both students and their professors are in an artificial literary situation. Unlike typical authors, students know less about their subject than their audience, although they are not supposed to let on that they do. Chapter 2 is a crash course on the basic concepts of logic. It contains background information required for understanding subsequent chapters. Those who are familiar with logic will breeze through it, while those with no familiarity with it will need to read slowly, carefully, and at least twice. Chapter 3 discusses the structure of a philosophical essay and forms the heart of the book. The well-worn but sound advice that an essay should have a beginning, a middle, and an end applies to philosophical essays too. Chapter 4 deals with a number of matters related to composing drafts of an essay. Various techniques for composing are discussed. Anyone who knows how to outline, take notes, revise, do research, and so on might be able to skip this chapter. Chapter 5 explains several types of reasoning used by philosophers, such as dilemmas, counterexamples, and *reductio ad absurdum* arguments. Chapter 6 discusses some basic requirements that the content of an essay must satisfy. Chapter 7 discusses goals for the form of your writing: coherence, clarity, conciseness, and rigor. Chapter 8 discusses some standard problems students have with the first few pages of an essay. Chapter 9 makes suggestions about how to read a philosophical essay. Chapter 10, new to this edition, describes properties of the web or network of beliefs of human beings. Understanding these properties fleshes out the idea that an author needs to know their readers; similarly, readers need to have some idea of the beliefs the author had in order to understand what the author means. Also new to this edition is chapter 11 about many of the properties that good, not necessarily correct, interpretations have. Judging an interpretation to be good is not merely something felt. Numerous appendices cover such topics as research and how to study for a test.

Like essays, most books have conclusions that either summarize or tie together the main strands of the work. However, it would have been artificial to do so in this case, since the book as a whole does not develop one main argument but consists of a number of different topics that should be helpful to the student. Appendix A, "It's Sunday Night and I Have an Essay Due Monday Morning," is included for those who bought this book but never got around to reading much of it, and can serve as a conclusion. Several of my students who used one of the first three editions let me know that this was the first part of the book they read, on a Sunday night about six weeks into the semester.

In order to serve the needs of a wide range of students, the level of difficulty varies from elementary to moderately advanced. Even within individual chapters, the level of difficulty can vary significantly, although each section begins with the simplest material and progresses to the most difficult. Thus, a chapter on a new topic might revert from complex material in the previous chapter to a simple level. I believe that intelligent, hardworking students can move rather quickly from philosophical innocence to moderate sophistication.

At various points, I have presented fragments of essays to illustrate a stylistic point. The topics of these essay fragments are sometimes controversial and the argumentation provocative. These passages are meant to keep the reader's interest and do not always represent my view. It would be a mistake to focus on the content of these essay fragments when it is their style that is important. Also, it is quite likely that the reader will disagree with a few or even many of the stylistic claims I make. If this leads readers to at least think about why they disagree and to discover what they prefer and why, then a large part of my goal will have been achieved.

Chapter 4 contains a section, "The Rhetoric of Philosophical Writing." Going back as far as Socrates, rhetoric has often had a bad name in philosophy. No negative attitude toward rhetoric is implied in this book. "Rhetoric," as I use it, contrasts with logic and refers to style, that is, to those elements of writing that facilitate communication. The right kind of rhetoric in writing is not antithetical to logic. Rather, the right rhetorical elements are important. After all, like any essay, a philosophical essay that fails to communicate fails in one of its central purposes.

Philosophical Writing is intended to be practical, to help you write better and thereby improve your ability to present your thoughts. Since almost any class may require you to write an essay that analyzes some concept or argument, the skills gained in learning to write about philosophical concepts may prove useful in writing other types of essays. When I described the structure of a philosophical argument to a friend and colleague, he said, "That's the structure of a historical argument."

A problem faced by English speakers who wanted to avoid language that favored male human beings is less severe now than it was 40 years ago because many clear-headed writers have suggested various ways to avoid the problem. Here are four ways:

(1) Delete the pronoun: "A professor should prepare [omit: his] lectures well before they are to be given."
(2) Change the pronoun to an article: "A professor should read the essays of the [instead of: his] students soon after they are submitted."
(3) Use plural nouns and pronouns: Instead of "A professor should prepare his lectures well before they are scheduled to be given," write "Professors should prepare their lectures well before they are scheduled to be given."
(4) Paraphrase the pronoun away: Instead of "If a student does not study, he cannot expect to do well on the tests," write "A student who does not study cannot expect to do well on the tests."

Another suggestion is to use "they" with "anyone," "someone," and "no one." That is, these sentences would be counted fully grammatical:

Anyone who fails *their* exam will be permitted to take a make-up exam.

If *someone* is tortured for a long time *they* will eventually suffer a breakdown.

Since *no one* studied hard, *those* who failed the test will not be permitted to take a make up exam.

The objection to this practice is that it is illogical. Since "anyone," "someone," and "no one" are singular, they should not be paired with a plural pronoun. This style of handling personal programs is widely enough used to make it acceptable. Also, excellent writers in past centuries have used plural pronouns in this way.

When for one reason or another, I have found it convenient to use generic pronouns that are grammatically male or female, I have used the following conventions. Male gender pronouns will be used for references to the professor. Female gender pronouns will be used for references to the student. Since this book is about students, I believe the female gender pronouns predominate. In any case, no hierarchical order is implied by these uses. Professors and students simply have different roles and responsibilities.

1
Author and Audience

It may seem obvious who the author and audience of a student's essay are. The student is the author, and the professor is the audience; that is true. However, a student is not a normal author, and a student's professor is not a normal audience. I expand on these two points in this chapter. I begin with the conceptually simpler topic: the abnormality of the professor as the audience.

1.1   The Professor as Audience

It's indispensable for an author to know who the audience is because different audiences require different ways of explaining. An author should not use the technical language of an electrical engineer to describe how electrons move through wires to electrical outlets. Section 1.3 says more about this matter, and chapter 10 discusses it in detail.

A student is not in the typical position of an author for several reasons. While an author usually chooses her intended audience, the student's audience is imposed on her. The student's predicament, however, is not unique. An audience usually chooses his author. But the student's audience, her professor, does not choose his author; it is his student. Both the author and the audience should make the best of necessity. And necessity often is the motivator for innovation. (The science of soil management developed to meet increased demand for food. Radar was invented to defend against enemy aircraft.)

Unless the student is exceptional, she is not writing to inform or convince her audience of the truth of the position she takes in her essay. So her purpose is not persuasion. Further, unless the topic is exceptional or the professor is unusually ignorant, the student's purpose is not straightforward

Philosophical Writing: An Introduction, Fifth Edition. A. P. Martinich.
© 2025 John Wiley & Sons, Inc. Published 2025 by John Wiley & Sons, Inc.
Companion website: www.wiley.com/go/Martinich5e

exposition or explanation either. Presumably, the professor already understands the material that the student is struggling to present clearly and correctly. Nonetheless, the student should not presuppose that the professor is knowledgeable about the topic being discussed for this reason. In the professor's role, he should not assume that the student understands the material about which she is writing. It's her job to show her professor that she understands what the professor already knows. A student may find this paradoxical situation perverse. But this is the existential situation into which the student as author is thrown. (An important part of understanding human beings is understanding that much of a person's life is not chosen but imposed on her. No one chooses their parents, even to be born.)

Notwithstanding the student's unusual position, the structure and style of her essay should be the same as an essay of straightforward exposition and explanation. As just mentioned, the student's goal is to show her professor that she knows some philosophical argument or position by giving an accurate rendering of it; that usually includes showing that she knows why the philosopher holds it. Doing so usually requires laying out the structure of the philosopher's arguments, the meanings of his technical terms, and the reasons or evidence for his premises. (One difference between the history of philosophy and the history of ideas is that the former cares about the structure and cogency of the arguments.) These matters are explained in chapter 2. The student needs to assume (for the sake of adopting an appropriate authorial stance) that the audience is (1) intelligent but (2) uninformed. The student must state her thesis and then explain what she means. She must prove her thesis or at least provide good evidence for it.

All technical terms have to be explained as if the audience knew little or no philosophy. This means that the student ought to use ordinary words in their ordinary senses. If the meaning of a technical term is not introduced or explained by using ordinary words in their ordinary meanings, then there is no way for the audience to know what the author means. For example, consider this essay fragment:

> The purpose of this essay is to prove that human beings never perceive material objects but rather semi-ideators, by which I mean the interface of the phenomenal object and its conceptual content.

This passage should sound profound for less than a nanosecond. In theory, it is not objectionable to use a technical term to explain a new technical term, but this is acceptable only if the prior technical term has already been explained in ordinary language. The term *semi-ideator* is a neologism and is unintelligible to the reader until its meaning is explained. In addition to neologisms, some ordinary words have technical meanings in philosophy, so their particular meaning may need to be made clear. Here are some examples:

ego
matter
pragmatic
realized
reflection
universal

If an author uses a word with an ordinary meaning in an unfamiliar technical sense, the word is ambiguous, and the audience will be misled or confused if that technical meaning is not explained in terms intelligible to the audience.

It is no good to protest that your professor should allow you to use technical terms without explanation on the grounds that the professor knows or ought to know their meaning. To repeat, it is not the professor's knowledge that is at issue but the student's. It is her responsibility to show that she knows the meaning of those terms. Do not think that the professor will think that you think that the professor does not understand a term if you define it. If you use a technical term, then it is your term and you are responsible for defining it. Further, a technical term is successfully introduced only if the explanation does not depend on the assumption that the audience already knows the meaning of the technical term! That is what the student has to show.

There is an exception. For advanced courses, a professor may allow the student to assume that the audience knows what a beginning student should know about philosophy, perhaps some logic, parts of Plato's *Republic*, Descartes's *Meditations*, or something similar. For graduate students, the professor may allow the student to assume a bit more logic, and quite a bit of the history of philosophy. It would be nice if the professor were to articulate exactly what a student is entitled to assume and what not, but he may forget to do this, and, even if he remembers, it is virtually impossible to specify all and only what may be assumed. There is just too much human knowledge and ignorance and not enough time to articulate it all. If you are in doubt about what you may assume, you should ask. Your professor will probably be happy to tell you. If he is not, then the fault is in him, certainly not in his stars, and you can find comfort in the knowledge that in asking, you did the right thing. That is the least that acting on principle gives us.

While I have talked about who your audience is and about how much or how little you should attribute to him, I have not said anything about the attitude you should take toward the audience. The attitude is respect. If you are writing for someone, then you should consider that person worthy of the truth, and if that person is worthy of the truth, then you should try to make that truth as intelligible and accessible to him as possible. Further, if you write for an audience, you are putting demands on that person's time. You are expecting him to spend time and to expend effort to understand what you have written; if you have done a slipshod job, then you have wasted his time and treated him unfairly. A trivial or sloppy essay is an insult to the audience in addition to reflecting badly on you. If a professor is disgruntled when he returns a set of essays, it may well be because he feels slighted. A good essay is a sign of the author's respect for the audience.

1.2   The Student as Author

The author should not intrude in her essay. This does not mean that she has to be invisible. Whether the author refers to herself or not should be determined by what is appropriate and idiomatic. Some decades ago, students were forbidden to use "I" in an essay. A phrase like "I will argue" was supposed to be replaced with a phrase like "My argument will be" (or "The argument of this paper" or "It will be argued"). Formal writing is more informal these days. "My argument will be" is verbose and stilted. "I will argue" is preferable for another reason. Although physical courage is widely admired and discussed in contemporary society, intellectual courage is not. Too few rational people have the courage of their convictions, yet convictions that are the result of investigation and reflection deserve the courage needed to defend them.

Ideas have consequences just as surely as physical actions do. Some are good, some are bad; some are wonderful, some are horrid. Own up to yours.

A person who writes, "It will be argued," is passive; he is exhibiting intellectual courage obliquely at best. By whom will it be argued? If it is you, say so. A person who writes, "I will argue," is active. She is committing herself to a line of reasoning and openly submitting that reasoning to rational scrutiny.

Philosophical writing is almost never autobiographical even when it contains autobiographical elements. (*The Confessions* of St. Augustine and those of Jean-Jacques Rousseau are notable but rare exceptions.) It is very unlikely then that you should expose your personal life or feelings in your philosophical writing, at least in those terms. No reader should care how you *feel* about the existence of God, freedom, abortion, or anything else,

11

presented merely as your feelings. Thus, the use of the phrase, *I feel*, is forbidden in essays because your feelings have no claim to universality and do not automatically transfer to your audience. You might feel that God exists, but that is no reason why anyone else should. The phrase, *I argue*, in contrast, does transfer. The phrase implies that the author has objective rather than merely subjective grounds for her position and thus that the audience ought to argue in the very same way.

Specific events in your life also have no place in your essay, considered as *your* events. Considered simply as *events*, they may have both relevance and force. Contrast the way the following two paragraphs make the same point.

> When I was 14, I wanted a ten-speed bike but needed $125 to buy one. The only way I could get the money legally was to work for it. I hired myself out at $4.00 an hour doing various jobs I hated, like cutting lawns, washing windows, and even baby-sitting. It took three months, but I finally had enough money to buy the bicycle. What I came to realize, often as I was sweating during my labors, was that money is not just metal or paper, it is control over other human beings. The people who hired me were controlling my life. I came to realize something else: if I have money and also respect someone, I shouldn't force him to do crummy jobs just so they can get my money.

> Suppose a young person wants to buy something, say, a ten-speed bicycle. She may hire out her services for money, perhaps at $4.00 an hour cutting lawns, washing windows, or baby-sitting. By hiring herself out, she is putting herself within the control of the person paying her. Money, then, is not simply metal or paper; it is a means of controlling the behavior of other human beings. Further, if a person respects others, she will avoid hiring people for demeaning and alienating labor.

Although the first passage is livelier and more appropriate in nonphilosophical contexts, for example, a newspaper or magazine article, its philosophical point is made more obliquely than in the second, in which the author's view of money is directly related to every human being and not just to the author. Thus, the second passage is preferable for a philosophical essay. The first passage is egocentric; the persona of the author is the student herself. In the second passage, the persona of the author is an objective observer of the human condition.

The notion of a persona is a technical one. The word *persona* comes from the Latin word for the mask that actors wore on the stage in theater productions. There were masks for comic and tragic characters, for gods and mortals. To have a persona is to play a role. An author plays a role and hence has a persona. The question is, What is that persona? or What should that persona be? because there are two possible roles an author can have in her essay.

An author inescapably has the role of creator, since she is responsible for the words of her essay. As the creator, the author has a transcendent perspective on her essay; she is outside it insofar as she is making it and is not made by it. If an author makes herself a character in one of her examples, then she takes on a second persona, that of a character who is in the example she is constructing. She is simultaneously the creator and the creature, an incoherent situation. The presence of two personas may confuse the reader. Consider the following passage:

> Suppose that Smith and I have our brains interchanged. And I think that I am Smith and he thinks that he is I. However, I think I remain myself because I am identical with my body at any given time.

It is difficult to understand this passage because the reference of "I" shifts between the author *as a creature in the scenario* and the author *as the creator of the scenario*. Contrast the original with this revision in which references to the author as a character are replaced with references to a purely created character:

> Suppose that Smith and Jones have their brains interchanged. Jones believes that he is Smith and Smith believes that he is Jones. Nonetheless, I argue that Jones remains Jones and Smith remains Smith, because a person is identical with his body at any given time.

Even this passage can be improved. There is something tendentious about saying "Jones remains Jones and Smith remains Smith" that was not obvious in the first passage. The following version is better:

> Suppose that the bodies of Smith and Jones have their brains interchanged. The body that had Jones's brain now has Smith's brain, and vice versa. The body that originally had Smith's brain now, with Jones's brain, says that it is Jones. And the body that originally had Jones's brain now, with Smith's brain, says it is Smith. I shall argue that the identity of the person is determined by the brain it has and not by the identity of the rest of the body.

The point is that the more objective the author's standpoint the better. (Recall that I am speaking about the style of the above passages not passing judgment on their cogency. Whether the duality of personas has philosophical consequences is a substantive issue; see Thomas Nagel, *The View from Nowhere*, New York: Oxford University Press, 1985.) There is never any need for an author to cast herself in her own examples: Smith and Jones,

White, Black, Brown, and Green, and Lee and Kee are versatile philosophical character actors.

What the characters in scenarios believe and do are determined by the authors who create them. If their beliefs are mistaken or their actions objectionable, it is because the author has made them so. When an author says, "Suppose Smith and Jones have their brains interchanged," Smith and Jones have their brains interchanged. And if an author says that a brain in a vat thinks that he is a scientist, the brain in the vat thinks that he is a scientist.

An author's will in constructing an example cannot be thwarted as long as what she says is coherent and has no doubts about what she is supposing. She transcends the situation she describes. In this way, the author's situation is inherently anti-skeptical. A story is told about an eighth grader who was having trouble learning algebra. The teacher said, "Suppose that x equals 2." The student became quite anxious because she thought the teacher might have been wrong or at least overlooking a possibility: "Teacher, suppose that x does not equal 2." The student did not realize that when a person supposes something to be true for the sake of argument, then it is true within the context of that discussion. For all intents and purposes, an author is omnipotent and omniscient. (I am speaking only of philosophical authors. Some fiction tries to undermine the privileged position of an author through the use of an "unreliable narrator.") However, the power of the author is limited by logical coherence. Be on guard against thinking that you have proven a point by constructing a logically contradictory scenario, as in this essay fragment:

> Suppose that there is a four-sided plane-figure, of which each interior angle is 90°. Further suppose that each point of its perimeter is equidistant from a point inside of it. It follows that there is a round square.

This scenario is defective because its supposition is contradictory.

Unlike the author, the characters in a philosophical example are subject to error and deception. This is a perfectly acceptable scenario:

> Suppose that Smith, who has known Jones for 20 years, sees someone who looks exactly like Jones walking across the plaza. Further suppose that Smith does not see Jones, but Jones's long-lost twin brother, although Jones himself is also walking across the plaza out of Smith's sight....

So far in this chapter, I have tried to explain the sense in which a student's audience, the professor, must be considered ignorant and the sense in which the student, a philosophical author, should maintain a transcendent perspective, from which she is omniscient and omnipotent. How is that for a Hegelian reversal?

1.3   Three Attitudes About Philosophical Method

A difficult issue for the student as an author is knowing what her professor thinks is a good way to tackle a philosophical problem. Some professors think that a person's intuitions are the best starting point; others think that one must begin with a theory; and others think that a combination of the two is best. I will discuss each of these attitudes in this section.

Since the word "intuition" is used in various ways, I need to explain what I mean by it here.[1] Intuitions are the pre-theoretical judgments that a person makes about something. They are her ordinary beliefs. They can be contrasted with the judgments the person makes after having considered the issue extensively. Often these reflective judgments are the result of adopting some theory. A theory is an explanation or description of a large class of things, events, or phenomena. The theory must consist of some general propositions that apply to all or almost all of the phenomena.

Our intuitions include the beliefs that the sun goes around the earth, that human beings act freely without being necessitated to act the way they do, and that some things are inherently morally right and others wrong. It is a matter of theory that the earth goes around the sun, that every action is causally necessitated, and that nothing is inherently morally right or wrong. To say that something is a matter of theory is not to say that it is true; it may be true or false, depending upon whether the theory is true or false. Phlogiston was part of an eighteenth-century theory of combustion, but statements about phlogiston were false. In philosophy, there are typically two or more incompatible theories for any topic; so not more than one of them can be true, but both can be false. (In chapter 4, *contraries* are defined as two things that cannot both be true but both may be false.)

---

[1] In one sense, an intuition is a faculty of knowing particular objects without being able to form a judgment simply on the basis of that knowledge. Think about seeing something red. This may be the result of intuition. This intuitive experience of red needs to be distinguished from a judgment that one might form on the basis of the intuition, for example, *This is red* or *Something is red*. Intuitive knowledge is knowledge known immediately, without inference, for example, that $1 + 1 = 2$. In ethics, intuitionism is the view that some ethical propositions are known without inference, for example, that pleasure is intrinsically good, and sometimes that ethical judgments are the result of a special faculty, ethical intuition.

Philosophers are split over the relationship between intuition and theory. Some ("intuitionists") believe that intuition is privileged and that theories are constructed in order to justify and explain intuitions. Wittgenstein, who in the later part of his life wrote that everything is all right as it is, is a paradigmatic case of an intuitionist in the sense specified above.

Other philosophers ("theorists") believe that the goal of philosophy is to develop a theory about a topic and that intuitions have little or no value. Bertrand Russell argued that sentences like "Socrates is wise" are actually not subject-predicate in form but really complex existential assertions, meaning something like:

> There exists an object x such that x philosophizes in fifth-century BCE Athens and is named "Socrates," and for all y, if y philosophizes in fifth-century BCE Athens and is named "Socrates," then y is identical with x, and x is wise.

Russell's argument is grounded in a theory: his famous theory of definite descriptions.

Privileging only intuition or only theory is an extreme position. The middle ground promotes what may be called reflective equilibrium. This view holds that philosophy should begin with intuitions; that theorizing should begin by trying to explain those intuitions; and that when intuitions and theories conflict, there should be a compromise between them, such that intuitions sometimes are given up to accommodate theoretical statements and sometimes theoretical statements are given up (or modified) to accommodate intuitions. Roughly, intuitions should give way when there are theoretical statements that explain a very large number of intuitions, and some related but not the central intuition is inconsistent with them. And theoretical statements should give way when numerous and well-attested experiences support an intuition.

It is not controversial that the intuition that the sun goes around the earth should give way to the consequences of the heliocentric theory. It is controversial that intuitions about the basic structure of a sentence like "Abraham Lincoln was a president" should give way to Russell's theory of definite descriptions.

There is no way to predict whether your professor will prefer intuitions or theories, or reflective equilibrium. It is important that you figure out which he does by paying attention to how he introduces a philosophical problem, and when you cannot figure that out, ask him.

2
Logic and Argument for Writing

A little logic is not a dangerous thing. It is crucial for understanding the substance of many philosophical essays. We will discuss a small part of formal logic in this chapter, a part of propositional logic, some categorical logic, and a little about modal logic.

In his *Poetics*, Aristotle remarks that a well-constructed dramatic plot must reflect an action that is "whole and complete in itself and of some magnitude." He goes on to define a whole action as "that which has a beginning, middle, and end." Though Greek tragedy and philosophical prose may seem like quite disparate fields of literary endeavor, Aristotle's advice applies to writing a philosophical essay. Just as the core of a dramatic work is its plot, the core of a philosophical essay is its argument in a broad sense of *argument*. Just as a good play will have a well-demarcated beginning, middle, and end, so too will a good essay. The beginning of a philosophical essay introduces the argument; the middle elaborates it; the end summarizes it. Every competent speaker of English has some idea of an argument in logic. It is not a quarrel; it is not a verbal fight. It is something connected with reasoning. In theory, philosophers engage only in the latter. Although there are several ways of reasoning, we are interested in this chapter only in a small part of reasoning.

2.1 What Is a Good Argument?

At the simplest level, there are two kinds of arguments: good ones and bad ones. A good argument is one that does what it is supposed to do. A bad argument is one that does not. A good argument is one that

Philosophical Writing: An Introduction, Fifth Edition. A. P. Martinich.
Companion website: www.wiley.com/go/Martinich5e

shows a person a rational way to go from true premises to a true con-clusion, as well as the subject allows (some subjects more easily or cer-tainly show the way than others, say, mathematics more than a esthetics). As explained here, a good argument is relative to a person. What might legitimately lead one person to a conclusion might not lead another person to the same conclusion because so much depends upon the person's background beliefs. (Chapter 10 says more about this.) What a contemporary philosopher or physicist would recognize as a good argument is often not what an ancient Greek, even Plato, Aristotle, Ptolemy, or Euclid, would recognize. Also, there may be good arguments that the ancient Greeks could recognize as good arguments that we cannot. For obvious reasons, I can't give an example. (Exercise: Why can't I give one? Can you?)

The notion of a "good argument" is an intuitive one. In this chapter, I want to make this intuitive notion progressively more precise by considering the following definitions:

Df(1) **An argument is a sequence of two or more proposi-tions of which one is designated as the conclusion and all the others of which are premises.**

Df(2) **A sound argument is an argument that is valid and that contains only true premises.**

Df(3) **An argument is valid if and only if it is necessary that if all the premises are true, then the conclusion is true.**

Df(4) **A cogent argument is a sound argument that is rec-ognized to be such in virtue of the presentation of its structure and content.**

Each of these definitions contains key technical terms and ideas that need to be explained, including *proposition* and *valid*. Let's begin by looking at Df(1), the definition of *argument*. Notice that an argument is characterized as a sequence of propositions. Although *proposition* could be given a more tech-nical formulation, for our purposes it is enough for us to understand this term as equivalent to "a sentence (or main clause) that has a truth-value;" that is, it is a sentence (or main clause) that is either true or false. (There are only two truth-values. Some systems of logic have a third value, but it is not a truth-value; they will not be discussed.) Propositions are sometimes contrasted with questions and commands, which cannot be true or false.

Proposition is often used interchangeably with *statement* and *assertion* even though the meanings of these words can be different in important ways.[1]

Returning to the definition of *argument*, we should notice that an argument is a *sequence* of propositions because the propositions are supposed to be related in some logically significant way. One of these propositions will be designated as the conclusion; that is, the proposition that is to be proven. Within the context of an essay as a whole, the conclusion is the thesis. Since subordinate propositions within the essay may have to be proved, these subordinate propositions may also be conclusions with their own sets of supporting premises. The premises are the propositions that lead to the conclusion. They provide the justification for the conclusion.

The above definition is abstract. Let's make it a bit less so by considering an extremely spare argument:

All humans are mortals.
Socrates is a human.
_____
Therefore, Socrates is mortal.

The first two sentences are premises. The third is the conclusion, as indicated by the word *therefore*. Other words in ordinary language that indicate the conclusion are *consequently, hence, it follows that,* and *thus.*

Exercise

Give two other words or phrases from ordinary language that indicate a conclusion.

The premises are supposed to provide the rational grounds for accepting the conclusion. While the argument about Socrates is good in some sense, it is rhetorically lame because no one would seriously argue for such an obvious conclusion. It rarely happens that three simple sentences constitute a rationally forceful argument. A rationally forceful argument, what is called in this book a *cogent argument,* typically requires elaboration and

_____

[1] Propositions, statements, and assertions can be true or false, but facts cannot be true or false. Facts are factual;, and a proposition that states a fact is true; a proposition that does not state a fact, that is, does not fit the facts, is false. Propositions that allegedly state facts or state alleged facts but are false are sometimes called "states of affairs" by philosophers. There are two kinds of states of affairs, those that are "realized" – these are the ones that are facts – and those that are not realized – these are the things that make false propositions false.

embellishment. Yet, at the beginning of our study, it is wise to keep the matter as simple as possible.

The definition of *argument* in Df(1) is neutral with respect to the issue of whether an argument is defective (bad) or not. Some arguments are defective and some are not. Our goal is to understand the nature of all arguments by concentrating on what constitutes a good one. We then understand what a defective argument is by identifying how it fails to measure up to the criteria for good arguments. As Parmenides said, "The ways of falsehood are infinite, while the way of truth is one."

To further refine the definition of a good argument, let's now consider the concept of a sound argument given in Df(2):

Df(2) A sound argument is an argument that is valid and that contains only true premises.

As this definition makes clear, there are two aspects to a sound argument: validity and truth. An argument is unsound in either of two cases: if it is invalid or if one or more of its premises are false. Thus, to show that your argument is sound, you must show that the argument is valid and show that the premises are true. Since a sound argument is partially defined in terms of the technical notion of validity, we need a definition of it:

Df(3) An argument is valid if and only if it is necessary that if all the premises are true, then the conclusion is true.

To put this in a slightly more colloquial form, the conclusion of a valid argument must be true whenever all its premises are true. The truth of the premises guarantees the truth of the conclusion.

In Df(3), validity is defined in terms of truth and necessity. Further, in Df(4) a cogent argument is partially defined in terms of a sound argument; a sound argument is partially defined in Df(2) in terms of an argument; and an argument is partially defined in Df(1) as consisting of premises and a conclusion. This process of defining one thing in terms of other things cannot go on forever; no more than the stability of the earth can be explained by saying that it sits on the back of an elephant that rests on the back of another elephant, that rests on the back of another elephant, *ad infinitum*. At some point, the process of explanation must end. (Under all the elephants is a tortoise, and that is the end of it.)

As regards validity (and hence soundness and cogency), the process of explanation ends with truth and necessity. These two concepts are being taken as basic and will not be defined. I am relying upon our common understanding of the notions of truth and necessity to carry us. This is not to say that these notions are not problematic; it is just that one must stop somewhere. Cogency, soundness, and validity could have been defined using some other terms, and then those other terms would have been basic and undefined.

It is not objectionable to leave some terms undefined. Indeed, some terms have to be undefined. In order to *say* anything, one must assume that the meanings of *some* words are understood. This may form the foundation for a paradox involving how it is possible for people to learn a language if one must already know words before one can say anything. A short answer is that language must have arisen among a group of people that had the practice of a person P_1, using some sounds or gestures to get another person P_2 to understand what P_1 wanted P_2 to do or to believe. These rudimentary gestures and sounds could be made more complex over time because human beings have sufficient imagination and intelligence to figure out the increasingly complex sounds and gestures. Something like this is true, I believe, and fortunately, I don't need to present and defend a complete account that will resolve the paradox.

In every enterprise, one eventually gets to a point at which something must be accepted without definition or argument. If the arguer and "arguee" cannot agree on any such point, there is a sense in which an argument cannot get started. However, although neither *truth* nor *necessity* will be defined, a little more can and will be said about validity in section 2.2 of this chapter. Let's approach this topic by treating sound arguments first.

A sound argument is a valid argument with true premises. As desirable as sound arguments are, many are unhelpful because they are not recognizable as good arguments. To incorporate the aspect of recognizability into our intuitive notion of a good argument, I introduce the idea of a *cogent* argument, as spelled out in Df(4):

Df(4) **A cogent argument is a sound argument that is recognized to be such in virtue of the presentation of its structure and content.**

There are many reasons why a rational person may not recognize a good argument. If its logical form is too complex for any human being to recognize or if the evidence needed to show that the premises are true is simply not available, a sound argument would necessarily fail to be cogent, because the condition of recognizability could not be satisfied. However, many sound arguments are, as a matter of fact, not cogent because they are not properly formulated and/or adequate evidence is not adduced in support of key premises. Proper formulation of an argument involves its structure: The argument must be valid, and the premises and conclusion must be set out in such a way that its validity is apparent. The matter of evidence, on the other hand, is related to an argument's content and involves once again the notion of truth. Each individual premise must be true, and the evidence presented must make this clear.

The intuitive notion of a good argument that we started with at the beginning of this chapter has now evolved into the notion of a cogent argument. We can now summarize by saying that a good (i.e. cogent) argument involves three things: formal validity (structure), true premises (content), and recognizability. This is what you should strive for in your writing. If any one of these elements is missing, your argument will not be cogent. All of these elements are individually necessary and jointly sufficient to produce a cogent argument. In section 2.3 of this chapter, we will examine the notion of cogency in more detail. For now, we need to return to a fuller treatment of the crucial notion of validity, the aspect of an argument related to its structure or form.

2.2   Valid Arguments

Recall the definition of a valid argument given in section 2.1:

Df(3)   An argument is valid if and only if it is necessary that if all the premises are true, then the conclusion is true.

To repeat what was said earlier, in a valid argument true premises guarantee a true conclusion. A valid argument *cannot* have true premises and a false conclusion. Validity preserves truth. The situation is different when one or more of the premises is false. In such cases, the conclusion might be true or false. In other words, there are valid arguments that have

(a)   true premises and true conclusion;
(b)   false premises and false conclusion;
(c)   false premises and true conclusion.[2]

---

[2] A related topic, bad arguments with a true conclusion, is treated in section 2.8 of this chapter.

Let's look at an instance of each of these possibilities (for the sake of illustration, exercise whatever tolerance is necessary to assume that the premises in the following examples are true or false as indicated).

Example of a valid argument with true premises and a true conclusion
Justice is fairness.

Fairness is distributing rewards according to merit and penalties according to blame.

Justice is distributing rewards according to merit and penalties according to blame.

Example of a valid argument with false premises and a false conclusion
Justice is what the strong desire.

What the strong desire is what is good for the strong.

Justice is what is good for the strong.

Example of a valid argument with false premises and a true conclusion
Justice is what the strong desire.

What the strong desire is distributing rewards according to merit and penalties according to blame.

Justice is distributing rewards according to merit and penalties according to blame.

In each of these examples of a valid argument, the conclusion is related to the premises in a fairly straightforward way. This need not be the case.

Exercise

Give an example of a valid argument (1) with true premises and a true conclusion; (2) with false premises and a true conclusion; and (3) with false premises and a false conclusion on some topic that has nothing to do with justice or fairness.

Although it is counterintuitive, there are valid arguments in which the premises and conclusion are not related in any plausible way. There are two types of valid arguments in which the conclusion is wholly unrelated to the premises. One type occurs when the conclusion is a *tautology*, a proposition that is trivial, uninformative, but still true, for example, "Either Aristotle is a great philosopher or he is not."[3] Every argument with a tautology as a conclusion must be valid, no matter how irrelevant the premises are to that conclusion. For example, the following argument is valid, even though the premise has no apparent topical or evidential relation to the conclusion.

Ima Hogg was a great philanthropist.

Either Aristotle is a great philosopher or he is not.

This argument is defective because the premise is irrelevant to the conclusion; it is not cogent. Yet, it is a *valid* argument.

The other type of valid argument with topically unrelated premises and conclusion is one in which the premises are contradictory. (Roughly, a proposition is contradictory when it asserts and denies the same thing, e.g. "Aristotle is a great philosopher and he is not a great philosopher." Obviously, two non-conjoined propositions can contradict each other, like these two: "Aristotle is a great philosopher" and "Aristotle is not a great philosopher.") Now consider this argument:

Aristotle is a great philosopher and he is not a great philosopher.

No philosopher has ever made a mistake.

This argument is valid because it satisfies the definition of validity even though the conclusion is unrelated to the premise. When an argument contains a contradictory premise, that premise is necessarily false, and hence it is not possible for all the premises to be true and the conclusion false. More generally, even if there is no single contradictory premise, so long as the premises are jointly contradictory, the argument is valid.

Many people consciously believe contradictory propositions and sometimes think that there is some merit in doing so. In "Song of Myself," Walt Whitman wrote, "Do I contradict myself? Very well then I contradict myself. (I am large, I contain multitudes.)" That makes for good poetry but bad philosophy. Ralph Waldo Emerson wrote, "A foolish consistency is the hobgoblin of little minds," and this has led some people to think that there is a wise inconsistency. The philosopher Hegel thought that contradictions were an indispensable part of philosophy. So what is wrong with having contradictory beliefs? The simple answer is that a person with contradictory beliefs is logically

---

[3] Ludwig Wittgenstein wrote that a person who knows that either it is raining or it is not knows nothing about the weather (*Tractatus Logico-Philosophicus*, paragraph 4.461).

committed to every proposition. This is bad because true (empirical) beliefs do not just mark off the part of conceptual space that is factual; they exclude the parts of conceptual space that are nonfactual. (The false ones are the negations of the true ones.) But by committing oneself to a contradiction, one allows all the false propositions to mingle among the true ones. Contradictory beliefs do not discriminate between the good ones from the bad ones. And that is bad.

Since standard beliefs are propositions, I will illustrate the problem with contradictions by taking advantage of the fact that contradictory premises entail all propositions. The valid argument below uses the contradictory premise that *Horses fly and horses do not fly* and proves that *cruelty is kindness*, but it should be obvious that any other contradictory premise and any other offensive false conclusion can be substituted for them, respectively. The rules that justify the inferences and the propositions to which they apply are listed in the column on the right. The names of the rules can be found below on pages 29 and 30.

1. Horses fly and horses do not fly.	(The contradictory premise.)
2. Horses fly.	(From (1) by simplification.)
3. Either horses fly or the best life is poor, nasty, and brutish.	(From (2) by addition.)
4. Horses do not fly.	(From (1) by simplification.)
5. The best life is poor, nasty, and brutish.	(From (3) and (4) by disjunctive syllogism.)

People sometimes find the above kind of proof "fishy" and unpersuasive, even though the form of the argument is valid. Where "p" and "q" represent propositions, & conjunction, and v disjunction, any argument of this form is valid:

1. $(p \,\&\, {\sim}p)$
2. p
3. $(p \lor q)$
4. ${\sim}p$
---
5. q

A person who believes contradictory propositions usually does not realize that she does, and she may draw what she believes are interesting consequences from her contradictory beliefs. But since anything can be proved from contradictory premises, the consequences she draws are actually not interesting.

Let's now say more about the fact that in a valid argument, the premises entail the conclusion. Upon what does entailment depend?

One answer is that entailment depends upon the meanings of the words making up the propositions of the argument. Two types of words might be distinguished: topic neutral and topic specific.

Topic-specific words include those that are typically first thought of as words, such as *dog, cat, walks, yellow,* and *happily,* as well as more emotionally charged words such as *disarmament, deficit, abortion,* and *fraternity.* What all these words have in common is that they specify or restrict some topic. A sentence with the word *dog* in it, for example, in some vague general sense, might be said to have a dog or dogs as one of its topics. The logic that is concerned with the entailment properties of topic-specific words might be called material logic. Thus, material logic is concerned with the entailment that holds between

This object is yellow

and

This object is colored.

Topic-specific words are central to the way people think about reality or our conceptual scheme. Very general concepts, for example, *goodness, truth, justice, beauty, person,* and *object,* are traditional topics of philosophy, and a large part of their contribution to the truth of various other propositions is a large part of what philosophy has been about. Thus, a philosopher might worry about the nature of knowledge by asking whether

x knows that p

entails

x believes that p.

And the philosopher may worry about the nature of truth by asking whether

"S" is true

entails

"S" corresponds to some fact.

Let's now consider some topic-neutral words such as *not, and, or, if ... then, if and only if, all,* and *some.* They are topic neutral in the sense that they do not restrict the topic or subject matter under discussion. Further, they are not restricted with regard to what topic-specific words they can combine with to form sentences. The logic that is concerned with the entailment properties of topic neutral words is called *formal logic.* For example, each of these arguments is valid for the same reason:

If John is rich, then Mary is happy.
John is rich.
Mary is happy.

If smoking causes lung cancer, then people should not smoke.
Smoking causes lung cancer:
People should not smoke.

If humans are aggressive by nature, then a strong government is needed to protect humans from themselves.
Humans are aggressive by nature.
A strong government is needed to protect humans from themselves.

It does not matter that each of these arguments concerns a different topic. Given the meaning of *if ... then,* any argument of this form is valid:

$$\text{If } p, \text{ then } q$$
$$\frac{p}{q}$$

where "p" and "q" represent propositions. Recall that propositions are sentences or main clauses that have a truth-value. This is important because a mistake in representing an argument can occur if certain words or phrases are translated as if they expressed a complete thought. The sentence:

Lee is standing and Sam is standing.

is a "conjunction" and expresses two propositions, "Lee is standing" and "Sam is standing." It might be represented as "(L and S)" or "(p and q)." Colloquially, we would say, "Lee and Sam are standing." This latter sentence expresses the same conjunction and so could be represented in the same way, as, say, "(L and S)." "L" translates "Lee is standing;" it does not translate "Lee," which is a proper name, not a sentence or main clause. Contrast these cases with

Adam and Beth stood together.

This sentence does not express a conjunction even though it contains the word "and." It is not colloquial for "Adam stood together" and "Beth stood together." So it would be a mistake to translate it as, say, "(A and B)."

The form of argument we have been looking at above is one of the most intuitive argument forms there is. It is called *modus ponens,* which loosely translated means *the mode (method) of affirming.* What is affirmed is that *p. Modus ponens* is one of a number of inference forms that constitute the core of *natural deduction systems of propositional logic.* Roughly, propositional logic, sometimes called *the propositional calculus,* can be defined as the logic of some uses of *not, and, or, if … then* and *if and only if.* These words figure crucially in some of the most basic forms of argumentation that people use. Here, they are presented schematically:

Modus ponens	*Modus tollens*
If p, then q	If p, then q
p	Not q
——	——
q	Not p
Disjunctive syllogism	*Hypothetical syllogism*
p or q	If p, then q
Not p	If q, then r
——	——
q	If p, then r
Constructive dilemma	*Destructive dilemma*
If p, then q, and if r than s	If p, then q, and if r then s
p or r	Not q or not s
——	——
q or s	Not p or not r
Simplification	*Addition*
p and q	p
——	——
P	p or q

Logic typically includes special symbols for the most important topic-neutral words. There is no one set of symbols that is used by a majority of logicians. Different logicians use different symbols for the same topic-neutral words. Here are some examples:

Propositional Connective	Symbol	Symbol	Symbol
Not	~	¬	−
And	&	·	∧
Or	v		∨
if … then	⊃		→
if and only if	≡		↔

If the symbols in the first column are substituted for their English equivalents, then the argument forms just presented look like this:

$$
\begin{array}{c}
\textit{Modus ponens} \\
p \rightarrow q \\
p \\
\hline
q
\end{array}
\qquad
\begin{array}{c}
\textit{Modus tollens} \\
p \rightarrow q \\
\sim q \\
\hline
\sim p
\end{array}
$$

$$
\begin{array}{c}
\textit{Disjunctive syllogism} \\
p \vee q \\
\sim p \\
\hline
q
\end{array}
\qquad
\begin{array}{c}
\textit{Hypothetical syllogism} \\
p \rightarrow q \\
q \rightarrow r \\
\hline
p \rightarrow r
\end{array}
$$

$$
\begin{array}{c}
\textit{Constructive dilemma} \\
(p \rightarrow q) \ \& \ (r \rightarrow s) \\
p \vee r \\
\hline
q \vee s
\end{array}
\qquad
\begin{array}{c}
\textit{Destructive dilemma} \\
(p \rightarrow q) \ \& \ (r \rightarrow s) \\
\sim q \vee \sim s \\
\hline
\sim p \vee \sim r
\end{array}
$$

Since these forms are of their very nature abstract, it may be helpful to give an example of each of them. Let's begin with *modus ponens*:

If Hobbes is an empiricist, then Hobbes holds that sense knowledge is the foundation for all knowledge.

Hobbes is an empiricist.

Hobbes holds that sense knowledge is the foundation for all knowledge.

Let's now consider an instance of *modus tollens,* which bears some similarity to *modus ponens.*

> If Hobbes is an empiricist, then Hobbes holds that sense knowledge is the foundation for all knowledge.
>
> Hobbes does not hold that sense knowledge is the foundation for all knowledge.
> _____
> Hobbes is not an empiricist.

Modus ponens and *modus tollens* are clearly related. Often a philosophical problem can be summarized as a dispute over whether the sound argument concerning a certain issue should be formulated as a *modus ponens* or a *modus tollens* argument. One could imagine a dispute involving the argument examples above. One person might be using the *modus ponens* argument to prove that Hobbes emphasizes the importance of observation in science. His opponent might use the *modus tollens* argument to prove that Hobbes is not an empiricist. There is a saying in philosophy: One person's *modus ponens* is another person's *modus tollens.* Obviously much more would be involved in the debate than merely these two arguments. Although both arguments are fairly obviously valid, it is not obvious which, if either, is sound, and hence neither argument is cogent. As a matter of fact, the instance of *modus tollens* is the sound argument and could form the core of a cogent argument if it were buttressed with evidence showing that Hobbes himself emphasized the deductive and *a priori* aspects of science.

Let's now consider an example of disjunctive syllogism:

> Either Hobbes is an empiricist or he is a rationalist.
>
> Hobbes is not an empiricist.
> _____
> Hobbes is a rationalist.

This argument is of course valid. Is it sound? A frequent defect of arguments that have the form of disjunctive syllogism is that not all the relevant alternatives are specified in the disjunctive proposition. If the disjunctive proposition does not exhaust all the possibilities, then it may well be false. For example, is every philosopher either an empiricist or a rationalist? Isn't it possible for a philosopher to be neither? A large part of this issue will depend upon how the terms *empiricist* and *rationalist* are defined. So, if our example of a disjunctive syllogism has any hope of forming the core of a cogent argument, it is necessary to define those terms even though this alone would not suffice (see chapter 5, section 5.1, "Definitions").

Hypothetical syllogisms are often used to line up series of dependencies, for example,

> If every human action is causally determined, then no human action is free.
> If no human action is free, then no human is responsible for any of his actions.
> ————————————————————————
> If every human action is causally determined, then no human is responsible for any of his actions.

Although the formal rule of a syllogism dictates that there be only two premises, as in the above example, several hypothetical syllogisms can, however, be strung together to yield a result like this:

> If every event is causally determined, then every human action is causally determined.
> If every human action is causally determined, then no human action is free.
> If no human action is free, then no human is responsible for any of his actions.
> If no human is responsible for any of his actions, then it makes no literal sense to praise or blame humans for their actions.
> ————————————————————————
> If every event is causally determined, then it makes no literal sense to praise or blame humans for their actions.

When propositions are linked in this sort of way and the conclusion is either counterintuitive or otherwise unacceptable, the challenge lies in determining where and how to break the chain.

Let's now consider the two rules of dilemma. Constructive dilemma might be thought of as two instances of *modus ponens* conjoined:

$$(p \rightarrow q) \,\&\, (r \rightarrow s)$$
$$\frac{p \lor r}{q \lor s}$$

Similarly, destructive dilemma might be thought of as two instances of *modus tollens* connected:

$$(p \rightarrow q) \,\&\, (r \rightarrow s)$$
$$\frac{\sim q \lor \sim s}{\sim p \lor \sim r}$$

Let's now consider a concrete example of each, beginning with constructive dilemma:

> If determinism is true, then actions are neutral with respect to praise or blame, and if humans have free will, then science is limited in what it can explain about reality.
> Either determinism is true or humans have free will.
> _____
> Either actions are neutral with respect to praise or blame or science is limited in what it can explain about reality.

Just as one person's *modus ponens* is another person's *modus tollens*, one person's constructive dilemma is another person's destructive dilemma. The above example of constructive dilemma is easily transmuted into an example of destructive dilemma:

> If determinism is true, then human actions are neutral with respect to praise or blame, and if humans have free will, then science is limited in what it can explain about reality.
> Human actions are not neutral with respect to praise or blame, or science is not limited in what it can explain about reality.
> _____
> Either determinism is not true or humans do not have free will.

Genuine philosophical examples of dilemmas typically conclude with a disjunction of unpleasant alternatives. That is what makes the argument a dilemma in the ordinary sense of the term, in contrast with the logical sense we have been discussing. Dilemmas will be discussed again in chapter 5.

Now that we have a better understanding of what constitutes a valid argument form, let's return to the main issue of this chapter, namely, what makes up a cogent argument.

2.3   Cogent Arguments

Recall the definition of a cogent argument in section 2.1:

(Df4)   A cogent argument is a sound argument that is recognized to be such in virtue of the presentation of its structure and content.

A cogent argument is one that compels the audience to accept its conclusion in virtue of his recognition that the argument is valid and the premises true. Cogent arguments are person relative. This would come out more clearly if we reformulated our definition like this:

An argument is cogent for an audience just in case that audience recognizes it to be sound.

The same argument might be cogent to one person and not cogent to another. All cogent arguments are persuasive to the audience that recognizes them. Yet not all persuasive arguments are cogent. People are often persuaded by bad arguments and fallacious reasoning.

An argument may be sound and yet fail to be cogent because its soundness is not recognized. An argument might be this way necessarily, either through the complexity of form that outstrips human comprehension or through the impossibility of gathering evidence needed to show that its premises are true. We are not really interested in these non-cogent arguments, since there is nothing humans can do about them. If humans *cannot* recognize the validity, and the evidence is *in no way* available, then that is the end of it. These arguments, however, should not be confused with others.

There are also some sound arguments that are in fact not recognized as such either because (1) although their logical structures are not recognized, they could be if they were explained, or because (2) although their premises are not recognized as true, they could be if the evidence that is available were provided. About these kinds of unrecognized sound arguments, something can be done: The author can provide for her reader an explanation of their logical structures and a description of the evidence for her premises.

This can be made clearer with an example. There is no doubt that it is easy to provide a sound argument for the proposition "God exists" (if he does exist). And there is no doubt that it is easy to provide a sound argument for the proposition, "God does not exist" (if he does not exist). Thus, one (*but only one*) of the following two arguments is sound.

First Argument
Either God exists or June 1 is Independence Day.

June 1 is not Independence Day.

God exists.

Second Argument
Either God does not exist or June 1 is Independence Day.

June 1 is not Independence Day.

God does not exists.

Now it should be obvious that *neither* of these arguments is cogent. The problem is that the sound argument, whichever one it is, is not apparent! Each argument is clearly valid. Both are instances of disjunctive syllogism. And the second premise of each argument is true. The locus of the problem is the first premise. If God exists, then the first premise of the First Argument is true in virtue of that very fact, and then the First Argument is sound. If God does not exist, then the first premise of the Second Argument is true in virtue of that very fact, and then the Second Argument is sound. But which is it?

Unfortunately, there is nothing in either argument that allows us to determine which is sound. There is nothing in either argument that rationally forces us to accept its first premise. Thus, neither argument is cogent. It is the author's duty to forge sound arguments into cogent arguments. Typically, this requires elaboration, explanation of the argument's validity, and/or evidence for the truth of the premises.

How might an author try to strengthen one of the above arguments? Although I will usually try to give examples of how to do things correctly, in this case, I will explain how things might go wrong. One can also learn from one's mistakes.

Since the same sort of strategies would apply to either argument, let's consider just the first one. What the First Argument needs is evidence that is sufficient to establish that the first premise is true. What kind of evidence would accomplish this goal? The premise is a disjunctive proposition. As such, it is true if either disjunct is true. We already know that the second disjunct is false. Thus, if the premise is true, it must be because its first disjunct is true. But that disjunct "God exists" is identical with the conclusion. Thus, any evidence for the truth of the premise is by that very fact *[eo ipso]* evidence for the truth of the conclusion. What this means is that evidence for the premise is superfluous. If one had evidence for the proposition "God exists," then one could apply it immediately to the conclusion without relying on the premises at all.

Suppose someone wanted to defend the cogency of this argument by claiming that the first premise is true because "God exists" is true and that "God exists" is true because it is self-evident. This defense does not work because it begs the question. That is, the purpose of the argument is to prove that God exists. So, it is not acceptable for the defender to assume that very thing to be self-evident. "Begging the question" is the fallacy of using a proposition both as the conclusion and as either a premise or as expressing evidence for a premise. (In recent years, the phrase "begging the question" has taken on a completely different meaning in American culture. It has come to mean "invites discussion," as in this example: "Saying that the US is the greatest nation because it has the most powerful armed forces begs the question of what property makes a nation great.") Here is a blatant example of begging the question in the sense used in logic:

The National Debt is too large.
—————————————————
The National Debt is too large.

No one is going to be misled by this argument. Most instances of the fallacy of begging the question, like all fallacies, are more subtle. Sometimes the fallacy occurs when the same proposition is expressed in two verbally different ways. For example, to argue

All humans are mortal.
—————————————————
Therefore, all humans will die.

is to beg the question since the premise and the conclusion mean the same.

A more complex and interesting example of begging the question is this:

Whatever the Bible says is true. For the Bible is the Word of God, and the Word of God is true. Further, we know the Word of God is true because the Bible tells us so.

The basic argument is this:

The Bible is the Word of God.
The Word of God is true.
—————————————————
The Bible is true.

The premise, "The Word of God is true," needs to be supported by evidence. But to use "The Bible says so" (that is, "The Bible is true") as expressing that evidence is to beg the question. For, in this context, "The Bible says so" is another way of saying "The Bible is true," which is just what is supposed to be proved. Thus, it cannot be used either as a premise or as evidence for a premise. (Many intelligent people in centuries past have in effect seemed to argue in this way. One might defend them by maintaining that they were not presenting the argument above but instead expressing a set of mutually supporting beliefs that they held. For more about this, see chapter 10.)

What makes the cogency of an argument recognizable? I suggest that it involves the relevance, informativeness, and connectedness of the propositions of the argument. A cogent argument contains premises that are relevant to the conclusion. Thus, the arguments about the existence of God that were discussed above are not cogent because not all their premises were relevant to the conclusions. (It's notoriously difficult to explain or define relevance.) A cogent argument must also contain premises that are informative. Sometimes premises are informative if they are novel in the sense that the audience was not aware of them until they were seen in the argument. Sometimes premises are informative in a derivative way such as by presenting them in a novel way. Thus, while it may not be informative for someone solely to assert, "I exist" – it seems trivial as a proposition standing alone – it is informative when a philosopher points out that this proposition can withstand the most skeptical attitude about knowledge. Taken in this novel way, "I exist" can be the foundation of all other knowledge. It may be further informative in proving the existence of God, as Descartes tried to do.

Finally, sometimes premises contribute to cogency, not because they are individually novel, but because they are shown to be connected to other premises or propositions. In his *Meditations*, Descartes shows a connection between the propositions "I am thinking" and "I exist." "I am thinking" either entails "I exist," or the latter is a necessary presupposition of "I am thinking" or the experience of thinking contains within itself the *I*'s existence.

A controversial and important example of begging the question is Immanuel Kant's claim that there must be a reality external to human, sensory experience because the elements of that experience are representations, and there cannot be representations unless there is something represented (but not sensed), call this *x*, the thing in itself. A critic will point out that the fact that elements of sensory experience are called "representations" does not prove that they are genuinely representations. The unknown *x* must include its not being known to exist. The concept of "objects causing representations" is like the concept of witches. Puritans thought they existed, mistakenly.

2.4 Fallacies

Some bad forms of reasoning are so common that they have been given names. Two formal fallacies, that is, fallacies that involve an invalid pattern of reasoning, are *affirming the consequent* and *denying the antecedent*. Compare the fallacy of affirming the consequent

Affirming the consequent

If p, then q $[p \rightarrow q]$

q

p

with the valid argument form affirming the antecedent, described above. One way to show that affirming the consequent is invalid is to construct an instance of the argument form with true premises and a false conclusion:

If Elon Musk owns one billion pounds of gold, then
Elon Musk is rich. (True)
Elon Musk is rich. (True)

Elon Musk owns one billion pounds of gold. (False)

Denying the antecedent is any argument of the form:

Denying the Antecedent

If p, then q $[p \rightarrow q]$

Not p $\sim p$

Not q $\sim q$

Exercise

Show that denying the antecedent is formally invalid by constructing an argument of that form with true premises and a false conclusion.

Some nonformal fallacies are clothed in a valid argument, for example, the fallacy of false dichotomy. Consider this short text:

American elections list a Democratic and a Republican candidate. Lee did not vote for the Democratic candidate. Therefore, she voted for the Republican candidate.

This argument has the valid argument form (loosely expressed) of disjunctive syllogism:

$(p \vee q)$

$\sim p$

q

but the first premise, "American elections list a Democratic and a Republican candidate," is false since it implies that every candidate is either a Democrat or a Republican. However, some candidates are Independents, members of the Green Party, or socialists. The conclusion is false if Lee voted for a candidate who is not a member of the Democratic or Republican Party or if she did not vote at all.

Exercise

Arguments in ordinary language usually have complicated components. Discuss the logical form and problems with the premises of the argument below as clearly as you can. The curly brackets are intended to help you identify the parts of the argument that bear on the truth of the premises, not the logical form.

The United States is either a republic or a democracy. The United States is not a democracy {because in a pure democracy, the business of the government is conducted by an assembly of all the citizens. The business of the United States is not conducted by an assembly of all the citizens.} Therefore, the United States is a republic {because the business of the republic is conducted by Congress, which consists of representatives of citizens.}

This argument appears to have the form of a disjunctive syllogism:

The United States is a pure democracy or it is a republic
The United States is not a democracy.
Therefore, The United States is a republic.

This appearance is deceiving. Why is this argument not sound?

In addition to formal fallacies, described above, there are nonformal fallacies that are at least as common. In this section, I want to discuss only one such fallacy, special pleading, because it is often overlooked even by intelligent people. The fallacy is using one principle or one kind of evidence for one kind of situation but not using that principle or evidence for another case when it should be. The exercise below involves some fictional countries:

Exercise

The nation Candu controlled the nation Kantdu for a century. It regulated Kantdu's borders and international commerce. Tired of being treated badly, a militia within Kantdu invaded Candu and brutally killed 1,000 civilians of every age. A third nation, Especial, condemned Kantdu for the slaughter of Candu's civilians according to the principle that *it is unjust to kill innocent civilians*. Candu then invaded Kantdu and brutally killed 3,000 civilians of every age. Especial did not condemn Candu. Especial is guilty of special pleading because it did not criticize Candu even though the same principle, namely, that *it is unjust to kill innocent civilians*, applied to Candu's action as much as to Kantdu's.

1 When Especial failed to criticize Candu's invasion of Kantdu, Especial was accused of special pleading. Especial defended itself by asserting that it applied the principle *that one country may invade a second one if the first is punishing the second for serious injustices*. Is Especial engaging in special pleading?

2 How could Especial have committed any fallacy when the scenario does not indicate that Especial drew any conclusion? (No conclusion, no argument.) If there is an implicit conclusion, what is it?

No example of a cogent argument has been presented in this section because the diversity of my readers precludes me from giving any. I leave the discovery of a cogent for the reader's own circle of friends, as an exercise.

The upshot of the chapter up to this point is that the notion of a sound argument does not fully capture the intuitive notion of a good argument.

2.5 Quantification and Modality

People sometimes talk about things in general and sometimes about only some things, for example, "Every politician lies," "Some [or: a few] politicians lie," "No politicians lie," and "Some [or: a few] politicians don't lie." Intuitively, people usually make the right inferences relative to such "quantified" sentences. But it is helpful to have a precise description of the logical connections between words like "all" and "some." A complete description would be complicated and take a lot of space. But it is worthwhile to have a rudimentary idea of these connections. The first thing that we need to do is to specify what forms of sentences will be discussed. Following Aristotle, we will take as our examples sentences that have these forms:

All Fs are Gs, Some Fs are Gs, No Fs are G, *and* Some Fs are not Gs,

where "F" and "G" can be replaced by most nouns and noun phrases.

None of the examples of "quantified" sentences given above have these forms. But it is easy to paraphrase them, so that they do: "All politicians are liars," "Some politicians are liars," and so on. (While people who tell only one or a few small lies are usually not considered liars, we are going to assume here that all it takes is one lie to be a liar.)

The logical connections that apply to sentences of the form mentioned above are set out in what is known as the square of opposition:

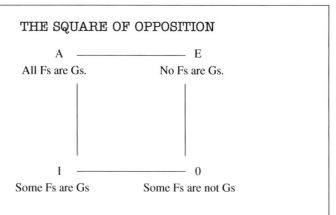

THE SQUARE OF OPPOSITION

A —————————— E

All Fs are Gs.   No Fs are Gs.

I —————————— 0

Some Fs are Gs   Some Fs are not Gs

Examples of A-sentences[4] are "All lawyers are educated people," "All good students are people who study hard," and "All liberals are communists." (Some of the preceding statements are true and some false, and the same is true of the sample sentences that follow. Their actual truth-values are irrelevant to their

---

[4] The names of the four types of propositions come from the Latin words "*affirmo*" ("I assert") and "*nego*" ("I deny"). These words help students who know Latin remember the appropriate place for the sentence forms that go in the square.

logic.) While the sentences "All lawyers have a lot of knowledge," "Every good student studies hard," and "If someone is a liberal, she believes in communism" are not strictly A-sentences, they can be paraphrased as A-sentences.

Examples of I-sentences are: "Some lawyers are officers of the court," "Some good students are people who study," and so on.

Examples of E-sentences are "No lawyers are educated people," "No good students are people who study hard," and "No liberals are communists." And while the sentences "No lawyers have a lot of knowledge" and "None who are good students study hard" are not E-sentences, it is obvious that they can be paraphrased into the form of E-sentences.

Examples of O-sentences are "Some lawyers are not educated people," "Some good students are not people who study hard," and "Some liberals are not communists." And while "A few lawyers are not educated people" and "Not all good students study hard" and "Many liberals are not communists" are not strictly O-sentences, it is obvious that they can be paraphrased into O-sentences.

A presupposition of the logic of these sentences is that there are actual instances of Fs and Gs. So given that unicorns do not exist, the square of opposition does not describe the logic of a sentence like "Some unicorns have two horns."

We can now state the principal logical relations between these four types of sentences:

(a) A-sentences entail their corresponding I-sentences.
(b) E-sentences entail their corresponding O-sentences.
(c) Corresponding A- and O-sentences are contradictory.
(d) Corresponding E- and I-sentences are contradictory.
(e) Not both an A-sentence and its corresponding E-sentence can be true.
(f) Both an I-sentence and an O-sentence can be true together.

41

Exercise

1   For (a) above, give an example of an A-sentence that is true and then another example in which the A-sentence is false.

2   For (b) above, give an example of an E-sentence that is true and then another example in which the E-sentence is false.

3   Do you know what the truth-value is of the corresponding I- and O-sentences of exercises (1) and (2) above? (Answer this for all eight(!) I- and O-sentences.)

4   Give one example of (d), and one of (e), and one of (f).

5   Does the sentence, "Some dogs are mammals" entail "All dogs are mammals"?

6   Does the sentence, "Some women are lawyers" entail "Some women are not lawyers"?

In addition to inventing the square of opposition, Aristotle noticed that similar logical connections are related to many sentences that include the words and phrases, "necessarily," "possibly," "necessarily not," and "possibly not." In the diagram below, the symbol "□" stands for "necessarily," "it is necessary that," and "must," and some other locutions too. Your knowledge of English is a generally reliable guide about when necessity is being expressed. The symbol "◊" stands for "possibly," "it is possible that," "can," and others. The symbol "~" indicates something expressing negation.

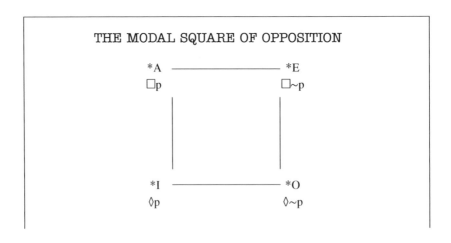

THE MODAL SQUARE OF OPPOSITION

*A ————————— *E
□p   □~p

*I ————————— *O
◊p   ◊~p

An important difference between the square of opposition and the modal square of opposition is that the propositions do not have to be categorical propositions. This fact is represented by the use of "p." It stands for complete sentences, just as it did when the logic of "not," "and," "or," and other sentence connectives were discussed.

Here are the principal logical relations between sentences in the modal square:

(a) *A-sentences entail their corresponding *I-sentences.

(b) *E-sentences entail their corresponding *O-sentences.

(c) Corresponding *A- and *O-sentences are contradictory.

(d) Corresponding *E- and *I-sentences are contradictory.

(e) Not both an *A-sentence and its corresponding *E-sentence can be true.

(f) An *I-sentence and an *O-sentence can both be true together.

Here are some instances of (a) through (c):

(a′) "Necessarily two plus two equals four" entails "It is possible that two plus two equals four."

(b′) "Necessarily it is not the case that two plus two equals four" entails "Possibly it is not the case that two plus two equals four." [Of course the two sentences mentioned in this example are actually false.]

(c′) "Necessarily two plus two equals four" and "Possibly it is not the case that two plus two equals four" are contradictory.

Exercise

Give an instance of (d) through (f).

One reason that necessity and possibility are so important to philosophy is that traditionally philosophy, in contrast with ordinary truths about the world or scientific truths, aimed to identify what is necessarily true, that is, what must be the case; and it also aimed to identify what was possibly the case because, by knowing what is possible, one identifies the outer boundaries of a concept.

So far, necessity and possibility have been discussed as if they had one sense. In fact, it is important to distinguish two senses of them. The first is logical or metaphysical necessity. Examples (a')–(c') above illustrate this kind of necessity. It has nothing to do with human knowledge. The other sense of necessity and possibility, epistemic, is intimately connected with what people know. If someone says, "It is possible that the president is currently in her office," and is using the epistemic sense of "possible," he is saying in effect, "I have no knowledge that leads me to believe that she is not in her office." If someone says, "She must be in her office," in the epistemic sense of "must," he is saying in effect, "I have conclusive proof that she is in her office."

While it is difficult to explain rigorously what logical necessity and possibility are without using technical notions, it is easy to explain what they mean in relation to each other. For example,

$\Box p = \sim\Diamond\sim p$ "Necessarily p" is logically equivalent to "It is not possible that it is not the case that p."

$\Diamond p = \sim\Box\sim p$ "Possibly p" is logically equivalent to "It is not the case that necessarily it is not the case that p."

Exercise

1. (a) Define "$\Box\sim p$" in terms of "$\Diamond$" and "$\sim$".
   (b) Define "$\Diamond\sim p$" in terms of "$\Box$" and "$\sim$".

2. (a) Do you think that "$\Box p$" entails "$\Box\Box p$"? Why or why not?
   (b) Do you think "$\Diamond p$" entails "$\Diamond\Diamond p$"? Why or why not?
   (c) Do you think "$\Box p$" entails "$\Diamond\Box p$"? Do you think "$\Diamond p$" entails "$\Box\Diamond p$"?
   (d) If "$\Box p$" entails "$\Diamond\Box p$," does "$\Box p$" entail "$\sim\Box\sim\Box p$"?
   (e) If "$\Box p$" entails "$\Diamond\Box p$," does "$\Box p$" entail "$\sim\Box\Diamond\sim p$"

In the three sections that follow, several other logical concepts will be explained: consistency and contradiction in section 2.6, contraries and contradictories in section 2.7, and the strength of a proposition in section 2.8.

I have presented nothing more than the most basic information about logic. A detailed presentation of simple deductive and informal logic is contained in Lewis Vaughn's *The Power of Critical Thinking*, 7th edn. (New York: Oxford University Press, 2021). Similarly, the examples of arguments that I have used have been like skeletons of the kind of argument you will find in philosophy in order to make it easier to understand the particular point that I wanted to convey. Genuine philosophical arguments are often difficult to identify in their original context. A superb book that makes the transition from considering bare bones arguments to the fully elaborated and often difficult arguments of professional philosophers is *Just the Arguments: 100 of the Most Important Arguments in Western Philosophy*, ed. Michael Bruce and Steven Barbone (Malden, MA: Wiley Blackwell, 2011). The authors of the individual arguments describe the argument discursively, but then explicitly identify the premises and the inference steps that lead to the conclusion.

2.6   Consistency and Contradiction

We have been talking about good and bad arguments. But people also care a great deal about the logical properties of clusters or sets of propositions. For example, the propositions, "George Washington was the first president of the United States" and "Abraham Lincoln was the sixteenth president of the United States" are consistent with each other. Both of them can be true at the same time, and in fact they are both true. Consistent propositions may be on the same or a related topic as the sentences about Washington and Lincoln are. But they may also be on completely unrelated topics, e.g. "George Washington was the first president of the United States" and "A friend of Turgenev gave him the idea for *Fathers and Sons*." One sentence is about the history of the United States, the other about a Russian literary figure. They are consistent with each other even though they are topically unrelated.

Propositions can be consistent with each other even if one, some, or all of them are false. The sentence about Turgenev is false but nonetheless consistent with the sentence about Washington, which is true.

Here is a set of sentences that are consistent and all of which are false:

Aristotle discovered America.
Descartes failed his college course in geometry.
Henry Ford signed the Declaration of Independence.
The Cleveland Indians won the 1995 World Series.

As this example shows, consistency is not a guarantee of truth. It is possible for propositions to be consistent with each other, yet not true. Still, it is important for propositions to be consistent. For if propositions are not consistent with each other (that is, if they are *in*consistent or contradictory), then one of them has to be false. And philosophers, and nonphilosophers, should avoid falsity like the plague.

The easiest sets of inconsistent propositions to identify are those that contain a proposition and its negation:

Turgenev is a novelist.
Turgenev is not a novelist.

It is not necessary to know anything about Turgenev to know that at least one of these propositions is false. The fact that at least one proposition in an inconsistent set must be false is an interesting feature that philosophers often exploit. They formulate sets of propositions, each of which seems true, but which are together inconsistent. Such sets of propositions may be called *paradoxes*.

The Paradox of Freedom and Causality

1 All events are caused.
2 Human actions are free.
3 Human actions are events.
4 Whatever is caused is not free.

The Paradox of Reference and Existence

1 Everything referred to must exist.
2 The name "Hamlet" refers to Hamlet.
3 Hamlet does not exist.

The Paradox of Promising

1 If a person promises to do something, then she has an obligation to do it.
2 If a person has an obligation to do something, then she can do it.
3 Some people sometimes make promises that they cannot keep.

Formulating a philosophical problem as a paradox helps focus the issue. Any purported solution to the problem must identify the proposition or propositions that are false and explain why; alternatively, the solution must explain why all the propositions are in fact consistent and why they appear to be inconsistent. It is not always easy to tell whether propositions that appear to be inconsistent with each other actually are. This is especially true when the seemingly inconsistent propositions are vague, like

British empiricists believed that minds exist.
British empiricists believed that minds do not exist.

It is not clear whether these sentences are inconsistent because it is not clear whether either sentence is talking about all British empiricists or just some of them. If one of the sentences is talking about all British empiricists, then the sentences are inconsistent. But if each sentence is about some British empiricists, then the sentences would both be true. My own view is that when sentences are vague, it should be said that they do not express a proposition at all, that they express only part of a thought. Since they do not express complete propositions, they do not have truth-values and are neither true nor false nor consistent or inconsistent with each other.

So far I have given examples of consistent and inconsistent sets of propositions that have contained at least two propositions. But these notions also apply to individual propositions. The proposition

Aristotle was a poet

is consistent because it is possible for it to be true, even though it is in fact false. And the proposition

Aristotle was a poet and Aristotle was not a poet

is inconsistent because it is impossible for it to be true. Inconsistent propositions are also called *contradictions*.

Consistency and inconsistency (contradiction) are obviously related ideas. Although it might not be obvious, they are also related to entailment. A proposition *p* entails a proposition *q* just in case *not q* is inconsistent with *p*.

Exercises

1   Choose one of the paradoxes above and explain why the set of the propositions is inconsistent.

2   Assume that there are some British empiricists. Are the following two propositions consistent or inconsistent with each other?

All British empiricists believe that the mind is a substance.
Some British empiricists believe that the mind is a substance.

3   Sets of inconsistent propositions can be converted into valid arguments that consist of the propositions of the set as premises and a proposition that is entailed by the premises and contradicts at least one of the premises. In the Paradox of Reference and Existence, such an argument is this:

The Paradox of Reference and Existence

1   Everything referred to must exist.
2   The name "Hamlet" refers to Hamlet.
3   Hamlet does not exist.
    Therefore,
4   Hamlet exists. From (1) and (2) by universal instantiation on (1)

Convert the Paradox of Freedom and Causality and the Paradox of Promising into arguments.

2.7   Contraries and Contradictories

In the last section, contradiction was defined in relation to consistency. A contradiction is a proposition that is inconsistent, and a contradictory set of propositions is a set of propositions that are together inconsistent. Contradiction can be defined in other ways, ways that do not mention inconsistency:

A (self-)contradiction is a proposition that cannot be true.
A set of propositions is contradictory just in case there is
no way to make all of them true.

For example, "Socrates is mortal and Socrates is not mortal" is contradictory, and the set of (two) propositions, "Socrates is mortal" and "Socrates is not mortal," is contradictory.

For the purpose of contrasting contradictions with contraries, it is convenient to restrict the discussion to pairs of propositions (I am assuming that each of the propositions is not analytic and not contradictory):

> Two propositions are contradictory just in case one must be true and one must be false.
> Two propositions are contrary just in case they cannot both be true (and neither is analytic nor contradictory).

These two propositions contradict each other:

The wall is blue.
The wall is not blue.

These two propositions are contraries:

The wall is (completely) blue.
The wall is (completely) red.

Although two contrary propositions cannot both be true, it is possible for both of them to be false. If the wall is yellow, then both of the propositions displayed immediately above are false.

It should be obvious that we can extend the idea of contradictions and contraries to predicates or properties (I am assuming that each predicate is neither analytic nor contradictory):

> Two properties are contradictory just in case one must be true of an object and one must be false of it.
> Two properties are contrary just in case they cannot both be true of an object (and they are not contradictory).

Being blue/being non-blue are contradictory properties. Being blue/being red are contrary properties.

The distinction between contraries and contradictories is important because they are often mistaken. Although it is unlikely that you will mistake being red and being blue for contradictory properties, you might mistake being rich and being poor as contradictory, or being generous and being stingy. Also it is easy to confuse being unjust (a contrary of being just) with being not just (its contradictory). A cabbage growing in a garden is not just but it is not unjust either.

Some philosophers have used the observation that *being just* and *being unjust* are contraries and not contradictories to help solve the problem of evil. Here is an example of that in an essay fragment:

A SOLUTION TO THE PROBLEM OF EVIL

The problem of evil is insoluble until and unless one realizes that justice and injustice are contrary terms and that neither one applies to God. To be just is to be subject to laws and to follow all of those laws that apply. To be unjust is to be subject to laws and not to follow all of those that apply. But God is neither just nor unjust because he is not subject to any law. In order to be subject to law, one must not have control over it. But God has complete control over law since he makes all of the laws and is subject to no constraint with regard to the content of those laws. That is part of what is meant both by the omnipotence and the absolute sovereignty of God. That is why God was not unjust when he told Abraham to kill his son Isaac and not unjust when he allowed Satan to torture Job. Since God can be neither just nor unjust but makes the laws that determine who will be, it is appropriate to say that he is above justice and injustice.

But what else should we say about God with respect to justice and injustice? Since every property has a contradictory and at least one property of each contradictory pair of properties is true of an object, the properties contradictory to being just and to being unjust must be true of God. Consequently, God is not just and not unjust.

Let's consider one last pair of terms. Subjectivity and objectivity are often simply assumed to be contradictories. Whether they are contraries or contradictories depends upon how they are defined. One way to guarantee that they are contradictories is to define one of them as not being the other. For example,

> **x is subjective if and only if x can be judged by only one person and on the basis of her immediate experience.**
> **x is objective if and only if x is not subjective.**

So defined, subjectivity and objectivity are contradictory. But sometimes both are defined independently of each other, such that they turn out to be contraries that are mistaken for contradictories.

x is subjective if and only if x can be judged by only one person and on the basis of her immediate experience.
x is objective if and only if x is publicly observable.

For example, abstract entities like truth, justice, government, numbers (not to be confused with numerals), and some physical entities like subatomic particles (only the effects of which can be seen) are neither subjective nor objective by the above definitions (see, further, chapter 5, section 5.1, "Definitions").

Exercises

1 Which pairs of the following propositions are contradictories, which are contraries, and which are neither?
   (a) All women are lawyers.
   (b) No women are lawyers.
   (c) Some women are lawyers.
   (d) Some women are not lawyers.
   (e) Some women are philosophers.

2 Is the following pair of propositions contradictory, contrary, or neither? Why?

   Snow is white.
   Coal is black or not black.

3 Which pairs of the following propositions are contradictories, which are contraries, and which are neither? (This exercise appeals to your intuitions about the ideas of necessity and possibility. Something was said about these ideas in section 2.5.)
   (a) Necessarily, all women are lawyers.
   (b) Necessarily, no women are lawyers.
   (c) Possibly, some women are lawyers.
   (d) Possibly, some women are not lawyers.
   (e) Probably, some women are lawyers.

4   Categorize the following pairs as contraries, contradictories, or neither:
    (a)   tall/short
    (b)   tall/non-tall
    (c)   just/merciful
    (d)   just/unjust
    (e)   red/tall
    (f)   rubber/iron
    (g)   merciful/unmerciful
    (h)   all-powerful/powerful
    (i)   happy/unhappy
    (j)   responsible/irresponsible
    (k)   lawful/unlawful
    (l)   male/female
    (m)   male/non-male
    (n)   Democrat/Republican
    (o)   poor/honest

5   Given the definitions below, are subjectivity/objectivity contraries or contradictories?

    x is subjective if and only if there is only one person who can experience x.

    x is objective if and only if the properties of x can be determined by more than one person.

2.8   The Strength of a Proposition

Philosophers often talk about the strength of a proposition. Some propositions are stronger and some are weaker than others. These notions of strength and weakness are technical ones and need to be defined. Although the definitions are not difficult – they require only that you understand the notion of entailment – without these definitions you would be surprised at what philosophers think about the strength or weakness of a proposition.

A proposition p is stronger than a proposition q if and only if p entails q and q does not entail p.

For example, "Most British empiricists believe that the mind is a substance" is stronger than "Some British empiricists believe that the mind is a substance."

A proposition *p* is weaker than a proposition *q* if and only if *p* does not entail *q* and *q* does entail *p*.

Obviously, "Some British empiricists believe that the mind is a substance" is weaker than "Most British empiricists believe that the mind is a substance." Two propositions are equally strong if each entails the other.

There are many propositions that cannot be compared with regard to strength, for example, "Plato was a philosopher" and "David Hume was a philosopher." Neither proposition entails the other. Thus, one is neither stronger nor weaker than the other. Further, although "Every Greek philosopher had an ethical theory" may sound stronger than "It is possible that some philosopher at some time believed some true proposition," in fact it is not, since it does not entail the latter. This does not mean that these two propositions are equally easy or difficult to prove. Indeed, the former would be more difficult to prove or would at least require much more evidence since it is making a claim about *all* Greek philosophers, while the latter is making a claim about *some* philosopher. Moreover, the evidence for each would be different. If one proposition is stronger than another, then it requires more or better evidence to prove it; but if they cannot be related to each other in terms of strength, then there is no general way of predicting which proposition will require more or better evidence.

It is important for you to know how strong propositions are for several reasons. You need to know how strong each of your premises needs to be in order to prove your case. Premises should not be stronger than you need them to be because the stronger they are the more evidence they require and typically the more difficult they are to prove. The weaker the proposition, the less evidence one is required to supply. But your premises should also not be too weak, because if they are, then they will not entail your conclusion. Your argument will be invalid. Further, if you try to prove something stronger than is necessary and fail, then either you or your audience may draw the false inference that your position is untenable, even though a weaker set of premises might have been sufficient to entail your conclusion.

Sometimes discovering that something can be proved using a weaker proposition can be a great philosophical discovery. Many philosophers have tried to prove the existence of God by using as a premise, "Something is in motion." John Duns Scotus, in the late thirteenth century, made a brilliant move when he constructed a proof that uses the weaker proposition "It is possible that something is in motion." This proposition is true so long as the idea of motion does not contain a contradiction. This proposition might be true even if what humans consider motion were an illusion and there were no actual motion in the world. Thus, this proposition has fewer presuppositions than the stronger proposition, "Something is in motion."

Suppose you want to write in favor of skepticism. For our purposes, let's say that it is the view that no human knows anything. Then it is important to decide (know?!) which of the following propositions you need to prove or provide evidence for:

1   Each belief humans have is dubious.
2   Each belief humans have might be dubious.
3   Each belief humans have is false.
4   Each belief humans have might be false.

Proposition 2 is weaker than 1; 4 is weaker than 3. (Is 3 weaker than 2? Is 2 weaker than 4?) A philosopher is in a better initial position if he can get away with proving the weaker of two propositions.

It is also important to know how strong your opponent's proposition is. If your opponent asserts "All British empiricists believe that the mind is a substance," then he is asserting something *quite strong.* This means that his position can be refuted by establishing a relatively weak proposition: "Some British empiricist does not believe that the mind is a substance." Thus, it would be sufficient for you to show that there is at least one person, for example, David Hume, who is a British empiricist who did not believe that the mind is a substance. On the other hand, if your opponent asserts "Some British empiricists believed that the mind is a substance," then he is asserting something relatively weak, and the truth of the proposition, "Some British empiricist did not believe that the mind is a substance" is *not* sufficient to refute him. Rather, you would have to prove the very strong proposition, "No British empiricists believed that the mind is a substance." I would advise against trying to prove this. In general, the stronger a thesis, the weaker a proposition needs to be to refute it, and the weaker a thesis, the stronger a proposition needs to be to refute it.

Abstractly considered, strong propositions require a lot of evidence, while weak propositions require little. In practice, how much evidence is required depends upon the needs of your audience. You must supply as much evidence as your audience needs to be informed and persuaded. Consider this argument for what is a rather strong proposition, namely, that no taxation is justified:

> Nonvoluntary transfers of property are violations of rights. A thief who steals property violates the owner's rights. Taxation is a nonvoluntary transfer of property from the individual to the government. Therefore, the government through taxation is no better than a thief.

Although it is possible that this argument is sound, it would not be cogent for most audiences. For it does not take into consideration any of the relatively obvious arguments against the premise that "taxation is a nonvoluntary transfer of property" (in books on critical reasoning and informal logic, this neglect to mention all the considerations relevant to an issue is called *the fallacy of suppressed evidence*). Consider an essay fragment that is written as a reply to the above passage:

> Taxation is not like thievery at all, but rather like a payment for services rendered. People rely upon the government for various services that are essential to the quality of their life, not just police and fire protection, but roads, traffic laws, utilities, civil and criminal courts, and so on. People in business rely on the government even more, e.g. for patent laws and import and export laws. Indeed, when a businessman uses currency as his mode of exchange, he is using something made by the government, and he thereby uses all the machinery of government, its full faith and credit, to guarantee that the paper has the value he supposes it has. Further, taxes are legislated by elected representatives of the citizens, at least in some countries. Since representatives have the right to act for their clients, they can vote for taxes which fall on the clients themselves. Representatives are authorized by their clients to commit them to certain courses of action. In short, taxation is a voluntary transfer of property from citizen to government for services rendered.

This essay fragment has a better claim to expressing a cogent argument than the first. This of course does not settle the issue of which view about taxation is correct. The opponent of taxation might have decisive replies to the objections raised by the proponent of taxation. The point to be made here is that a person's essay will not be cogent unless she does raise and then answer exactly these sorts of objections. Moreover, the position of the tax opponent will actually be strengthened by this process, because it will force him to articulate further grounds for his view that cannot be shaken by the objections already raised.

These same remarks apply to the proponent of taxation. He should explain why there is opposition to taxation, reply to that opposition, explain how an opponent of taxation might respond, and then again reply. Each set of objections and replies ought to be deeper, subtler, and more revealing than the last, if the process works correctly. That is how progress in philosophy often occurs. For more about this method of reasoning, see chapter 5, section 5.8, "Dialectical Reasoning."

Exercises

Consider the relative strengths of the propositions within each of the following sets. Which, if any, proposition is the strongest *true* proposition of the set? (Of course, there will be disagreement about the answers.)

1 (a) All empirical statements are based upon observation and nothing else.
   (b) All empirical statements are based upon some actual observation.
   (c) All empirical statements are based upon some possible observation.

2 (a) Lying is always wrong.
   (b) Lying is usually wrong.
   (c) Lying is sometimes wrong.
   (d) Lying is never wrong.

3 (a) Lee is at home.
   (b) It is not the case that Lee is not at home.
   (c) Lee is not at home.
   (d) Lee is homeless.

2.9   Bad Arguments with True Conclusions

It is provable that for every true proposition, there are an infinite number of bad arguments for it. For example, here are two obviously bad arguments that have a true conclusion:

It is not the case that Plato is a philosopher.

Plato is a philosopher.

Either Descartes is a philosopher or Plato is not a philosopher.

Descartes is a philosopher.

Plato is a philosopher.

Given these two obviously bad arguments, it should be easy to see that there are an infinite number of bad arguments for any true proposition. Thus, a bad argument for a proposition does not show that the proposition is false. Hence, although the above argument for abortion is not cogent there may well be other arguments that are.

3

The Structure of a Philosophical Essay

3.1 An Outline of the Structure of a Philosophical Essay

Socrates was no friend of rhetoric, as he understood it. Still, he was willing to concede this much: "Any discourse ought to be constructed like a living creature, with its own body, as it were; it must not lack either head or feet; it must have a middle and extremities so composed as to suit each other and the whole work" (*Phaedrus* 264C). To extend the metaphor, just as body parts have different shapes and functions – arms, legs, wings, and horns – essay parts have different forms and functions. Further, just as different animals have different anatomies, philosophical essays have different anatomies. Some are more complex and unusual than others, yet all evolve from a basic form.

In this book, the most basic form and its immediate evolutionary descendants will be discussed. These forms all have a head, trunk, and tail. In prosaic terms, every essay should have three parts: a beginning, a middle, and an end. It was Winston Churchill, I believe, who put it this way: Say what you are going to do; do it; say what you have done. You may have heard this before, for a good reason: It is true. As a first shot at specifying the structure of an essay, it is valuable. Yet, this truism may become objectionable if more is not said about what goes into the structure of an essay and how a writer might construct one. A more informative guide is needed.

In the more informative guide, the first element, "Say what you are going to do," and the third, "Say what you have done," are substantially unchanged. They appear below as segments I and V. The second element, "Do it," however, divides into three segments: II–IV.

Philosophical Writing: An Introduction, Fifth Edition. A. P. Martinich.
© 2025 John Wiley & Sons, Inc. Published 2025 by John Wiley & Sons, Inc.
Companion website: www.wiley.com/go/Martinich5e

The Structure of a Philosophical Essay
A Simple One

I   State the proposition to be proved.
II   Give the argument for that proposition.
III Show that the argument is valid.
IV   Show that the premises are true.
V   State the upshot of what has been proven.

Segment I, stating the proposition to be proved, is the beginning of the essay. The statement to be proved is often called "the thesis sentence," or, more simply, the thesis. The thesis might be a statement like "Justice is rendering each person what is due to him," or it might be a historical thesis like "Descartes's method of doubt is the same as Sextus' skepticism."

Aristotle said, "A speech has two parts: you must state your thesis; and you must prove it." Although an essay is not exactly a written speech, what Aristotle says about a speech can be applied to an essay. The most basic division of an essay is into a statement of the thesis and its proof. The statement of the thesis comes before the proof. If you begin your essay with your first premise, rather than with a statement of your thesis, the reader will likely have difficulty understanding the relevance of the premise. One reason for this is that from any proposition, an infinite number of propositions follows. (It is easy, but not relevant here, to prove this. Anyone who has taken a course in logic should be able to do it. Those without a course in logic might ask their professor to do it some rainy day.) Although virtually all of the infinite possible propositions will have an absurdly low probability of being drawn by the author, it is unfair and irrational for an author to expect the reader to anticipate which of these she might draw. Even if it appears that 10 propositions are likely to be the conclusion, it is somewhat uncooperative to make the reader engage in a guessing game.

Compare writing an essay with an automobile trip to a previously unvisited location. If the traveler can look at the destination and the planned path to be taken, she will more easily remember the roads leading to the destination during the drive. Each turn and traffic signal will be organized in relation to that destination. Since philosophy can be difficult, it is important to make as clear as possible what you are trying to prove in your essay. There should be no surprises in philosophy, except those caused by an insight, expressed with brilliant clarity. Do not confuse rhetorical pyrotechnics for philosophical light.

Of course, your principal purpose in writing a philosophical essay is Truth for the sake of Truth (*Veritas gratia Veritatis*). Another purpose, however, is to show your professor your mastery of the material. Before reading your essay, your professor will assume neither that you do nor that you do not know the material; but once he does begin reading it, the burden of proof is on you to show that you do know the material. An unclear essay is evidence of unclear thought.

Segments II–IV constitute the middle of the essay. Concerning segment II, it is good practice to state your argument as soon as possible. This gives the reader the opportunity to see the general structure of your argument. The reader has a chance to see the overall picture of how you are going to get to your thesis. It is not necessary to state each premise that will be used when the full argument is discussed. It is sometimes good to state a premise that will need one or more sub-arguments to support it.

With the initial statement of your argument finished, you proceed to show your argument to be valid in segment III. Recall that a valid argument is one that shows that the conclusion must be true as long as all the premises are true (or are contradictory). Explain how your premises entail your conclusion.

Once you have finished showing that your argument is valid, you should provide in segment IV sufficient evidence to rationally convince your reader (your professor) that each premise is true, and typically, your audience will have doubts about one or more of your premises. State the evidence for your premises. You should also think about objections your reader might have. Raise them yourself. It will help clear the air of that doubt. If you can answer those objections, your argument is stronger, or at least it will look stronger to your reader.

Segment V is the end of your essay. There are several ways to end an essay. One way is to summarize your argument. This is in line with the notion "say what you have done." Because it comes at the end of your careful explication, your summary can assume a lot. You may use technical terms freely and assume that the meanings of your propositions are clear. Another way to end an essay is to explain what further implication it has, or you might say what the next step in your research is. This last conclusion is ill-advised if you are submitting your final essay for a course.

Still another way to end an essay is to explain why your results are important, if their importance could not be appreciated by stating them earlier in the essay. Typically, you should explain why your results are important near the beginning of your essay to pique your reader's interest. Sometimes, however, the importance cannot be appreciated before one goes through the argument, or the relation between the results and the importance is implausible without the argument. In these cases, it is both justified and advisable to explain the importance of your results at the end.

I have briefly described the simplest structure a philosophical essay can have. Typically, the structure of a philosophical essay will be much more complicated. To help reflect this additional complication, let's look at a more complicated outline of the structure of a philosophical essay.

The Structure of a Philosophical Essay
A Slightly More Complex One

I   Beginning: State the proposition to be proved.
- A. Orientation
  1. Specify what general topic will be discussed.
  2. Report what previous philosophers have thought about this topic.
- B. State what is to be proved; state the thesis.
  1. Report who has held the same or a similar view.
  2. Report who has held the opposite or a different view.
- C. Motivation: Explain why this thesis or topic is interesting or important.
- D. State what you will assume in your essay without argument.

II   Give the argument for the proposition to be proved.
- A. Explain the general force of the argument.
- B. Explain what the premises mean.

III Show that the argument is valid.
- A. Explain those terms that are used in a technical sense or that are ambiguous; resolve the ambiguity.

    B.   Explain how the conclusion follows from the premises.
       1.   The inference to intermediate conclusions will have to be explained as part of the complete explanation.
       2.   Sometimes one can explain the inferences by citing rules from a natural deduction system, e.g. modus ponens or modus tollens. More often the explanation concerns explaining the conceptual relations between the concepts expressed in the premises.
    C.   Give the rules that justify the inferences that are not apparent from the initial statement of the argument.

IV   Show that the premises are true.
    A.   Give the evidence for the premises.
       1.   Explain the premises, and explain the meaning of those terms that might be misunderstood and that bear upon the truth of your premises.
       2.   Adduce the intuitions of the audience; supply examples and subsidiary arguments that lend support to the truth of your premises.
    B.   Raise objections.
       1.   Raise objections that have actually been raised against your position.
          a.   Raise the objections that historically significant philosophers have already raised to that problem.
          b.   Raise the objections that your professor or fellow students have raised.
       2.   Raise objections that no one else has raised and that, when answered, further explicate and shore up your thesis.
    C.   Answer the objections.

V   Conclusion:
    A.   State the upshot of what you have proven.
    B.   Indicate further results that one might try to get.

The outline is in large part self-explanatory. Still, other things need to be said about it, since it is an abstract and schematic entity. First, not every essay will contain every element of the outline. Second, not every essay will contain these elements in the order in which they are given here.

The order given is a standard order, but it should not be considered invariable. Your material should dictate the order. Third, some items in the outline are roughly the same, e.g. I.A.2. and I.B.1. One reason for this is that essays typically unfold one step at a time. It is often rhetorically more effective to follow this procedure: Provide some general background, then state your own position, then provide a more detailed background, and so on. Another reason why the same general topic is listed in more than one place in the outline is, again, that your material should dictate your order, and sometimes that means discussing a topic in one place and sometimes in another. Finally, parts of this outline – even the whole of it – can be embedded as subordinate elements within other parts of the outline. For example, at the beginning of an essay, in the course of explaining what previous philosophers have thought about this problem, you might want to introduce the argument that some other philosopher gives for his position. In other words, you would want to introduce segments II–IV of the "Outline" as an element subordinate to I.A.2. If you were to do this, then the outline for the early part of your essay would contain embedded elements. (See the accompanying box on p. 48.)

Of course, this kind of embedding can occur at almost any other place in your essay, and it can occur an indefinite number of times, even with one embedding within another. For example, for segment IV "Show that the premises are true," the truth of some premise may depend upon some argument that contains a premise that itself depends upon some argument that needs to be explained, so one will need to revert to segments II–IV as many times as is necessary to explicate each premise. Although it may seem complicated to have several embeddings, in fact, it is not. The human brain is quite capable of multiple embeddings of diverse types. If you signal each successive embedding for your readers, they will not be confused by the apparent complexity. The "basic" outline suggests that a philosophical essay contains only one argument. This is not correct, as we just saw in discussing the need for embedded arguments in supporting one's premises. Furthermore, though an essay might have one *main* argument, most essays contain other subordinate arguments that will relate to the thesis in various ways. The author will subscribe to some of these arguments, but in many cases she will merely be reporting arguments of those opposed to her view or "flawed" arguments made by those who will have supported her main thesis. In writing your own essay, you should attempt to show your opponents' views to be faulty while overcoming the problems of previous arguments in support of your thesis.

I   Beginning: State the proposition to be proved.
    A. Orientation
        1. Specify what general topic will be discussed.
        2. Report what previous philosophers have thought about this topic.

> II   Give the argument for the proposition to be proved.
> III Show that the argument is valid.
>   A. Explain those terms that are used in a technical sense or that are ambiguous; resolve the ambiguity.
>   B. Give the rules that justify the inferences that are not apparent from the initial statement of the argument.
> IV Show that the premises are true.

    B. State what is to be proved; state your thesis.
        1. Report who has held the same or a similar view.
        2. Report who has held the opposite or a different view.
    C. Motivation: Explain why this thesis is interesting or important.
II   Give the argument for the proposition to be proved.
III Show that the argument is valid.
IV Show that the premises are true.
V   Conclusion.

3.2 Anatomy of an Essay

Printed below is a sample essay, "Hobbes's Divine Command Theory of Morality," which illustrates most items in the structure of a philosophical essay discussed in the previous section. Passages within the text have been numbered [1]–[22] as references to the commentary provided below the text of the essay. For best results in using the commentary, skim the entire essay first (it is quite brief). Then return to the beginning of the essay; read each numbered item and the accompanying footnote.

[1] Hobbes's Divine Command Theory of Morality

[2]The central problem in Thomas Hobbes's moral philosophy is answering the question, "Why are humans obligated to follow the moral laws?"

[3]There are two basic ways of interpreting Hobbes's answer to this question. [4]One interpretation is that humans must obey moral laws because God commands them to obey. [5]This is generally

---

[1] The title is an extremely important part of an essay because, if it is aptly formulated, it helps to satisfy the two most important parts of the beginning of an essay. Since the title is always the first thing a reader sees, even before the author's name, it creates the first impression. The title should convey a narrow range of topics from which the actual topic is selected. This delimitation of the range orients the reader. The title, "Hobbes's Divine Command Theory of Morality," obviously indicates that the main topic of discussion will not include elephants or geological ages. It restricts the topic to the intersection of topics about Hobbes and the Divine Command Theory of Morality. Of course, understanding the title also relies upon a great deal of background information. The title is more informative to someone who knows who Hobbes is and what the divine command theory of morality is.

[2] The first sentence must effect a transition from the abstractness and sketchiness of the title to the concreteness and specificity of the essay itself. The transition is very smooth in this essay since the phrase, "Hobbes's moral philosophy," in the first sentence echoes two of the key words in the title. Item [2] satisfies I.A.1: Specify what general topic will be discussed. (The difference between I.A.1 and I.B.1. and I.B.2 is solely in the relation the sentences have to other parts of the essay. I.A.1 is a report of the history of the problem without relating that history to the author's own thesis; I.B.1. and I.B.2 report that history in relation to the author's own thesis.)

[3] This sentence introduces I.2: Report what previous philosophers have thought about this topic. Item [3] is also *proleptic*; that is, it sets forth in a general way something that needs to be related in detail. Proleptic sentences are like implicit promises to say more about the topic. Such promises need to be kept as soon as possible. In this case, the promise is kept in the sentences immediately following: [4]–[7].

[4] This sentence is the first part of specifying the claim made in [3].

[5] This sentence names the interpretation referred to in [4]. It would be appropriate to introduce a note here that would give references to the scholarly work of Taylor, Warrender, and any other scholar the author thinks provides relevant background to the issue. Such a note is not provided here for simplicity's sake.

known as the Taylor–Warrender Thesis. [6]The other interpretation is that humans must obey moral laws because these laws are rational, in the sense that they are deducible by reason.

[7]This might be called the Secular Thesis.

[8]In this essay, I present an interpretation that is a version of the Taylor–Warrender Thesis. [9]Its claim is that according to Hobbes, an action is moral when God

---

Item [5] also marks the place where a discussion of the work of Taylor and Warrender could be inserted, if the author wanted to expand the essay. For example, sentence [5] could easily be expanded into three:

> [5] This is generally known as the Taylor–Warrender Thesis. [5a] A. E. Taylor first presented the thesis in these words: "I can only make Hobbes's statements consistent with one another by supposing that he meant quite seriously what he so often says, that the 'natural law' is the command of God, and so to be obeyed *because* it is God's command" (A. E. Taylor, "The Ethical Doctrine of Hobbes," in *Hobbes Studies*, ed. Stuart Brown, Oxford: Basil Blackwell, 1965, p. 49). [5b] Howard Warrender later elaborated a variation of it in this way: "[According to Hobbes] the reason why I *ought* to do my duty is that God commands it" (H. Warrender, *The Political Philosophy of Hobbes*, Oxford: Clarendon Press, 1957, p. 213).

These three sentences ([5]–[5b]) could be further expanded into a dozen or more if needed or desired, preferably by describing their views rather than by quoting them.

Quoting or otherwise indicating what scholars have thought about some philosophical view provides background for the ideal reader and evidence for your professor that you have done research on and are well informed about your topic. There are many other places in this essay that could be expanded in various ways. For example, see the note to [11].

[6] This and the next sentence complete the discussion of I.A.2. Notice the parallel structure of [4], which begins "One interpretation," and [6], which begins "The other interpretation." This kind of structure ties together different sentences and contributes to what is called "coherence" or "cohesion" in an essay.

[7] This sentence is co-ordinate with [5]. It completes the discussion of I.A.2: "Report what previous philosophers have thought about this topic."

[8] This sentence satisfies I.B: "State what is to be proved; state the thesis."

[9] This sentence partially satisfies I.B. It further explains the thesis. It slightly repeats the information given in [6], but the repetition is worthwhile if the author thinks that the audience might not be very familiar with Hobbesian scholarship. The repetition saves the reader from looking back to see what the Taylor–Warrender Thesis is.

commands it. [10]But my interpretation also incorporates the main feature of the Secular Thesis, since what God commands is deducible by reason.

[11]Hobbes often asserts that moral laws, which he identifies with dictates of reason, are divine laws (Leviathan, ed. C. B. Macpherson, Penguin Books, 1962, c. 31, p. 399). He also says "The Word of

---

[10] This sentence continues to satisfy I.B. Like [9], it slightly repeats earlier information.
[11] The sentences of this segment satisfy both II: "Give the argument for the proposition to be proved" and IV: "Show that the premises are true," especially IV.A: "Give the evidence for the premises." The argument is so brief and simple that its premises are not even stated in the essay. One consequence is that there is no need to include in the essay anything that would satisfy item III: "Show that the argument is valid."

If the argument were spelled out, it would look like this:

> If Hobbes says that laws of nature are divine laws, then
>   Hobbes believes that laws of nature are divine laws.
> Hobbes says that laws of nature are divine laws.
> ---
> Hobbes believes that laws of nature are divine laws.

(Some philosophers would claim that [11] does not express an *argument* but only a proposition and the evidence for its truth. I do not wish to argue the point here and ask that it be accepted as an argument for the sake of exposition.)

There is a good reason to spell out this simple argument here, though not in the essay itself. Some scholars think the argument is unsound; depending upon how "say" is defined, it is either the first or second premise that is false. For example, Leo Strauss thinks that for political reasons Hobbes, like many other philosophers, wrote words that he did not intend to be taken literally. In an essay as short as this one (two pages), there is no room to discuss Strauss's interpretation or even to mention it.

If the essay were expanded into a 10- or 20-page version, then it would be appropriate to introduce Strauss's views at this point. (For further discussion of this issue, see chapter 4, section 5, "Successive Elaboration.")

Let's now consider how [11] satisfies item IV. In the first sentence of [11], the author gives a reference to *Leviathan*, which purportedly substantiates her position. In the next sentence, the author actually quotes Hobbes's own words as evidence for her view and also provides a further reference to Hobbes's work. The last sentence of the paragraph claims that other evidence could be provided although it does not provide any of it. The author has presented a fair amount of evidence for the truth of the premise, "Hobbes says that the laws of nature are divine laws." However, in a longer essay, more evidence and some discussion of the evidence would have to be provided.

God, is then also to be taken for the Dictates of reason, and equity" (Leviathan, p. 456; see also De Cive 4.1). From the many passages that could be cited, it is clear that Hobbes's adherence to this doctrine is genuine; it was not asserted only once or half-heartedly.

[12]The view that the moral laws must be obeyed because they are commanded by God can also be proven by an argument that Hobbes has to accept. Moral laws are laws. All laws require a lawgiver. There is no lawgiver for moral law other than God. Therefore, God is the lawgiver of moral law.

---

[12] This paragraph develops a second argument for the author's thesis. Although in theory one sound argument for a proposition is sufficient to prove it, in practice it is often necessary to develop more than one sound argument in an essay in order for the author to succeed in her purpose. There are at least two reasons for this. First, an audience will often not recognize an argument as sound if it is the only sound argument presented for the conclusion. It seems to be a psychological fact about humans that it is easier for them to see some argument as sound if there are several other arguments, even logically independent of the first, that have the same conclusion. Second, an author's audience is diverse. Different people will recognize different arguments as sound. One person may be persuaded by one sound argument, while another person by another, depending upon each person's previously held beliefs and principles of evidence. Thus, in order to persuade a lot of people, it is typically necessary to develop several arguments for the same conclusion. To say this, however, is not to encourage an author to present her arguments too briefly or with insufficient detail. It is also not to encourage the author to present as many arguments as she can, no matter how bad or seemingly bad. Presenting a bad argument, or even one that appears to be bad, might be detrimental to the author's goal. Even though an unsound argument for a proposition does not indicate that that proposition is false, it may have the psychological effect of causing the audience to think that the proposition is false. So far as the persuasiveness of an essay is concerned, presenting 20 bad arguments for a thesis might do more harm than simply presenting one sound argument. It should still be emphasized that a conclusion is true if there is even one sound argument for it, and the existence of a million bad arguments in support does not prove that the conclusion is false.

If the argument of item [12] were made explicit, it would look like this:

Moral laws are laws.
All laws require a lawgiver.
There is no lawgiver for moral law other than God.
God is the lawgiver of moral law.

[13]One objection to my thesis is that Hobbes makes no appeal to God when he deduces the moral laws.

[14]My reply to this objection is that it is not necessary for Hobbes to mention God in the deduction of the moral laws. [15]The first step in understanding why this is correct is to draw a distinction between the form and the content of a law. [16]For Hobbes, as for any command theorist, a law has two parts: there is its content, which expresses what is to be done, and there is its form, which expresses the authority that obliges that it be done. [17]For example, the sentence, "I command that anyone who borrows something returns that thing in the same condition that it was lent," is properly used to express a law, when it is uttered by a sovereign.

---

[13] This sentence introduces item IV.B: Raise objections. It is the topic sentence of the paragraph. It invites the question, "Why doesn't Hobbes mention God in his deduction of the moral law?" The question is answered in the immediately following sentences.

The objection is a standard one raised by opponents of the Taylor–Warrender Thesis. Thus, this objection fits more specifically under section IV.B.1.a. In a longer essay, it would be appropriate to give a reference to at least the most important of these opponents and even to describe their objection at some length. If this essay were a draft of a longer essay that the author was composing by the method of "Successive Elaboration," then this would be an appropriate place for expanding the essay in the way just described. Because this essay is brief, even the references to the opponents of Taylor and Warrender have been omitted. It expresses in an unqualified way the general view of the author. This general view needs elaboration, which is presented in the following sentences.

[14] This sentence begins the answer to the objection expressed in [13]. It thus begins to satisfy item IV.C.

[15] This sentence continues item IV.C. Although it is not obvious – and it needn't be – from this sentence that the distinction between form and content is a very important one, it will become obvious in due course. It is important for an author not to rush her exposition. She shouldn't try to say everything that needs to be said in one or two sentences; she needs to uncover her thought step by step in neither a hurried nor a dawdling way.

The most important point of an essay should not be introduced as a reply to an objection, for a reply is by its nature a subordinate part of the essay. Nonetheless, it is often legitimate to introduce somewhat important points as replies. If all the replies were relatively unimportant, then the essay would be rather boring to read.

[16] This sentence continues item IV.C. Further, although it begins by relating to Hobbes ("For Hobbes"), it immediately broadens its importance by generalizing it ("as for any command theorist"). The rest of the sentence then characterizes the difference between the form and content of a law. A characterization is always general and abstract.

[17] This sentence gives an example of what is characterized in [16]. It makes the characterization less abstract.

[18]It is divisible into two parts. [19]The phrase, "I command," expresses the form of the law; or, as Hobbes says, "The stile of a Law is, *We command*" (*Leviathan*, p. 588; see also p. 317). [20]The rest of the sentence expresses its content.

[21]Although the form of moral laws is immediately clear ("I, God, command"), the content is not. For humans have no direct access to God, since He is invisible and otherwise unable to be sensed. Nonetheless, humans do know some things about God, such as that He is rational. Further, laws must be rational. An irrational or contradictory law is an impossibility. Now, since whatever is rational is deducible by reason, the content of the moral law is deducible by reason.

[22]The upshot of this discussion is that the content of the moral law is deducible by reason but not from our knowledge of the nature of God; and God's command is what makes this content a law and hence obligatory.

---

[18] This sentence begins with an explanation of the example. It is proleptic and finds its realization in the following two sentences, items [19] and [20].

[19] This sentence explains which part of the example concerns the form of a law and relates it to Hobbes's own words ("as Hobbes says"). There is a certain redundancy in the information given in [19], but it is justified, because the author's point is not one that is likely to be familiar to the reader and having it explained in two different ways makes the reader's burden lighter.

[20] This sentence is co-ordinate with [19]. But [20] is much briefer than [19]. More, it seems, needs to be said, and it is said in the next paragraph.

[21] The phrases "the form of moral laws" and "the content" in the first sentence of this paragraph tie this paragraph to the immediately preceding one. Again, this creates cohesion. Most of this paragraph presents a reconstruction of how Hobbes relates the content of a moral law as rational (or deducible) to the form of a moral law.

This completes the discussion of IV.C.

[22] This paragraph satisfies V: Conclusion. It summarizes the argument of the entire essay.

3.3   Another Essay

There is no need to follow the outline structure that I have given. Here's a well-structured essay that does not tightly fit "The Structure of a Philosophical Essay." Comments are in footnotes, in order to avoid having them confused with the numbered propositions in the essay.

The Great Fear and Ignorance Argument[1]

The single most impressive argument in the philosophy of Thomas Hobbes is what I shall call "The Great Fear and Ignorance Argument."[2] It is a crucial part of his argument that human beings need an absolute sovereign to govern them.[3]

(1) Some people in the state of nature are dangerous. (2) It is very difficult to know who these people are. Therefore, (3) It is necessary to be afraid of everyone.[4]

The argument occurs in *De Cive*, the second of Hobbes's three books on political philosophy.[5]

---

[1]   Titles are important. They should always be informative, and sometimes they can be catchy too, as this one is supposed to be. How could fear and ignorance be the topic of an interesting argument in philosophy? Perhaps the word "ignorance" indicates that the essay has something to do with skepticism. Is the argument about great fear, or is it a great argument? The essay itself will show that the author intends both. At this point, the title is simply provocative.

[2]   This first sentence orients the reader by giving him background information. The essay will be about an important argument in the philosophy of Thomas Hobbes.

[3]   This second sentence continues to orient the reader by giving information about the immediate context of Hobbes's argument.

[4]   The author is not wasting any time in presenting the argument. She is confident that this brief argument is intriguing and will incline the reader to continue reading. It also gives the reader the opportunity to stop reading if he thinks that there is no hope of this argument being interesting.

[5]   A student author provides this kind of information in order to show her professor that she has some wider knowledge of Hobbes's philosophy than just the argument of *De Cive* and also to provide context.

The argument is impressive because it is very brief and yet cogent. It begins with an indisputable[6] premise. The state of nature is the condition human beings are in when there are no laws.

In addition to its importance for proving the necessity of government,[7] another reason for holding that the argument is powerful is that it is easily adapted to explain the reasoning of other social phenomena. Every schoolchild is instructed in the program "Stranger Danger." Here is its underlying argument:

(SD-1) Some strangers are dangerous.
(SD-2) You, child, cannot be sure which strangers are dangerous.
Therefore, (SD-3) You must be afraid of all strangers.

Notice its similarity to the Great Fear and Ignorance Argument.[8] The Stranger Danger Argument may be even more forceful than the original argument because children are more vulnerable in our society than adults are.

But the general argument form has many more applications. Here are two that may be called "The Policeman's Argument" and "The Feminists' Argument."[9]

(PA-1) Some motorists who are stopped for a traffic violation are dangerous.
(PA-2) A policeman cannot be sure which motorists are dangerous.

---

[6]   The author was tempted to write "incontrovertible." That would have been a very good word to use in the seventeenth century, but since "indisputable" is more familiar and does the same work, it is better. Don't use unfamiliar words unnecessarily.

[7]   This opening phrase connects this paragraph with the earlier statement of the importance of Hobbes's argument. So the phrase contributes to the coherence of the essay.

[8]   This sentence contributes to both the logical and rhetorical coherence of the essay.

[9]   The form of Hobbes's argument is given wider application. Notice that the essay unfolds in stages: Hobbes's argument, an argument of the same form about strangers, and two arguments of the same form about policemen and feminists. Contrast this with giving all four arguments at once or Hobbes's argument followed by the three others. Readers need to be given time to process the information being presented.

> Therefore, (PA-3) A policeman must be afraid of all motorists.
> (WA-1) Some males are rapists.
> (WA-2) A woman cannot be sure which males are rapists.
> Therefore, (WA-3) A woman must be afraid of all males.

Other forms are easily constructed using the fears that African Americans have about White Racists.[10]

Let's now introduce an additional aspect of Hobbes's Great Fear and Ignorance Argument.[11] Each person I in the state of nature is intelligent enough to construct the argument for himself and will know that every other person is constructing the same argument with respect to I. That is, every person thinks that I is dangerous. So each person has a good reason to launch a preemptive strike against I. Knowing this, I also has a good reason to launch a preemptive strike against everyone else.

But this is the same as being in a state of war with everyone else, for, as Hobbes said, war does not require actual fighting, but any tendency to fight. That is why the relations between the United States and the Soviet Union during the second half of the twentieth century were called a Cold War. It was a war with little actual fighting.

The Policeman's Argument invites introducing another aspect of Hobbes's original argument.[12] What attitude will a motorist take when she realizes that the policeman is suspicious of her behavior? It will be negative and probably something that includes anger and resentment. This will make relations between the policeman and motorists worse.

---

[10] It's unnecessary to spell out the premises and conclusion for these arguments since the form of the previous arguments makes it clear how it should be done.

[11] Another aspect of the original argument, or something related to it, is now being presented. Uncover your argument step by step.

[12] The essay concludes with a provocative question and a comment about the practical implication of two of the arguments discussed. A further generalization of that implication is straightforward.

> The point of Hobbes's argument is to get people
> to see that unrestricted freedom is not a good thing
> and that government is necessary for a decent life.
> Government reduces the number of dangerous people
> and the occasions when they can act. But the power
> of government is always limited; and even within civil
> societies, children, women, some minorities, and even
> policemen have reason to be afraid.[13]

---

[13] The concluding paragraph repeats the main point of Hobbes's argument and describes the importance of the related arguments.

4

Composing

There are various stages of composing an essay. The first stage may involve preliminaries that only minimally involve writing; note taking and writing down initial thoughts are commonly a second stage, followed by writing a first draft, followed by successive drafts. Among the preliminaries are selecting a topic and tentatively outlining your essay. Writing successive drafts includes writing second and third drafts and polishing. Not all of these topics will be discussed in this chapter. You can find discussions of all of them in any number of general books on writing. Yet, there is one point to underscore: Writing must be done in stages. Do not expect to produce an essay of high quality if you write it straight through in one draft. Some students think that they have a genius for writing. Most are wrong. Few people are geniuses, and people with a genius for writing are fewer still. Thomas Edison's adage, "Genius is 1 percent inspiration and 99 percent perspiration," is close to correct. Writing is a kind of labor. After Adam sinned, God said to him (Genesis 3:17):

> Because you have listened to your wife
> and have eaten from the tree which I forbade you,
> accursed shall be the ground on your account.
> With labor you shall win your food from it
> all the days of your life.
> And with labor you shall write your essays
> all the nights of your life.

It is tragic that some scribe, cosmically depressed by his fate, omitted the last two lines at some stage of transmitting the Bible to later generations. I have written at some length about the stages of composing an essay, because too many authors neglect these stages.

Philosophical Writing: An Introduction, Fifth Edition. A. P. Martinich.
© 2025 John Wiley & Sons, Inc. Published 2025 by John Wiley & Sons, Inc.
Companion website: www.wiley.com/go/Martinich5e

For most of the stages of composing, nothing more needs to be added since most of the stages of philosophical composing are the same as those of other disciplines. However, there are some techniques of composing philosophical essays that pose some special problems for students. I have developed some techniques that have benefited my students and are not discussed in other books. These techniques are the topic of this chapter.

4.1   How to Select an Essay Topic

Before setting out to write, you need to select a topic. Your professor may have given you very specific topics from which to choose or he may allow you to shape your own topic from a general one. Since this latter possibility is the more troublesome, I will assume that you are in that situation. Some general topics are:

the problem of universals;
the nature of free will;
the problem of determinism;
the relationship between mind and body;
Plato's theory of the Good;
Anselm's ontological argument;
the meaning of Descartes's *cogito, ergo sum*.

It is virtually impossible to write a good essay if your topic is not more specific than these are. Notice that these topics are formulated as noun phrases. They do not commit the author of an essay to any particular position. For example, the first topic listed, the problem of universals, is neutral between the belief that universals exist and the belief that they do not. Essay topics should not be neutral. The author of an essay should commit herself to some position. Whether it is true or false, asserting some position gives the student a place from which to begin. In order to ensure that your topic expresses some position, formulate it as a declarative sentence:

Universals do not exist.
No humans have free will.
Determinism is true.
Mind and body are identical.

For our purposes, it is not important whether you argue that there are universals or that there are not; what is important is that you commit yourself to one position or another. For it will be that commitment from which your essay will develop.

The topics listed above may be appropriate for essays in introductory classes in philosophy. In advanced classes, they are too broad. The more advanced the study of some topic is, the narrower the topics are. One reason for this is that in introductory classes, students have less to say about topics because they know less; thus the topics are broader. In advanced courses, students know more and have more to say about topics; thus the topics can be narrower. People who complain that professional philosophy is too narrow do not realize that this is a sign of progress in philosophy. How many of them would complain about the narrowness of most scientific research projects?

4.2   Techniques for Composing

There are a number of techniques that you can use to begin the process of drafting your essay:

Outlining your ideas (see section 4.3)
Successive elaboration (see section 4.5)
Conceptual note taking (see section 4.6)

None of these techniques is inherently better than any other. The best technique is the one that works for you, the one that gets the essay written. Yes, written. If something is worth doing, it is worth doing badly. It goes without saying that writing a good essay is even better than writing a bad one. Which technique is best is relative to the author and to the occasion of her writing. Students write more or less on demand: "Your assignment for Monday is to write a 1,000-word essay on 'The influence of Indian mysticism on Plotinus' doctrine of the descent of the soul'." That's probably not a topic that you would have wanted to write about in the normal course of events.

On some topics, your thoughts may be sufficiently well ordered to allow you to outline your ideas immediately. On other topics, you may know only that you want to defend a certain proposition and need to elaborate it during successive drafts. On still other topics, you may have nothing more at the beginning than a number of half-formed thoughts that need to be written down without being censored by your critical faculties.

These techniques are not mutually exclusive. Two or even all three can be used in the composition of an essay, and two or all three might be used on some segments of the essay, and not others. When several techniques are used, it is not important in what order they are used. Further, one technique can be used more than once; you can use one technique, then another, and then return to the first.

4.3   Outlining

Outlining serves the same purpose as the "Outline of the Structure of a Philosophical Essay" in chapter 3. It makes the content of your essay clearer by making its structure clearer. During those initial efforts at composing, outlining can be as helpful for figuring out *what* you want to say as *how* you should say it.

When I was an undergraduate, the culmination of "History of English Literature: *Beowulf* to *The Waste Land*" (a yearlong course required of *all* sophomores, engineers, and business students included) was the submission of a research paper, 6,000–7,000 words. In addition to the paper itself, all the note cards students had accumulated in the process of research, all preliminary drafts, and an outline of the paper had to be submitted as supporting evidence. (There were stories about this material being submitted in bushel baskets by the more ambitious students. I never saw this done.)

The outline was supposed to have been written prior to the writing of the paper. I cheated. Not being skilled at writing outlines, I wrote the outline *after* I had written the paper. I justified this violation with the sophomoric – or was it Platonic? – argument that I couldn't know what the outline of the paper would be until after it was written. Nonetheless, writing the outline after the paper is written is not a bad idea, as a means of checking for coherence and intelligibility. If you *can* write a plausible outline from your paper, then you are sure that it has an intelligible structure. If you find that you cannot do so, then something is wrong with its structure, and you should fix it.

4.4   The Rhetoric of Philosophical Writing

Rhetoric is often described as the art of persuasion. Since a person can be persuaded by bad reasoning and insufficient, misleading, or false evidence, it has often been contrasted with philosophy, which is supposed to aim exclusively at truth and valid reasoning. Nonetheless, an aspect of philosophical writing that is essential to cogent argumentation (see chapter 2, section 2.3) is aptly termed "rhetoric" because it concerns how to construct the language that is supposed to get the reader to recognize the sound argumentation.

Quite a bit has already been said about the rhetoric of philosophical writing in chapter 3, "The Structure of a Philosophical Essay." By stating one's thesis near the beginning of the paper, then by laying out the argument, and finally raising and answering objections, the author has gone a long way to getting the reader to recognize a sound argument, if it is sound.

There are some other things to keep in mind in order to present your argument in the best way.

Don't let a text dominate your essay. Many of your essays will give an exposition of some philosopher's argument. Often, following the order in which the philosopher has presented the argument is the order in which you should present it. But not always. In a debate on free will between Thomas Hobbes and John Bramhall, Bramhall began by stating what kind of freedom ("liberty") he was not going to defend: not liberty not to sin, not liberty from misery, and so on. Only later does he say something positive about what he means by liberty. If an author follows Bramhall's exposition, she might write this:

> Bramhall initially described his doctrine of liberty in negative terms. What he advocates is "neither a liberty from sin, nor a liberty from misery, nor a liberty from servitude, nor a liberty from violence." A bit more informative is his denial that human actions are necessitated: "I understand a liberty from necessity or rather from necessitation, that is, a universal immunity from all inevitability and determination to one." Bramhall is in effect saying that Hobbes is wrong. Later Bramhall explains his view more clearly in positive terms by committing himself to "liberty of election," where election is an "act of judgment and understanding."

The author at least implies that Bramhall's negative assertions are not as helpful as his positive assertions that come later. But the author reproduces Bramhall's unhelpful order. The author can improve on Bramhall's own statement of his position by beginning with the positive characterization and then adding the negative ones in order to give a complete exposition of what Bramhall wrote:

> Bramhall describes his doctrine of liberty as "liberty of election," where election is an "act of judgment and understanding." This liberty needs to be distinguished from what he calls "a liberty from sin, ... a liberty from misery, ... a liberty from servitude, [and] ... a liberty from violence." A bit more informative is his denial that human actions are necessitated: "I understand a liberty from necessity or rather from necessitation, that is, a universal immunity from all inevitability and determination to one." Bramhall is in

effect saying that Hobbes is wrong in holding that every event is necessary. Bramhall then goes on to commit himself to two concepts of liberty: "a liberty to do this or that good" and "a liberty to do and not do good and evil."

The author's revised paragraph has control over Bramhall's text.

Collect your thoughts. "Collect your thoughts" means that the sentences in a paragraph should follow a logical order. You need to take some additional time to figure out how they should be rearranged. If you repeat the same points in different paragraphs, you probably have not collected your thoughts. The following passage does not have its thoughts ordered correctly:

> Although [1]Kant thought people did not have a right to revolt, [2]he approved of the French Revolution. [3]Revolution would upset the system of laws.

Comment: The "although"-clause talks about Kant's opposition to revolution, as does the second sentence, [3] which begins *Revolution....* But the clause in between these two, [2], is about his approval of the French Revolution and interferes with the point of the clauses [1] and [3]. Here is a coherent ordering of thoughts:

> [2a]Kant did not think that people have a right to revolt because [3a]revolution upsets the system of laws. However, [1a]he approved of the French Revolution.

Comment: Notice that this revision suggests that the author should continue this paragraph by talking about why Kant made an exception of the French Revolution. [2a] and [3a] provide background to the exception of the French Revolution.

Exercise: Rewrite the first draft to make the essay about Kant's reasons for thinking that people did not have a right to revolt.

4.5 Successive Elaboration

One technique that students have found very helpful for improving their writing is what I call "successive elaboration." With this technique, you begin by stating *in one sentence* the thesis or main point of your essay. When formulating that single sentence, think about the possible background information your readers might need, and you should feel free to use technical terms. The required background information and explanation of technical terms should be supplied in the successive elaborations. For example, you might know that you want your essay to prove this:

Some human actions are free.

Your next step is to build upon this one sentence, perhaps, by supplying the premises that you think prove it:

Some human actions are free, for humans are held responsible for some actions, and persons can be held responsible only for free actions.

Now this essay fragment should be elaborated. It can be elaborated in a number of ways that are *suggested by the essay itself*. What is an action? What is it for an action to be free? What is responsibility? Not all of these questions need to be answered in the next elaboration. Here's one possible elaboration:

Some human actions are free, for humans are held responsible for some actions and persons can be held responsible only for free actions. In order to understand this argument, several terms need to be explained. By a free action, I mean an action that is not caused by any event other than an act of will. By being responsible for an action, I mean an action for which a person might be praised or blamed appropriately. And by an action, I mean any change that that is caused by a motion internal to it.

This elaboration suggests other questions and issues: Why is the issue of free will important? Why do some philosophers think that no actions are free? The elaboration of the essay fragment proceeds by trying to answer these questions, either partially or wholly. Notice that the essay, as developed so far, begins abruptly; it does not yet have an introduction. Both the question "Why is the issue of free will important?" and the notion of responsibility in the central argument suggest an appropriate introduction. Although students often think that the introduction must be the first thing they write and the conclusion the last, it seems to me that the opposite is true more often than not. You cannot introduce a reader to where you want to take him unless you already have a clear idea of where you want to go. Now read this elaboration:

One of the most important issues for human beings is also one of the central issues in philosophy. It concerns freedom and responsibility. In this essay, I will argue that some human actions are free, for humans are held responsible for some actions and persons can be held responsible only for free actions.

In order to understand this argument, several terms need to be explained or defined. By "free action," I mean an action that is not caused by any event other than an act of will. By "being responsible for an action," I mean an action for which a person might be praised or blamed. And by "action," I mean any change in a body or mind that is caused by a motion internal to it.

The biggest obstacle to the view that some human actions are free is the belief in universal causation, that is, the view that every event is caused by some other event.

In this example of successive elaboration, I have added text to both the front and the back of the essay fragment. Often sentences need to be inserted between the existing sentences, and those sentences modified in order to accommodate the new text.

The great advantages of this method are order and control of the way the essay develops. The method is orderly because every addition is justified and is invited by some part of the text. The method is controlled because at each stage of the elaboration the author knows what has dictated the additional text; at each stage, the author knows what is earlier and hence more basic than other parts.

A student might balk at the process of successive elaboration on the ground that it overcommits her at too early a stage of her writing. A student might protest, "But what if I make a mistake? What if the proposition I formulate as my main thesis is wrong? What if I formulate bad arguments for my wrong thesis? And how could I know my thesis is wrong and my arguments bad unless I first have good arguments?"

My reply is that even if an author *begins* drafting an essay with a thesis that she later finds out is false, and even if she constructs arguments for it that she later determines to be spurious, she has lost little or nothing. For, in discovering that a thesis is false, she has indirectly discovered the truth: the negation of her original thesis. Further, she has discovered some arguments that might lead or have led other people to believe the false thesis, namely, the very arguments the author had devised for her original thesis.

These are fruitful discoveries. For, if nothing else, the author can recast the essay she originally intended to write in a very simple way. Suppose she originally intended her main thesis to be "unicorns exist." Suppose her basic argument was such and such. But then she discovered that her reasoning was faulty for such and such reason. Then she might reformulate her essay in this way:

> It is plausible that unicorns exist. For such and such. However, this argument is not cogent. For so and so.

Often what an author discovers in drafting is not merely that her original thesis was wrong but that it was simplistic and needed some qualification or other restriction in order to make it true. For example, in her desire to refute determinism, a student might first formulate her thesis too strongly as "All human actions are free," and then, thinking that digestion and salivating are human actions, she might weaken her thesis to "Some human actions are free." (Alternatively, the student will realize that "human action" does not include nonvoluntary events like digestion and salivating.)

Here are some elaborate examples of successive elaboration. Three short essays about the proper way to interpret the Second Amendment of the US Constitution are given. These are followed by longer versions of each of the three essays. Study how each gets expanded.

First Interpretation (First Version)

ONLY ARMS USED BY THE MILITIA ARE CONSTITUTIONALLY GUARANTEED

The proper interpretation of the second Amendment to the US Constitution requires some historical information about it in order to understand it. In the eighteenth century, American colonists were worried about being dominated by a standing army; that is, a permanent, professional army, which could consist of mercenaries to a greater or lesser degree. In contrast to an army, a militia was an occasional force, made up of nonprofessional soldiers. The difference between an army and a militia is maintained in the United States between the army, governed by the federal government, and state militias, although state militias today are more professional than they were in the eighteenth century.

This historical information makes sense of the preamble to the second amendment, "A well-regulated militia being necessary to the security of a free State." It means that the citizens of states must have the right to form militias; and in the eighteenth century, this required citizens, more particularly, males of a certain age, to keep a gun because militias depended on the private firearms of its members.

The circumstances of the eighteenth century no longer exist. State militias have weapons stored in secure locations in militia camps. As long as arms are available to citizens who serve in the militia when called upon, there is no need to allow private citizens in their private capacity any gun or rifle at all. (226 words)

Second Interpretation (First Version)

OWNERSHIP OF ALL WEAPONS IS CONSTITUTIONALLY GUARANTEED

The meaning of the second amendment is clear on its face. Private citizens have the right to bear arms. No more would need to be said about this interpretation if opponents of the second amendment did not confuse the issue with irrelevancies.

Granted that in the eighteenth century, American colonists who would serve in militias if the need to defend a town or colony arose, kept their own guns because there was no safe, central place in which to store them; and granted that in the twenty-first century militias do store weapons in a safe place, the meaning of the operative clause does not change its meaning. Private citizens have a right to keep and bear arms. Moreover, the amendment does not state any limit on the number or nature of the weapons a citizen may own. That means that a citizen has a constitutional right to own rocket propelled grenades and their launchers, heavy machine guns, tanks, and fighter jets. Few if any people have the money or the desire to own such things. But they are protected by the Constitution. Remember, the justification for the constitutional right to bear arms was to protect citizens against a tyrannical government. Restricting the amendment to the possession of handguns, shot guns, and hunting rifles is inconsistent with the purpose of the amendment.

If an owner of a weapon uses it illegally – and not against a tyrannical government – then they are subject to criminal penalties. (243 words)

Third Interpretation (First Version)

THE SUPREME COURT MUST DECIDE WHAT
THE SECOND AMENDMENT ALLOWS

The meaning of the second amendment appears to be clear on its face: private citizens can own and bear weapons. But it is not so clear, as an understanding of other Constitutional amendments makes even clearer. The first amendment says that Congress shall make no law abridging the right of free speech. Supporters of this amendment often emphasize the word "no." they say that the amendment categorically and absolutely prohibits all abridgment of free speech.

Their view is obviously wrong. The Supreme Court a century ago declared that one does not have the right to shout "fire!" in a crowded theater if there is no fire. People do not have the right to maliciously print or speak false things about a private person who leads a private life. What appears to be an unrestricted right is not an unrestricted right. Similarly, the right to own and bear arms is restricted. Private citizens may bear arms when they are operating as part of a state militia. But it is not clear in what other situations they may have the right to keep and bear arms. The supreme Court has to decide this by using their best judgment. (196 words)

In what follows – the expansions and revisions of the essays above – deleted words and phrases are struck through and additions are in bold-face type.

First Interpretation (Expanded)

ONLY ARMS USED BY THE MILITIA ARE
CONSTITUTIONALLY GUARANTEED

The Second Amendment to the US Constitution is only 27 words long: A well-regulated Militia, being necessary to the security of a free State, the right of the people to

---

keep and bear arms, shall not be infringed. Nonetheless, its correct interpretation ~~the proper interpretation of the second Amendment to the Us Constitution~~ requires some historical information **in order to know what the American People meant by it**. In the eighteenth century, American colonists were worried about being dominated by a **government that kept a** standing army; that is, a permanent, professional army, which could consist of mercenaries to a greater or lesser degree. In contrast to an army, a militia was an occasional force, made up of nonprofessional soldiers. The difference between an army and a militia **today** is maintained in the United States ~~between the army,~~ **by having the regular armed forces** governed by the federal government, and ~~state~~ militias, **governed by the individual states.** ~~although state militias today are more professional than they were in the eighteenth century.~~

This historical information makes sense of the preamble to the second amendment, "A well-regulated militia being necessary to the security of a free state." it means that the citizens of states must have the right to form militias; and in the eighteenth century, this **often** required citizens, more particularly, males of a certain age, to keep a gun because militias depended **to a large extent** on the private firearms of its members.

The circumstances of the eighteenth century no longer exist. State militias have weapons stored in secure locations in militia camps. As long as arms are available to citizens who serve in the militia when called upon, there is no need to allow private citizens in their private capacity any gun or rifle at all. (268 words)

Second Interpretation (Expanded)

OWNERSHIP OF ALL WEAPONS IS
CONSTITUTIONALLY GUARANTEED

The meaning of the second amendment is clear on its face. Private citizens have the right to bear arms: **"the right of**

the people to keep and bear arms, shall not be infringed."
No more would need to be said about this interpretation if
opponents of the second amendment did not confuse the
issue with irrelevancies.

Granted, ~~that~~ in the eighteenth century American
colonists who ~~would~~ serve**d** in militias ~~if the need to
defend a town or colony arose~~ kept their own guns
because there was no safe, central place in which to
store them; **further** ~~and~~ granted, ~~that~~ in the twenty-
first **century** militias do store weapons in a safe place.
Nevertheless, the meaning of the operative clause does
not change its meaning. Private citizens have a right to
keep and bear arms. Moreover, the amendment does not
state any limit on the number or nature of the weapons
a citizen may own. That means that a citizen has a
constitutional right to own rocket propelled grenades
and their launchers, heavy machine guns, tanks, and
fighter jets. Few if any people have the money or the
desire to own such things. But they are protected by
the Constitution. Remember, the justification for the
constitutional right to bear arms was to protect citizens
against a tyrannical government. Restricting the
amendment to the possession of handguns, shot guns,
and hunting rifles is inconsistent with the purpose of
the amendment.

If an owner of a weapon uses it illegally – and not
against a tyrannical government – then they are subject
to criminal penalties. **So the literal meaning of the
Second Amendment does not threaten the safety of US
citizens. (276)**

Third Interpretation (Expanded)

WHAT THE SECOND AMENDMENT ALLOWS

The meaning of the second amendment appears to be
clear on its face: private citizens can own and bear
weapons: **"the right of the people to keep and bear arms,
shall not be infringed."** But it is not so clear; **and we can
show this by considering our**, ~~as an~~ understanding of

86

other Constitutional amendments. ~~make even clearer~~.
The first amendment says that Congress shall make no
law abridging the right of free speech. Supporters of
this amendment often emphasize the word "no." they
say that the amendment categorically and absolutely
prohibits all abridgment of free speech.

Their view is obviously wrong. The supreme Court a
century ago declared that one does not have the right
to shout "fire!" in a crowded theater if there is no fire.
People do not have the right to maliciously print or
speak false things about a private person who leads a
private life. What appears to be an unrestricted right is
not an unrestricted right.

Similarly, the right to own and bear arms is
restricted. Private citizens may bear arms when they
are operating as part of a state militia, **as the preamble
makes clear**.

**Perhaps a surprising consequence of this
interpretation is that the Constitution does not give
citizens unrestricted right to keep or bear even
handguns. Prohibiting citizens who are not actively
serving in a militia the right from keeping and bearing
guns does not contradict the purpose of the Second
Amendment: "A well-regulated Militia ... [is] necessary
to the security of a free State."** (256 words)

Exercises

1 Choose one of the expanded versions and further expand it to
form an essay of between 400 and 500 words. (Hint: One way to
expand the essays is to consider objections to the interpretation
that were raised in one of the other theories or that might have
been raised by them.)

2 This exercise has three parts:
   (a) State the main point of an article or chapter assigned by
        your professor in 35 words or less.
   (b) Restate the main point of the article or chapter described
        in (a), this time in 60–85 words. This short essay must

incorporate the sentences written for the answer to (a) almost verbatim; only minor stylistic changes, such as punctuation or the insertion or deletion of transitional phrases are permissible. Interlacing new sentences between the sentences of (a) is permissible.

(c) Restate the main point of the article or chapter described in (b), this time in 140–165 words. The same constraints specified in (b) apply to this essay.

4.6 Conceptual Note Taking

The two techniques already discussed, outlining and successive elaboration, assume that the author has a good grasp of the structure and direction of the essay before she begins writing. Often, this is not the case. As I was writing this, artificial intelligence produced a powerful app that can be put to good use if you have writer's block. Use ChatGPT to stimulate your thoughts. The answers that it may give you to simple questions may put you on track of an essay topic. I don't recommend using ChatGPT as a substitute for writing your essay. It should help you walk through an essay and not be a pony you ride.[1]

ChatGPT does not exclude other ways of forestalling writer's block such as *conceptual note taking*, a kind of uncensored writing that is similar to what some have called *free writing* and others *brainstorming*. Students sometimes mistakenly transform causes for not writing into justifications for not writing. That is unfortunate. Conceptual note taking undercuts writer's block because it is a process in which nothing that is written counts as wrong. Indeed, whatever is written contributes in some way to whatever becomes the final product, even if what is written is discarded at some point. Moreover, even the thought that the author has nothing to say counts as a legitimate thought to be expressed. Once the sentence

I have nothing to say about the problem of universals

---

[1] In April 2023, it was reported that ChatGPT scored in the 91st percentile in microeconomics and in the 91st percentile in macroeconomics compared to economics majors. For philosophy questions, it occasionally performed badly; in addition to mistakes, often odd ones, some of the references were mistaken. However, submitting the same questions two weeks later produced a much better but still not wholly reliable answer. I believe it is self-correcting.

is written, another suggests itself:

I don't even know what a universal is.

And others:

Professor Rebus argued in this way: Suppose a piece of paper called
A is white and another piece of paper called *B* is also white. Then
they have something in common, whiteness, and it is not identical
with *A* or *B*. Such things are universals.

Conceptual note taking objectifies your philosophical stream of consciousness, which remains mysterious, haunting, and impenetrable until it
is externalized.

The second purpose of conceptual note taking is to provide you with
materials to be organized and evaluated in preparation for writing a good
first draft. Typically, conceptual note taking does not yield a good draft,
nor is it supposed to.

Often when you begin writing with nothing more than some scattered
thoughts on your essay topic, you may have some sentences or examples
that you know should appear somewhere in the essay even though these
sentences do not state the central thesis, and your examples need to be
put into the right context. What you need to do is write down your first
thoughts about the topic. The thoughts you have needn't be precise and
needn't be complete. You may have only a word or phrase in mind that
you will want to think further about and develop later. The thoughts also
needn't be in any particular order. At this stage, what is important is getting half-formed thoughts out of your head and onto paper so that they
can be observed objectively. It is better to write down the thought that
you have, no matter how inchoate and incoherent, than to wait for these
thoughts to coalesce. There will be plenty of time later to figure out
where they go and how they might advance your argument. You might
come to see that you want to hold just the opposite of what you write
down initially. That does not present a problem. For those initial thoughts
present either something to argue against or the basis for demonstrating
and eliminating confusions others may have shared with you. Even if
you decide to discard those initial thoughts, little or nothing has been
lost, as I said above. You might not have been able to write your brilliant
essay if you had not traversed the path paved with your initially obscure
thoughts. Since one of the principal purposes of this exercise is to objectify
your thoughts so that they can be studied, elaborated, and rearranged,

it is often helpful to use relatively small pieces of paper and to put down just one thought on each. You can use 3×5-inch or 5×7-inch filing cards, or 5×7-inch or 9×12-inch tablets. If you use a word processor, put in a "new page" command often. After you have completed your note taking, it is easy to rearrange these cards or pages into a more logical order. Ideas written down at relatively distant times are easily brought together when they exist on separate cards or pages.

4.7   Research and Composing

Many essays require some sort of research, some investigation of the books or articles that scholars have written about your topic. The temptation is to do the research before you begin your own writing, and you may have been taught that this is the recommended procedure. In most cases, I do not recommend this.

Doing research keeps you from writing, and starting to write is typically the hardest thing to do; delaying the start seems most attractive to people. Further, research can inhibit your writing. If you fill your head or your note cards with what other people say, it may seem that no room is left for thinking of what you want to say. Put simply, first write down what you think about the topic; write as much as you can without relying upon what other people have thought. Doing this will force you to think about the topic.

Once you have exhausted your own thoughts, begin your research. It's likely that you will use the internet for much, if not all, of the research. The quality of the information you can find varies from excellent to poor. Three excellent sites are the Stanford Encyclopedia of Philosophy, The Internet Encyclopedia, and Wikipedia. The Stanford Encyclopedia is the best source, but many of its articles require nontrivial knowledge of the topic in order to be appreciated. The Internet Encyclopedia is very good and, in my experience, requires less philosophical knowledge. Wikipedia is good on most topics, but is the least authoritative. For upper-division undergraduates, articles in professional journals are often indispensable or at least valuable. There are so many excellent journals that it is best to ask your professor for guidance.

As you are drafting your essay, be sure to provide documentation for the material according to these rules of thumb:

If something you have written has been written before by someone else, footnote it.

If something you have written has been written better by someone else, quote and footnote it.

If something you have written has been written in more detail elsewhere, adapt it to your essay and footnote it.

If someone has said something relevant to your essay that you think is mistaken, use his view as an objection to yours; footnote and refute it.

In short, don't delay; write first; footnote later.

There is one more case of research impinging on your writing to consider. If you discover that someone else has refuted the position in a draft of your essay, then use it to your advantage. For example, suppose you wrote "such and such" and some scholar, say, Professor Wisdom, has shown that such and such is false; then your draft can be revised as follows:

> One might think that such and such. But, as Professor Wisdom has shown, such and such is incorrect because ....

Since you yourself thought such and such, it probably has some initial plausibility or at least is not intentionally a straw-man argument. Profit from your mistakes and credit the person who got you to see that you were mistaken.

If your writing has become bogged down and you are not able to make any progress, research can sometimes get you writing again. When you run out of ideas or do not know how to go on from some point, read or browse through some books relevant to your topic. Some item in them may stimulate your thinking and hence your writing. It is quite likely that you will need some sort of footnote to acknowledge the help you received from the book if you borrow something substantive from it. For more about footnotes and research, see Appendix C, "Scholarship: Notes, Citations, and References."

As I am writing this, ChatGPT is causing waves in schools and universities. How good is it? How should it be monitored? Should students be allowed to use it? I wish I had good answers. As a practical matter, your professor will answer them, largely based on his or her attitudes and values. If your professor allows it, I think that ChatGPT can be used to edit what you think is a final draft. It will probably smooth out your prose, making it more homogenous than it was. But too much homogeneity is not good. It makes sense to consult the changes that ChatGPT made and then use your own judgment about what if anything to change.

I will give you some idea of what ChatGPT did in April 2023. The first two paragraphs of section 4.8 are the same as those in the 4th edition of *Philosophical Writing*. They are followed by the rewrite performed by ChatGPT.

4.8   Sentences and Paragraphs

Every well-crafted sentence and paragraph has a structure that effectively conveys the idea in it. Let's begin with sentences. Some contain too many ideas, and some not enough. Students often begin an essay that does little or no work: "Descartes was a great philosopher," and "The problem of free will has challenged the greatest minds of philosophers for centuries, even for tens of centuries." Your professor will already know that you know that Descartes was a great philosopher because he said it several times in class, and he knows that you know that the problem of free will has been around for a long time.

Sentences often contain too many ideas. There are two general reasons for this. One is that you want to guard against the professor's thinking that you will not discuss some topic or that you are not aware that the main idea of your sentence involves some problem that needs to be discussed. What you need to understand is that all the relevant issues need to be introduced and dealt with in a deliberate and orderly way. The other reason that too many ideas appear in one sentence is that it makes it easy to write a syntactically complex sentence, and you hope that the complexity will be taken for profundity. I believe it was from John Searle that I first heard the adage, "Whatever can be thought clearly can be said clearly."

Here are the preceding two paragraphs rewritten by ChatGPT:

> The effectiveness of a sentence or paragraph hinges on its structure, which conveys the idea it expresses. Sentences can suffer from containing too few or too many ideas. A common mistake in essays is to begin with a sentence that fails to establish a clear purpose, such as stating the obvious fact that "Descartes was a great philosopher," or offering a trite observation like "The problem of free will has challenged philosophers for centuries." Your professor already knows these facts and expects you to offer a more insightful and substantive analysis.
>
> One reason why sentences may contain too many ideas is to avoid leaving out relevant topics or overlooking a crucial aspect of the main idea. However, it is important to introduce and address all relevant issues in a clear and organized manner. Another reason why sentences can become cluttered with ideas is to create syntactically

complex structures, which may give the impression of profundity. Nonetheless, it is important to remember the maxim of John Searle: "Whatever can be thought clearly can be said clearly." Therefore, strive to express your ideas in a concise and intelligible way.

Exercise

1 The two paragraphs rewritten by ChatGPT are about 20% shorter. It is then more concise. Does this mean that the ChatGPT paragraphs are better than the original paragraphs? Do the ChatGPT paragraphs leave anything out?

2 Write an essay of 75 words or less in which you answer the following questions: Which version do you think expresses Martinich's ideas better? Which paragraph is easier to understand? Which paragraph is more enjoyable to read?

3 Expand the essay you have just written to 125–300 words. Include in it examples of words, phrases, and grammatical functions, that illustrate and support your answers.

Another common problem in paragraphs is the occurrence of sentences that do not advance the argument. They needlessly repeat information that has already been provided, often in the immediately preceding sentence. Here's an example:

[1]The solution to the problem of negative existentials is, I think, extremely simple. [2]If one thinks about the language out of which the problem arises, the solution is not difficult to see.

One way to see that sentence [2] does not advance the essay is to compare its main clause, "the solution is not difficult to see," with the main clause of [1], "The solution … is … extremely simple." They say almost the same thing. What sentence [2] contributes is the idea in the subordinate clause,

"If one thinks ..." Thus, the essay can be given more momentum by including the subordinate clause of [2] with the main clause of [1]:

> The solution to the problem of negative existentials is, I think, extremely simple, ~~. I~~ if one thinks about the language out of which the problem arises, ~~the solution is not difficult to see.~~

Sentences that do not sufficiently advance the argument of the essay are usually the result of drafting. Because the author is not quite sure what she wants to say or how to say it, the same thought is written down more than once, in slightly different terms. It is probably a mistake to try to avoid these kinds of repetitions, because it will probably inhibit the free thinking needed to get the essay right. The solution is to write down what you think is needed at the time of drafting and then eliminate what is repetitious when you are revising the essay.

Example 1

Original: Eli Hirsch was drawing on Edmund Husserl's theory of intentionality. Hirsch followed Husserl in holding that "meaning is an affair of consciousness not of words."
Revision: Drawing on Edmund Husserl's theory of intentionality, Eli Hirsch held that "meaning is an affair of consciousness not of words."
Comment: The 24 words of *Original* are reduced to 19, about a 25% reduction. More importantly, the reader does not have to be slowed down by the idea that Hirsch drew on Husserl's philosophy, when this is implied in what follows.

Example 2

Original: Hirsch's line of reasoning was an inference not just to the best explanation but to the only explanation. According to him, the only way to account for the objectivity of the text is to hold that the author's intentions make it objective.

> *Revision*: Hirsch's line of reasoning was an inference to the best explanation for objective interpretation. Only the author's intentions can make the text objective.
>
> *Comment*: *Revision* is 40% shorter than *Original*. The idea of "to the only explanation" adds nothing to what is important about Hirsch's view.

The objectionable sentences in the two examples above are not doing their fair share of the work in moving the essay forward.

Notice that the sentences that were problems followed sentences that were clear enough on their own. Sometimes a sentence is unavoidably ambiguous or subject to misunderstanding, possibly because it expresses a difficult idea or involves a technical term. In such cases, the sentence may need to be followed by a sentence or clause that says just about the same thing in order to disambiguate or otherwise clarify it.

Example 3

By a physical object, I mean any object that has a place in space or time. Rainbows and shadows are physical objects, not to mention rocks, trees, dogs, and human beings.

Miss Grundy (or was it Mr. Thwack), your seventh-grade teacher, no doubt told you that every paragraph has to have a topic sentence. She was right. Each paragraph is like a mini essay. It contains some main theme, and it should be easy for the reader to find that theme. That means in part that the main theme should be expressed in the main clause of a sentence, not a subordinate clause, unless there is some good overriding reason to do that.

One reason many paragraphs lack unity is that the student keeps shifting her focus. Focus often shifts when the student is not clear about the focus of the entire essay.

4.9 Polishing

At some stage, your essay has an introduction, a fully worked-out middle, and a conclusion. Before typing your essay in its final version, you need to polish it. There are stylistic burrs that need to be sanded and grammatical gouges that need to be patched before it is presentable. Concerning grammar, I will say only that I strongly recommend it. (There are many books and websites that you can consult for help with grammar.) Concerning stylistic adjustments, they are best reserved for the final draft. Although there is nothing wrong with making obvious improvements in style as your composition progresses, you should go through your penultimate draft with just stylistic modifications in mind. There are all sorts of simple adjustments that can be made to improve your essay.

1   Try to find an active, vigorous verb to replace a phrase consisting of some form of "to be" and a noun phrase, especially an abstract noun: "My argument will be" → "I will argue that."

2   Change passive constructions into active ones: "The existence of universals was proven by Plato" → "Plato proved the existence of universals."

3   Transform prepositional phrases with abstract nouns into clauses: "The reconstruction of Kant's argument is difficult" → "Reconstructing Kant's argument is difficult."

4   Use participial phrases to subordinate a thought expressed in a main clause: "Aristotle tried to devise a more naturalistic theory of universals. He came up with his theory of immanent universals." → "In trying to devise a more naturalistic theory of universals, Aristotle came up with his theory of immanent universals."

5   Avoid needless or uninformative qualification: "Plato's position is not really contradictory" → "Plato's position is not contradictory."

6   Eliminate needlessly complex phrases: "Russell makes use of this construction" → "Russell uses this construction." "Quine gives vent to his belief that" → "Quine believes."

7   Make the antecedents of pronouns clear. Consider this fragment: "Aristotle struggled long and hard to devise a more naturalistic view of Plato's theory of universals. This is the topic of this essay." What is the topic? Is it Plato's theory, Aristotle's view, or Aristotle's struggle to devise a view? If we assume that it is the latter, then a suggested revision is: "Aristotle struggled long and hard to devise a more naturalistic view of Plato's theory of universals. This struggle is the topic of this essay."

8   Replace a phrase with a synonym: "The word *substance* has two meanings." → "The word *substance* is ambiguous."

9   Be sure your sentences literally say what you want them to say. Sometimes authors do not connect the right verb with the right subject. This sentence about a person in Hobbes's state of nature, "According to Hobbes, people fear the state of nature will kill them," should have been "According to Hobbes, people fear *that they will die if they stay* in the state of nature." The italics indicate what was left out.

Notice that the grammatical object of "fear" is no longer a noun phrase but a "that"-clause. The state of nature does not kill anyone, but conditions in the state of nature will. Often the problem is caused by the author's desire to be concise. The sentence, "The sovereign is the only way to survive the state of nature," needs to be expanded to "*Being protected* by a sovereign is the only way to *escape the dangers of* the state of nature." The italics indicate added words. Notice that when the sentence is filled out, the word "survive" gets replaced by the phrase, "escape the dangers."

10 Simple and direct. A sentence can sometimes be turned around to yield a simpler, more direct one: Change "There exists no need for rebellion on the people's part because ..." to "The people do not need to rebel because." Be wary of sentences that begin with, "There is."

11 Odd phrases, looped writing. Why would an author write, "Locke's view is ludicrous to the point of being laughable"? My guess is that the author thought that Locke's view was highly implausible but wanted to say it more colorfully. The author could not choose between "ludicrous" and "laughable" and so used both when one would have been sufficient. The phrase "ludicrous to the point of being laughable" is acceptable in a draft of an essay – you want to get your thoughts down without unnecessary hesitation – but in the final copy, at least one phrase should have been deleted. However, it is better to avoid words like "ludicrous" or "laughable" because they are insulting. It is better to say that a view is (highly) implausible and explain why. Other phrases, such as "Locke's blatant disregard for," should also be avoided and replaced with something like, "Locke does not consider."

These are only some examples of the kind of stylistic improvements you might make in a penultimate draft. Different people are subject to different stylistic burrs. When a friend or teacher marks infelicitous phrases and constructions, try to figure out whether this sort of infelicity regularly appears in your prose. If it does, keep on the lookout for it. Different people prefer different techniques for eliminating stylistic burrs. These techniques to some extent determine the person's *style*.

4.10   Evolution of an Essay

Printed below are three versions of a short essay. They are versions of an interpretation of a philosophical position. Argumentation is secondary to clear exposition. That is, the principal goal is not presenting a cogent, deductive argument, but an explication of some very brief, but important, passages in a work by Immanuel Kant.

Below "A Rough Draft: Kant and the Problem of Lying" should not be considered a first draft, but a good rough draft, the result of outlining, successive elaboration, or conceptual note taking and revision. Since only the author herself could appreciate the genuine fits and starts of her essay, "A Rough Draft: Kant and the Problem of Lying" is a relatively cleaned-up version. "A Rough Draft with Improvements" contains some substantive, but mostly stylistic, modifications. "The Final Draft: Kantianism, Lies, and Excuses" is the final version, the result of incorporating the modifications indicated in "A Rough Draft with Improvements." A good exercise for you would be to make your own corrections on "A Rough Draft: Kant and the Problem of Lying" and compare them with the corrections on "A Rough Draft with Improvements." You should expect the corrections to be different because there are an infinite number of ways to modify an essay.

You should think about why certain changes were made in the following drafts. Many of them are instructive and instantiate advice given earlier in the book. Ideally, these changes will be discussed with your professor or several students. Some of the changes that were made are controversial; you or your professor might disagree with them. If you do, it is important to explain why and to suggest alternatives. The final version of the essay might be further improved. How?

A Rough Draft

KANT AND THE PROBLEM OF LYING

Kant's philosophy is notorious for holding that lying is never permissible and is never right. Counterexamples to this rigorous position usually have the following form: suppose a strong, cruel, ruthless person is following someone. The person comes to your house and begs you to hide him. You agree to do so. The strong, cruel, ruthless person comes to your door and asks you whether you have seen the person being pursued. According to Kant, it is wrong for you to lie, because on his theory, moral principles are categorical imperatives. They do not admit of exceptions. If it is wrong to lie on any occasion, it is wrong to lie on all occasions.

Someone might try to evade this issue by observing that it is part of the meaning of the word "lie" that it is wrong. So, if the homeowner lies to the pursuer, he is doing something wrong.

This evasion is easily made irrelevant. Suppose that the homeowner previously promised the ruthless person to tell the truth and even stipulated that if the homeowner were to tell the ruthless person something he knew to be false, then that falsehood would count as a lie.

The question now recurs, "is it permissible or right to tell a lie?" the intuitions of most people are that it is permissible. They hold this position even when they believe or at least say that people ought not to lie, that lying is wrong, and they do not qualify their principles about lying.

I believe that the standard counterexample is not a genuine one. It is possible to adhere to Kant's categorical imperative that lying is always wrong and to explain why the homeowner ought to lie to the ruthless person. The explanation uses a concept already available in ethics, but underused.

Most people think that every bad action ought to be punished. Or that every person who does something bad ought to be punished for that bad action. But that is not correct.

Some bad actions are inexcusable, and others are excusable. Further, excusability is a matter of degree. People who act under some impairment, for which they are not to blame, have some of their culpability diminished; that is, they are partially excused.

The example of [the lie told to] the cruel person at the door is an example of a bad action that is completely excusable.

So, I have shown how a Kantian can continue to hold categorical imperatives and still account for our intuition that the homeowner is not culpable for lying.

One might object that this explanation of the cruel person at the door example is too weak, because the intuition that people have is not simply that the homeowner is not culpable for lying but that he morally must and morally should lie. That lying is the right thing to do.

In reply, I say that this objection indicates that people sometimes speak in a sloppy or imprecise way, as when they say a bigamist is married twice. Technically, no one can be married to more than one person at a time. The bigamist tries to have two marriages or two spouses; but when the bigamy is discovered, the apparent second marriage is declared invalid; that is, it is held that it never was a marriage. To say that lying is the right thing to do is, again, to say something self-contradictory. A lie, by definition, is wrong; it is better to keep the meaning of the word "lie" as it is, preserve our categorical principles, and use the concept of excuses, which we already have, to dissolve the paradox of thinking that some lies are good.

A Rough Draft with Improvements

The following is a revision of the draft above, with explanatory notes. Words that have been added are in boldface type.

KANTIANISM, LIES, AND EXCUSES[2]

Immanuel[3] Kant's philosophy[4] is notorious for holding that lying is never permissible and is never **morally**[5] right. Counterexamples to this rigorous position usually have the following form: **Here is a standard counterexample to his position**:[6] Suppose a strong,

---

[2] After writing her draft, the author thought this new title was more informative than the original, which only states the problem.
[3] With some exceptions, the first time a real person's name is introduced, the first name should be included.
[4] It is Kant, not his philosophy, that literally holds that lying is never morally right.
[5] Although one might assume that "right" means "morally right," it is advisable at the beginning of the essay to make explicit that it is moral, not practical or theoretical, right that is at issue.
[6] There's no need to talk about the "form" of a counterexample, when a specific example is going to be given.

~~cruel, ruthless person is following someone~~ a **Nazi** is **pursuing Stern, who has escaped from a labor camp.**[7] ~~The person~~ **Stern** comes to ~~your~~ **the** house **of Gutmann**[8] and **asks to be hidden** ~~begs you to hide him. You agree to do so.~~ **Gutmann, knowing that the victim is innocent and that the Nazis are cruel, hides Stern.** ~~The strong, cruel, ruthless person~~ **When the Nazi** comes to **the** ~~your~~ door and asks ~~you~~ **Gutmann** whether ~~you have seen the person being pursued.~~ **he has seen Stern, Gutmann says "No."** According to Kant, ~~it is wrong for you to lie,~~ **Gutmann has acted wrongly**, because ~~on his theory,~~ moral principles are categorical imperatives. They do not admit of exceptions. ~~if it is wrong to lie on any occasion, it is wrong to lie on all occasions.~~ **If it is ever wrong to lie, it is always wrong to lie.**[9]~~someone might~~ **A Kantian may**[10] try to evade[11] this ~~issue~~ **problem**[12] by observing that it is part of the meaning of the word "lie" that it is wrong. so, if the homeowner lies to the pursuer, he is doing something wrong. ~~{??some people even think that lying is the morally right thing to do.)~~[13]

---

[7] The use of "Nazi" and "labor camp" make the example concrete. The author can safely assume that the reader will have enough background information to understand that the Nazi is evil and that Stern is in great danger. The original phrase, "strong, cruel, ruthless, person," is abstract and wordy. Using a proper name "Stern" for the escapee makes future reference to him simpler and more concrete than "the escapee." Also, referring to Stern eliminates the needless presence of "you" in the scenario.

[8] Again, the proper name is more concrete than "the homeowner," making future reference simpler, and the name "Gutmann" suggests a good person.

[9] It is arguable that this sentence commits "the quantifier-shift fallacy." It seems to say, "If there exists one occasions on which it is wrong to lie, then on every occasion it is wrong to lie." But this kind of inference is not generally valid, e.g. "If there is one occasion on which it is wrong to take money from a bank [as a robber], then on every occasion it is wrong to take money from a bank [as a client withdrawing money from her account]." But we are not concerned with the soundness of this argument, and in any case, certain propositions of Kant's philosophy may warrant the inference about lying.

[10] There's no need to use the vague "Someone." Kantians and their views are being discussed. A traditional view of grammar holds that "may" is the present tense and "might" the past tense.

[11] The word "evade" has some pejorative connotation. "Avoid" is neutral. I have left "evade" because it is expressing the view of a critic. Also, see note 13.

[12] "Problem" is more precise.

[13] The author did not know whether she would use this sentence of the original. She decided against it. She deals with the objection implicit in the sentence later in the essay.

This evasion[14] is easily made irrelevant **by changing the scenario slightly**.[15] Suppose that ~~the homeowner~~ **Gutmann** previously promised the ~~ruthless person~~ **Nazi** to tell the truth and even stipulated **at the same time**[16] that if ~~the homeowner~~ **Gutmann** were to tell the ~~ruthless person~~ nazi something he knew to be false, then that falsehood would count as a lie.

So,[17] ~~T~~the **original**[18] question now recurs, "is it **ever** permissible or right to tell a lie?" the intuitions of most people are that it is permissible. They hold this position even when they believe or at least say that people ought not to lie, that lying is wrong, and they do not qualify their principles about lying.

I believe that the ~~standard~~ **Nazi** counterexample is not a genuine one. It is possible to adhere to Kant's categorical imperative that lying is always wrong and to explain why the homeowner ought to lie to the ~~ruthless person~~ **Nazi**. The explanation uses a concept already available in ethics, but underused.

Most people think that every bad action ought to be punished.~~Or~~[19] **or** that every person who does something bad ought to be punished for that bad action. But that is not correct. **While**[20] ~~S~~some bad actions are inexcusable, and others are excusable.[21] Further, excusability[22]

---

[14] "Evasion" ties this sentence to the preceding paragraph, which contains "evade." This is another reason to keep "evade" and not substitute "avoid." "Avoidance" is stilted.

[15] This phrase makes the sentence more explicit.

[16] This phrase makes the sentence more explicit.

[17] The "So" explicitly indicates the point of the revised example.

[18] "Original" ties this sentence to the earlier part of the essay.

[19] The "or"-clause is a sentence fragment, not a complete sentence.

[20] The first draft begins a new paragraph here. But that is unnecessary. So the revision makes two paragraphs one.

[21] In the original sentence, which was a conjunction, each conjunct was rhetorically equal to the other. But the author wants to emphasize the fact that some bad actions are excusable. So, it ought to be emphasized. This emphasis is achieved by using "while," which makes the clause it begins subordinate to the main clause, "others are excusable."

[22] As far as I know "excusability" is a neologism. But I'm letting it stand.

is a matter of degree. People who act under some impairment,[23] for which they are not to blame, have ~~some of their~~ **reduced** culpability ~~diminished~~;[24] that is, they are partially excused. **In Tudor England, it was against the law for one person to kill another person, even in self-defense. However, the king would completely excuse murders performed in self-defense**.[25] The example of ~~[the lie told to]~~[26] ~~the cruel person~~ **the Nazi** at the door is an example of a bad action that is completely excusable.[27]

So, I have shown how a Kantian can continue to hold categorical imperatives and still account for our intuition that the homeowner is not culpable for lying.

One might object that this explanation of the ~~cruel person~~ **Nazi** at the door example is too weak., ~~because~~[28] **T**he intuition that people have is not simply that the homeowner is not culpable for lying but that he morally must and morally should lie. ~~that~~ **L**ying is the right thing to do.[29]

In reply, I say that this objection indicates that people sometimes speak ~~in a sloppy or imprecise way,~~ **imprecisely,**[30] as when they say a bigamist is married twice. **Bigamy is a crime where it exists. In these places,** technically, no one can be married to more than one person at a time. The bigamist tries to have

---

[23] The commas after "impairment" and "blame" are deleted because the clause, "for which they are not to blame," is a restrictive (not a nonrestrictive) relative clause. See a grammar book for these terms.

[24] The changes contribute to succinctness.

[25] This example makes the claim more vivid, and shows that excuses can completely eliminate blame.

[26] In the original, the author thought she might want to include this phrase. She finally decided that the additional explicitness was not needed.

[27] In the original, this sentence began a new paragraph because the author wanted to emphasize it and thought it might need to be moved. Putting it alone made it easier to locate if repositioning was advisable.

[28] The sentence that forms this paragraph is too complex and perhaps not grammatical. So the author has broken it up into three sentences. Also, as a general rule, no paragraph should consist of one sentence.

[29] What had been, in the original draft, a clause that was not a complete sentence has been turned into one by deleting "That."

[30] The original sounds a bit harsh. There's no need to insult ones opponent.

two marriages or two spouses; but when the bigamy is discovered, the apparent second marriage is declared invalid; that is, it is held that it never was a marriage.[31] To say that lying is the right thing to do is, again, to say something self-contradictory.[32] A lie, by definition, is wrong.; It[33] is better to keep the meaning of the word "lie" as it is, preserve our categorical principles, and use the concept of excuses, which we already have,[34] to dissolve the paradox of thinking that some lies are good.

In conclusion, I have shown that Kant's moral principle that lies are never good has not been refuted, and that supposed counterexamples can be explained away by using the concept of excuses.[35]

The Final Draft

KANTIANISM, LIES, AND EXCUSES

Immanuel Kant is notorious for holding that lying is never morally right. Here is a standard counterexample to his position: suppose a Nazi is pursuing Stern, who has escaped from a labor camp. Stern comes to the house of Gutmann and asks to be hidden. Gutmann, knowing that the victim is innocent and that the Nazis are cruel, hides stern. When the Nazi comes to the door and asks Gutmann whether he has seen Stern, Gutmann says "no." According to Kant, Gutmann has acted wrongly, because moral principles are categorical imperatives. They do not admit of exceptions. If it is ever wrong to lie, it is always wrong to lie.

---

[31] The author is going on about this example at some length in order to indicate its importance for her solution.

[32] The author is repeating an earlier point to indicate that there was some initial plausibility for her view and against the opposite one.

[33] The author turned one complex sentence connected by a semicolon into two simpler sentences. The result is two sentences with more impact than the one sentence.

[34] The author decided it was not necessary to repeat this point.

[35] The author has added an explicit conclusion.

A Kantian may try to evade this problem by observing that it is part of the meaning of the word "lie" that it is wrong. So, if the homeowner lies to the pursuer, he is doing something wrong.

This evasion is easily made irrelevant by changing the scenario slightly. Suppose that Gutmann previously promised the Nazi to tell the truth and even stipulated at the same time that if Gutmann were to tell the Nazi something he knew to be false, then that falsehood would count as a lie.

So, the original question now recurs, "is it ever permissible or right to tell a lie?" the intuitions of most people are that it is permissible. They hold this position even when they believe or at least say that people ought not to lie, that lying is wrong, and they do not qualify their principles about lying.

I believe that the Nazi counterexample is not a genuine one. It is possible to adhere to Kant's categorical imperative that lying is always wrong and to explain why the homeowner ought to lie to the Nazi. The explanation uses a concept already available in ethics, but underused.

Most people think that every bad action ought to be punished or that every person who does something bad ought to be punished for that bad action. But that is not correct. While some bad actions are inexcusable, others are excusable. Further, excusability is a matter of degree. People who act under some impairment for which they are not to blame have reduced culpability; that is, they are partially excused. In Tudor England, it was against the law for one person to kill another person, even in self-defense. However, the king would completely excuse murders performed in self-defense. The example of the Nazi at the door is an example of a bad action that is completely excusable.

So, I have shown how a Kantian can continue to hold categorical imperatives and still account for our intuition that the homeowner is not culpable for lying.

One might object that this explanation of the Nazi at the door example is too weak. The intuition that people have is not simply that the homeowner is not culpable for lying but that he morally must and morally should lie. Lying is the right thing to do.

In reply, I say that this objection indicates that people sometimes speak imprecisely, as when they say a bigamist is married twice. Bigamy is a crime where it exists. In these places, technically, no one can be married to more than one person at a time. The bigamist tries to have two marriages or two spouses; but when the bigamy is discovered, the apparent second marriage is declared invalid; that is, it is held that it never was a marriage. To say that lying is the right thing to do is, again, to say something self- contradictory. A lie, by definition, is wrong. It is better to keep the meaning of the word "lie" as it is, preserve our categorical principles, and use the concept of excuses to dissolve the paradox of thinking that some lies are good.

In conclusion, I have shown that Kant's moral principle that lies are never good has not been refuted, and that supposed counterexamples can be explained away by using the concept of excuses.

Exercises

1 Which of the following two drafts, "A Paradox of Promising—1" or "A Paradox of Promising—2" is better? Why? Revise the better draft to further improve it.

A PARADOX OF PROMISING – 1

Philosophers have long argued about whether "ought" implies "can." philosophers have argued about whether, if a person ought or has an obligation to do something, then that person can do that thing. No doubt, it is usually the case that if a person has an obligation, then he or she can fulfill it by doing what is required. But there also seem to be cases in which a person has an obligation to do an action A and cannot do A.

This problem is neatly illustrated by what has been called "the paradox of promising":

(1) Whenever a person makes a promise to do an action A, he thereby puts himself under an obligation to do A.
(2) If someone has an obligation to do A, then he can do A.
(3) Some people sometimes make promises they cannot keep.

This paradox is not an argument but a set of inconsistent propositions. From (1) and (2) it follows that

(4) Whenever a person makes a promise to do an action A, then he can do A.

And (3) and (4) are inconsistent with each other, because (3) in effect says (3′) some people sometimes make a promise they cannot keep.

Each proposition is well supported. It is part of the meaning of a promise that making a promise creates an obligation to do what is promised. If someone has an obligation to do something then he can do it. This is the thesis that "ought" implies "can." it is irrational to require a person a do something that he or she cannot do. People are responsible for their actions and what is created by their actions. If a person cannot do something, then that thing is not within the domain of the person's actions. It seems to be a fact that some people sometimes make promises they cannot keep. Suppose Betty borrows 10 dollars from Carol on Monday because she needs to buy lunch. Her parents have promised to give her 50 dollars on Tuesday for living expenses. However, on Monday night, the parents are robbed of all their money and hence cannot send the money to Betty on Tuesday. We have a case here in which Betty has an obligation to pay Carol the 10 dollars, but she cannot pay.

A PARADOX OF PROMISING – 2

Does "ought" imply "can"? Philosophers have argued about this for centuries. Usually people do what they have to do. But sometimes they don't.

Here's a problem. Whenever a person makes a promise to do something, she has an obligation to do it. If someone has an obligation to do something, then she can do it. But sometimes people make promises and cannot keep them.

This problem involves an inconsistency. The first two sentences entail that whenever a person makes a promise to do something, then she can do it. But if she can do it, then it can't be right that sometimes people make promises and cannot keep them.

It's hard to know how to solve this problem. It is part of the meaning of a promise that promising creates an obligation to do what is promised. If someone has an obligation to do something then she can do it. This is the thesis that "ought" implies "can." you can't require a person a do something that she cannot do. If a person cannot do something, then she cannot do it. Pretend that Betty needs to buy lunch. She borrows 10 dollars from Carol on Monday. Her parents are rich and have more money than they need. They have promised to give her 50 dollars on Tuesday for living expenses. However, on Monday night, the parents are robbed of all their money and hence cannot send the money to her on Tuesday. Betty has an obligation to pay Carol 10 dollars, but it cannot be paid.

2   Revise the following essay fragment:

There are three main theories of ethics. The first is deontology, according to which there are certain things that a person ought or is required to do. The second is utilitarianism. Utilitarianism is a kind of consequentialism. Consequentialism is the view that the goodness or badness of an action is determined by the goodness of its consequences. According to utilitarianism, people should aim at achieving the greatest good for the greatest number. However, it is impossible to maximize two values simultaneously, the greatest good and the greatest number of people. Virtue ethics is the view that a good person is a virtuous person. Temperance, justice, honesty and courage are virtues. There are two forms. Intrinsic virtue ethics holds that virtues themselves make a person morally good. Instrumental virtue ethics holds that virtues are indispensable means to being a good person.

5
Tactics for Analytic Writing

Various tactics are used in analytic writing. Eight of the most important ones are discussed in this chapter: (1) definitions, (2) distinctions, (3) analysis (in a narrow sense), (4) dilemmas, (5) scenarios, (6) counterexamples, (7) *reductio ad absurdum* arguments, and (8) dialectical reasoning.

5.1 Definitions

In ordinary life, people use many words competently but are not able to state exactly what the words mean. Dictionaries usually do this quite well, but philosophers often want more. They want to know what something is necessarily or essentially: "A square is a plane figure with four equal sides and four right angles." and "A human being is a rational animal." Some philosophers want a definition to take a particular form or to be expressed with certain favored words. Thomas Hobbes wanted definitions to be expressed in terms of motions of bodies or terms reducible to motions of bodies. For example, he defined *will* as the last desire a person has before acting, and desires as imperceptibly small motions toward an object.

Generally, definition is needed when there is good reason to believe that the reader does not already know the meaning that the author intends the word to have. This may also happen when philosophers think the ordinary meaning of a word does not quite express what he means. The more precise definition has been called a "precising" definition. Sometimes a philosopher will want to be sure that the reader

Philosophical Writing: An Introduction, Fifth Edition. A. P. Martinich.
© 2025 John Wiley & Sons, Inc. Published 2025 by John Wiley & Sons, Inc.
Companion website: www.wiley.com/go/Martinich5e

understands which of the various senses a word has is understood in only one of those senses.

In philosophy, words often have more than one technical senses; so it is especially important to define them, for example, *knowledge, intuition, person, property,* and *transcendent.* If a word has an ordinary meaning, for example, "mind" or "person," but the author is going to use that word in a technical sense, the reader will not know what the author means unless the author tells him so. Sometimes a philosopher coins a new word, for example, whoever coined the term "sense datum." Giving a definition is essential here; otherwise, the reader has no way of knowing what is meant.

Students often think that they do not need to define terms, even technical terms, because they think that the professor must know what the words mean since the professor is an expert. That reason is beside the point. The student's goal is to show the professor that she knows what she is talking about, as explained in chapter 1. So, in addition to the fact that authors in general need to define technical and other terms needing explanation, student authors bear the burden of proving that they know what they are talking about.

A definition has two parts: the definiendum (the word to be defined) and the definiens (the words that give the meaning of the definiendum). A good definition is one in which the words in the definiens are easier to understand than the words in the definiendum. If they are not, the author is not helping the reader to understand the definiendum. The definiens cannot contain the key word in the definiendum. If the key word occurs in the definiens, then the definition is circular, for example, this one:

A human being is a being that is human.

I said "key" word because sometimes a definiendum contains several words. Here's a definition of "empirical argument":

An argument is empirical = df it contains at least one empirical premise

or

Something is an empirical argument = df it contains at least one empirical premise.

111

The key word here is *argument*. The definition is supposed to be what "empirical argument" means. It explains it as containing an empirical premise. If the process of definition ends here and the reader does not know what counts as an empirical premise, then the definition is defective. But if the definition is followed by another,

> A premise is empirical = df the most direct way of establishing its truth is by sensation

then the definition is acceptable.

Here are some examples of how definitions can be introduced in essays:

> The main point of W. V. Quine's article "Two Dogmas of Empiricism" is that the distinction between analytic and synthetic propositions has no theoretical justification. Analytic propositions *are defined as* those that are true in virtue of the meaning of their words. Synthetic propositions *are defined as* those that are made true by empirical facts.

> I shall argue that God is omnipotent and omniscient. I define "*x* is omnipotent" as "*x* is able to do everything that can be done" and "*x* is omniscient" as "*x* knows everything that can be known."

> According to Thomas Hobbes, God is neither just nor unjust. By *justice* he means not breaking any covenant, and by injustice, he means breaking a covenant.

> According to Thomas Hobbes, God is neither just nor unjust. By "*x* is just," he means "*x* has not broken any covenant," and by "*x* is unjust," he means "*x* has broken a covenant."

Definitions have been categorized in various ways. Implicitly in the discussion above, I divided definitions into descriptive (how a word is usually used), precising (how a word with a vague meaning will be used in a more precise way), stipulative (inventing a new meaning for a word), and technical (giving a precise definition of a word for use in the construction of a theory). These categories are not mutually exclusive. Although it is not useful for our purposes to give a neat categorization of kinds of definitions or even to discuss all the kinds that there are, one kind of definition deserves special mention: definition by genus and species.

This method is generally credited to Aristotle. We have already seen a stock example of this type of definition:.

A human being is a rational animal.

Other examples are:

A beast is an animal without reason.
An animal is a living being that can move itself from place to place.
A plant is a living being that cannot move itself from place to place.

Certain facts about genera and species are best illustrated by what is known as the Tree of Porphyry, attributed to Porphyry, a neoPlatonic philosopher. Each capitalized word or phrase in the diagram below designates either a genus or species.

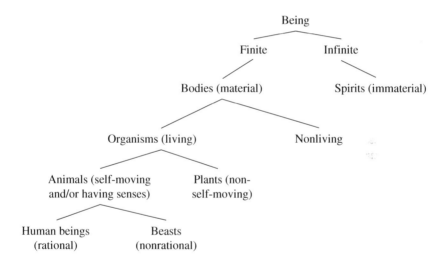

The concepts of genus and species are correlative; one has to be explained in terms of the other. A (direct) genus is the immediately higher general kind of a species. A (direct) species is an immediately lower kind of thing. Some genus will be the highest one (*Being*) and not be a species of any other genus. Each genus has more than one species falling under it. For example, *organism* has the species *animals* and *plants*. Each item that is immediately lower than another item (for example, *animals* is lower than *organism*) is a species of the higher item, the genus. Every genus has at least two species, and some species will be the lowest ones and will not be a genus of anything. *Human beings* is a species with no subspecies in

Aristotelian and scholastic philosophy. However, in contemporary anthropology, *Human Beings* (*homo* in Latin) is a genus because it does have various species below it, such as *homo erectus*, *homo habilis*, and *homo sapiens*.

What generates a species under a genus is something that some things of the species have that other things in the genus do not have. This thing, call it a *property*, distinguishes the members of one species from those of another species of the same genus. This distinguishing property is called *the specific difference* because it is the difference that separates one species from another. Although not quite sensible, it may help to remember the term by thinking that it is the difference that is specific to the species. Definitions by genus and species consist of a statement of the relevant genus and specific difference. The definition

A human being is a rational animal

consists of the genus *animal* and the specific difference *rational* in the definiens.

What form should a definition take? Philosophers often deal with abstract objects or at least often talk about objects abstractly like truth, beauty, and goodness. Traditionally, this has led them to try to define *truth*, *beauty*, and *goodness*. But starting with an abstract noun often resulted in definitions that were stilted or obscure, for example,

To be just is for one person to give another person what the first person owes to the second.

Inspired by certain developments in formal logic, philosophers in the twentieth century came to see that many nouns were abstracted from predicate expressions and that the predicate expressions themselves presented more perspicuous definienda. This led to the following changes:

Original form	New form
Justice	x is just
Knowledge	x knows that p
Truth	x is true
Promise	x promises that p to an addressee y
Excuse	x excuses y for an action a

Using the predicative form, the above definition of justice becomes the smoother:

x is just to y if and only if x gives to y what x owes y.

By this definition, we know what any sentence like "Adam is just to Beth" or "Carol is just to David" means. One simply substitutes the appropriate names in the places marked by "x" and "y." Let's consider another example: The new formulation of the classical definition

knowledge is justified true belief

becomes

x knows that p if and only if it is true that p and x is justified in believing that p.

And when this is made more explicit, it becomes:

x knows that p if and only if
(1) it is true that p;
(2) x believes that p; and
(3) x's belief that p is justified.

This last definition makes the components of knowledge stand out more starkly than the first.

One last point. It often turns out that philosophers need to define pairs of terms that they want to be contradictories, such as truth/falsity or objectivity/subjectivity (see chapter 2, section 2.5). The appropriate way to do this to guarantee that the defined terms are genuinely contradictory is to define one term and then to define the other as simply everything that is not the first. Here are two examples:

"x is war" means "x is a stretch of time during which one civil state is inclined to attack another civil state"
x is peace if and only if x is not war
"x is a bachelor" means "x is an unmarried, adult, male, human being"
"x is a nonbachelor" means "x is not a bachelor."[1]

It is not possible to define every word. If it were, then even the words used in the definiens would need to be defined, and then those words would need to be defined, ad infinitum. If definition could actually go on

---

[1] The subject expressions of predicates are often restricted to semantically acceptable words and phrases. So, acceptable subject expressions for "x is a bachelor" are names and descriptions of human beings that can replace x. Such restrictions are assumed for these and other examples.

forever, then the "ad infinitum" phrase would not be a problem. But definition cannot go on forever for at least two reasons. First, people know the meanings of many words even though they have not learned their meanings through definitions. Second, if some words in the definiens always needed to be defined, then there would be no foundation for meaning, no starting point. One may wonder, then, what the foundation for meaning is. In a word, it is the interaction between interlocutors (people who alternate between speaking and listening) in a context. The context of course is always some part of the world, in addition to the interlocutors themselves. Since this issue gets us into very deep water not essential to understanding how to write, no more will be said about it.

5.2   Distinctions

Philosophy students during the Middle Ages allegedly were given the following rule of thumb: When faced with a contradiction, make a distinction. That rule encouraged the abuse of distinction-making and eventually led to the bad reputation of scholastic philosophers, so-called "logic-choppers," "hairsplitters," and "dunces" (after the late thirteenth-century philosopher John Duns Scotus). Distinctions should be made only when they are necessary.

A principal reason for making a distinction is to avoid confusing or conflating two things. Ancient astronomers used the term *the evening star* for the first heavenly body to appear in the night sky and the term *the morning star* for the last body to disappear in the morning sky. It was a great discovery to learn that the two terms were used for the same object (Venus). This example strongly suggests that when people talk about the world with phrases, a distinction must be made between the sense (in German, *Sinn*) of the term and the object referred to (in German, *Bedeutung*). The two terms seem to give directions to the audience for identifying the object that is being talked about. Sense and reference was one of the most important distinctions in twentieth-century philosophy.

Sometimes a distinction is made that confuses an issue. In ordinary talk, the United States is described as a democracy or as a republic without any confusion. However, certain politicians in this century have claimed that it is crucial to distinguish between the two forms of government. Here is how these politicians might explain the distinction. A democracy is a government ruled by the people. (Usually, a democracy also requires majority rule.) A republic is a government in which some citizens represent other citizens. (Usually, a republic also requires its citizens to have political virtues such as experience, integrity, discretion, and courage.) Politicians who make this distinction often argue that since the United States has representatives, it cannot be a democracy, and if it is not a democracy, it must be a republic.

This distinction causes confusion. Nothing in the definition of a democracy preludes a democracy from having citizens represented by some citizens. It is reasonable to have representatives when the territory of a country is vast or the population is high. As for republics, nothing precludes them from being elected by majority rule and having all adult citizens participate in their government by voting, petitioning, and otherwise influencing the representatives who act on their behalf. The upshot is that although there is a distinction to be drawn between democracies and republics, there can be democratic republics or republican democracies. In other words, the distinction is not "a proper one."

A *proper distinction* (a technical term) has two characteristics: Its terms are exhaustive, and they are mutually exclusive. A pair of terms is exhaustive when at least one of them applies to each object of the group to be distinguished, like the terms even and odd, applied to the positive integers between, say, 1 and 1,000,000. The terms of this distinction are also mutually exclusive because none of these numbers is both even and odd. Our discussion of the distinction between democracies and republics indicates that it is easy to think that a distinction is proper when it is not.

The way to ensure coming up with a proper distinction is to use contradictory pairs of terms:

red/non-red
blue/nonblue
human/nonhuman
animal/nonanimal
just/non-just
merciful/non-merciful

The great advantage of proper distinctions is that they give a neat categorization of objects. There is a place for everything and everything is in its place. This can be seen in the Tree of Porphyry in section 5.1. One of Søren Kierkegaard's *personae* reports a classification of mankind into "officers, servant girls, and chimney sweeps" (*Repetition*, ed. and tr. by Howard V. Hong and Edna H. Hong, Princeton: Princeton University Press, 1983, p. 162). These terms are obviously not exhaustive – it leaves out scientists – and are not mutually exclusive either (if, for example, some officer is also a chimney sweep). An even more elaborately improper distinction is the one Jorge Luis Borges supposedly reports in his essay "The Precise Language of John Wilkins." In an obscure Chinese encyclopedia, the following distinctions are made between animals: "(a) those that

117

belong to the emperor, (b) embalmed ones, (c) those that are trained, (d) suckling pigs, (e) mermaids, (f) fabulous ones, (g) stray dogs, (h) those that are included in this classification, (i) those that tremble as if they were mad, (j) innumerable ones, (k) those that are drawn with a very fine camel's hair brush, (l) others, (m) those that have just broken a flower vase, (n) those that resemble flies from a distance" (*Other Inquisitions, 1937–1952*, tr. Ruth Simms, New York: Washington Square Books, 1965, p. 108). I leave it as an exercise for the reader to explain why the terms are neither exhaustive nor mutually exclusive.

While it is easy to see that some distinctions are not proper, for example, red/blue or dog/animal, others are not. Consider just/unjust. Certainly, what is just is not unjust. But is what is not unjust always just? Suppose you are sitting in a room alone. Your elbow begins to itch, and you scratch it. Did you do something unjust? No. Did you do something just? No. In scratching your elbow, you did not pay anyone what you owed to that person; you did not fulfill a duty you had; and you did not fulfill an obligation. Your head scratching was non-just, not unjust. Think about the three terms: just, unjust, and non-just. The terms just/non-just are contradictory terms – they express contradictory properties, and so the distinction between them is a proper distinction. But the terms just/unjust do not yield a proper distinction. Some things are neither just nor unjust, as indicated above.

The mistake of thinking that two terms are contradictory when they are not is sometimes philosophically important, for example, the distinction between a sense-datum and a material-object. A shadow is neither.[2] Another philosophical distinction that is not a proper one is that between appearance and reality. The appearance of shadows, mirror images, afterimages, and rainbows is their reality.

Exercises

1 What does the fact that there can be citizens who are Independents, or Libertarians, or Environmentalists (the Green Party) tell us about the terms democrat and republican (small *d* and *r*)?

---

[2] See J. L. Austin, *Sense and Sensibilia*, ed. G. J. Warnock (New York: Oxford University Press, 1964) pp. 55–61. For another example, see *John Searle and His Critics*, ed. E. Lepore and R. Van Gulick (Oxford: Blackwell Publishers, 1991) p. 141.

2   Let the set of things to be divided up be human actions. Why precisely is the distinction between just and unjust actions *not* a proper one? Because … (circle the letter of the sentence that gives the correct reason):
    (a)   No action can be just and unjust;
    (b)   Some actions are not just and not unjust;
    (c)   No action is just and unjust, and some actions are not just and not unjust.

3   Is the distinction between female and nonfemale a proper one? Why or why not?

Let's now consider the two ways of drawing a distinction: by characterization and by example. We begin with the latter. A distinction can be drawn by giving enough examples to get the reader to understand what the distinction comes to. Here is an example of an author explaining a distinction by giving examples:

> There are two kinds of labor: alienated and unalienated. The labor of a peasant, the labor of an auto worker, and the labor of a bureaucrat are alienated. The labor of an artisan, a poet, and a statesman is unalienated.

The drawback of characterization by example is that it may not be obvious what the principle of division is. Certainly, this is the case in Borges's Chinese classification. It is easy for the disseminator of a distinction to be misled herself. If she relies only upon examples, it is possible that the author will conflate two different distinctions.

Characterization then is theoretically the better method of drawing a distinction because it specifies the principle or property that differentiates the terms. Here is an example of characterizing the distinction between alienated and unalienated labor:

> There are two kinds of labor: alienated and unalienated. Labor is alienated when the laborer does not have full control over his work or does not receive its full benefit. Labor is unalienated when it is not alienated.

It is often advisable to combine both methods, as in this passage:

> There are two kinds of labor: alienated and unalienated. Labor is alienated when the laborer does not have full control over his work or does not receive

its full benefit, for example, the labor of peasants, auto workers, and bureaucrats. Labor is unalienated when it is not alienated, such as that of the self-employed, poets and statesmen.

As this discussion of characterizing a distinction suggests, every distinction depends upon the existence of some property that all the terms of one group or category have and that all the things in the other group lack, even if the author is not able to articulate that difference.

Without a difference, there would be no distinction at all. Sometimes people try to draw a distinction and fail because they think they specify a difference but do not. This is what is meant by the somewhat inaccurate phrase *a distinction without a difference*. (It is inaccurate because without a difference there is no distinction at all, only the attempt or appearance of a distinction.) For example, in Woody Allen's film *Mighty Aphrodite*, an ineffectual father tries to save face by purporting to distinguish between the head of the family (himself) and the decision maker (his wife). But in fact this is a distinction without a difference. His wife is the head of the family because she is the decision maker. (At best, he would be a *titular* head; that is a person with the title of "Head" but without the power of one.) A related example concerns the English Church in the sixteenth century. When the Act of Supremacy needed to be reformulated, some clerics were reluctant to call Queen Elizabeth I the "Head of the Church," as King Henry VIII had been called, because she was a woman. They wanted to make a distinction. So the term *Governor* was settled on. But the Act of Supremacy restored to her exactly the powers held by Henry VIII, and it described her as "supreme ... in all spiritual or ecclesiastical things." So the alleged distinction between Head and Governor is a distinction without a difference. Also, there was a tradition in England of distinguishing between the king's two bodies: his physical body and his political body. The rebels of the English Civil War claimed to be trying to liberate the political person, King Charles I, by defeating the natural person Charles Stuart. The royalists thought this alleged distinction between the royal and natural bodies of their king was a distinction without a difference.

Permit me one final example. A French defense minister once tried to defend his country's decision to resume nuclear testing by in effect saying the following: "The French government is not testing nuclear bombs. A distinction must be made between bombs and devices that explode. The French government is testing nuclear devices that explode, not bombs." The minister was ridiculed because he was trying to draw a distinction without a difference. But the testing continued.

5.3 Analysis

Analysis is analogous to definition. Definitions are explicitly about giving the meanings of words. Analyses are explicitly about giving the necessary and sufficient conditions for concepts. Since words express concepts, definitions are the linguistic counterparts to analyses. Much of what was said about definitions applies to analyses. Perhaps both topics could have been treated together, but I think that pedagogically it makes sense to treat them separately.

Every analysis, like every definition, consists of two parts, an analysandum and an analysans. The analysandum is the notion that needs to be explained and clarified, because there is something about it that is not understood. The analysans is the part of the analysis that explains and clarifies the analysandum, either by breaking it down into parts or by specifying its relations to other notions.

An analysis tries to specify in its analysans *necessary and sufficient conditions* for the concept expressed in the analysandum. Necessary conditions are those that the analysans must contain in order to avoid being too weak. Being an organism is a necessary condition for being a human, because a human must be an organism. But being an organism is not a sufficient condition. Dogs and cats are organisms but not humans. Sufficient conditions are those that are enough to guarantee that the concept in the analysans is satisfied. Having twenty million dollars of Berkshire-Hathaway stocks is a sufficient condition for being rich. But it is not a necessary condition, because a person can be rich without having that much Berkshire-Hathaway stock. Having ten thousand pounds of gold is also a sufficient condition for being rich.

There is one further preliminary point to make. Let's consider this tentative analysis of bachelorhood:

Something is a bachelor if and only if
(1) it is unmarried;
(2) it is adult;
(3) it is male.

This is a pretty good first shot. It is not, perhaps, adequate. One might think that since only humans are bachelors, a fourth condition needs to be added:

(4) it is human.

However, young adult seals that have not yet mated are also called bachelors. For two reasons it is not necessary for us to argue here about whether

121

or not to add the fourth condition. First, my intention is to give an example of an analysis, not to defend that analysis. Second, what should be noticed here is that setting out an analysans as explicitly as I have just done makes the terms of the disagreement between the pro-seal-bachelors and the anti-seal-bachelors clear. And when the terms of disagreement are clear, debate about which side is correct is much easier.

Let's now consider a genuinely philosophical analysis of a concept:

A person S knows that p if and only if
(1) it is true that p;
(2) S believes that p;
(3) S is justified in believing that p.

This analysis is very attractive (compare it to the definition of "x knows that p" in section 5.1). It makes at least one element of knowledge very clear: It is not possible to know something that is false. Sometimes people say that they know something when in fact what they say they know is false. This does not show that it is possible to know something that is not true. It simply shows that sometimes people are mistaken about what they think they know. Our analysis of knowledge also assimilates knowledge to belief. Knowledge is a kind of belief according to the above analysis. This is more debatable. There have been some powerful arguments with the conclusion that knowledge and belief are different psychological states. Again, it is not to our purpose to argue whether the above analysis or some other is correct or not. Finally, condition (3) is surely not adequate as it stands. In order to be a satisfactory analysis, it is necessary to specify what being justified in believing something means. Again, it is not to our purpose to argue about this matter. It is enough to point out that the analysis makes the issues that need to be debated clear.

There are three ways in which proposed analyses commonly go wrong: An analysis may be defective by (1) being circular, (2) being too strong, or (3) being too weak. These kinds of defects will be discussed in order.

An analysis is circular if the analysandum, or its key term, occurs in the analysans. For example, if one is trying to analyze "freezing," it is a mistake to propose as the analysans "something that happens to a liquid when it freezes." The problem is obvious: If someone needs an analysis of freezing because he does not know what it is, then it does no good to tell him that it is something that happens to a liquid when it freezes. This does not make the notion of freezing any clearer or more understandable because, since the analysans includes the notion of freezing, one must understand *that*, before one can understand the analysandum: freezing. If, on the other hand, someone already understands what freezing is, then he has no use for an analysis of freezing in the first place. In either case, to the extent that the understanding of an analysans depends upon understanding the analysandum, the analysis is uninformative and unhelpful.

However, the above analysis is not totally uninformative. It does convey that freezing is something that happens to liquids, and the person in need of the analysis may not have known this before being presented with the circular analysis. But notice that this informativeness is due to the part of the analysans that did not depend upon any prior understanding of the analysis of freezing.

It is important to distinguish this kind of circularity from a related phenomenon that sometimes goes under the same name. Suppose that A, B, C, ..., Z are analysanda; further suppose that A occurs as part of the analysans of B, B as part of the analysans of C, ..., and Z as part of the analysans of A.

Now it may at first seem that someone who did not understand any of these notions would not be helped by any of these analyses. If she doesn't understand any of the analysanda and if each analysans contains one of the analysanda, then she cannot understand any analysans either; she has no entry into the circle. In extreme cases, this may be true. Usually, however, someone who encounters such a group of analyses has a fairly good understanding of at least one of the notions involved. If so, she can get at least a partial understanding of the other notions and a better and clearer understanding of the one she started with by going around the circle and seeing how it is connected with related notions. Thus, if circularity is spread over a great many analyses (the more, the better), it may cease to constitute a defect.

You might wonder how someone can get any understanding of a concept by seeing its connections with other concepts. The answer, I think, is that basic concepts are learned through interactions with what is normally called the world, the nonlinguistic and nonconceptual part of reality. These events and actions of everyday objects get conceptualized in various ways. This idea is inspired by Immanuel Kant's adage, "Concepts without perceptions are empty; perceptions without concepts are blind."

The ideas of analysis discussed so far presuppose that the goal of analysis is understanding. Not all philosophers take this view; some regard the goal to be *reduction*. The idea behind reductionism is that understanding something problematic is less problematic if a complex phenomenon is broken down into simpler things. This is common in science. Water is better understood when its simpler elements, hydrogen and oxygen, are understood. Hydrogen, oxygen, and other elements are better understood when their simpler elements, electrons, protons, and neutrons, are understood. But reductive analysis adds something to the concept of analysis. The more complicated things, such as water, are eliminated, no longer thought of as significant.

Reduction as elimination does not require just simpler things; the things also have to be of a different kind. Water gives way to chemical elements; chemical elements give way to atoms, and atoms to subatomic particles. Many philosophical theories are similar. One philosophical theory is preferable to another if it requires fewer different kinds of objects to explain reality. Thus, if one theory requires two kinds of objects, then it is usually considered superior to another that requires 13 kinds. (The principle that entities should not be multiplied beyond what is necessary is known as "Ockham's razor," after William of Ockham, a fourteenth-century English philosopher, to whom it is credited.) However, monism, a theory that posits or reduces everything to one thing, either mental entities or material entities, should be more attractive than dualism. Why then the dominance of dualism during most of the seventeenth century and even for much of the twentieth century? The reason is that philosophers found it difficult to give a plausible and adequate account of both mental and physical things. Since at least the beginning of this century, monism has been favored. Many philosophers believe that cognitive science has provided substantial evidence for materialism. Naturalistic panpsychism, the view that every genuine entity includes a mental dimension, is a kind of monism. In general, monism is more attractive than dualism unless it has some drawbacks that outweigh its simplicity.

When the analysans of an analysis of concept c does not contain anything like c, then it is tempting to think that c has not only been explained by the analysans but also that c can be eliminated as a genuine kind of thing. For example, suppose that the natural numbers 1, 2, 3, and so on seem to be genuinely existent things because people talk as if they are things like "Three is odd" and "Seven plus five equals twelve." These sentences seem to be true because the numbers referred to seem to have properties. However, because numbers cannot be sensed, some philosophers have tried to devise a way of analyzing numbers, addition, of being prime, and so on, entirely in terms of the characteristics of physical objects. If any of these attempts were successful, then the assumption that numbers exist could be eliminated. A statement that "two plus two equals four" would really be a statement about physical objects in a greatly abbreviated form.

In many cases, the reduction takes more than one analysis. For example, Thomas Hobbes, who proposed to reduce all phenomena to the motions of material particles, analyzed governments in terms of the actions of human beings, the actions of human beings in terms of the motions of their limbs and organs, and the motions of their limbs and organs in terms of tiny motions of tiny bits of material particles.

Clearly, a group of *reductive* analyses must never be allowed to form a circle, however large. An analysandum that creeps back into a subsequent analysans has not been eliminated from the philosophical theory, and the reductionist's whole project is vitiated. This fact has certain paradoxical consequences. There are many cases in which it is obvious that A can be analyzed in terms of B and B in terms of A, but neither of the two is simpler or more basic than the other. The reductionist who takes Ockham's razor seriously will presumably want to adopt one of these reductions, but she cannot adopt both of them without forming a circle. How is she to choose? That is a genuine question.

Let me now turn to other ways in which an analysis might be defective, namely, how an analysis might be too strong or too weak. An analysis is too strong just in case it is possible to give an example of the notion being analyzed (the analysandum) that does not satisfy all the conditions specified in the analysans; conversely, an analysis is too weak just in case it is possible to describe something that satisfies all the conditions set down in the analysans but is not an instance of the analysandum. Consider this analysis of bachelorhood:

Something is a bachelor if and only if
(1) it is unmarried;
(2) it is male; and
(3) it is human.

This analysis is too weak, because children satisfy all three conditions, but we consider only adults to be bachelors.

Let's now consider a stronger analysis of bachelorhood:

Something is a bachelor if and only if
(1) it is unmarried;
(2) it is male;
(3) it is human;
(4) it is adult; and
(5) it plays tennis.

This analysis is too strong; bachelors who do not play tennis do not meet condition (5), so (5) should not be part of the analysans.

It is possible for a single analysis to be both too strong and too weak. For example, we can combine the defects of the analysis that was too weak with the defects of the analysis that was too strong:

Something is a bachelor if and only if
(1) it is unmarried;
(2) it is male;
(3) it is human; and
(4) it plays tennis.

Since there are bachelors who don't play tennis, the analysis is too strong. Since there are male, unmarried children who play tennis and are not bachelors (because they are too young), the analysis is too weak. Too strong and too weak.

Here are two more examples of philosophical analyses that are too strong and too weak. These analyses are supposed to explain how private property comes to exist. It assumes the background condition of "the state of nature," that is, the condition in which there is no civil government. It also assumes that no object has previously been owned. Here's the first analysis:

An object O becomes the property of a person P if and only if P mixes P's labor with O.

This analysis is too strong because a person can own something without mixing their labor with it. We will present a situation in which the left-hand side of the analysis is true and the right-hand side of the analysis is false. Suppose a tree contains an apple and a person controls the apple by guarding it against all others. Then that person owns the apple. But that person has not mixed her labor with the apple. The person may have exerted herself by fending off would-be takers of the apple, but she has not touched the apple and hence could not have mixed her labor with it. This is a counterexample, that is, an example that shows that some claim or proposition is false. (See also section 5.6.) But a defender of the analysis of property might object to this supposed counterexample in various ways. One is to deny that guarding an object is the same as owning it. Another is to extend the concept of mixing one's labor to include guarding an object. Are there replies to these objections?

The next counterexample is supposed to show that the analysis is too weak. We will present a situation in which the right-hand side of the analysis is true and the left-hand side of the analysis is false. Suppose that someone squashes an apple underfoot. The person has mixed her labor with it but does not own it.

Let's now consider the second analysis; this one is about how value in an object originates. The concept of mixing one's labor is used again:

An object O has a value if and only if a person P mixes P's labor with O.

The analysis is too strong. Suppose two hungry people see a ripe apple. The apple has a value because they want it. But neither has mixed his labor with it.

The analysis is also too weak. Suppose again that a person intentionally squashes an apple. The person has mixed his labor with the apple but the apple has no value because no one wants a squashed apple.

It is usual to hold that the terms in the analysans are more basic or primary than the terms in the analysandum. However, there are correlative terms that are equally primary. (Two terms are correlative terms just in case the simplest analysis for each term is in terms of the other.) That is, it is incorrect to say that one is more basic or primary than the other. Most alleged correlative terms are contestable. For example, some (witty) philosopher has defined the terms *mind* and *matter* in this way:

Mind: no matter.
Matter: never mind.

It is easy to be a dualist if mind and matter are genuinely correlative terms. The terms *particular* and *universal* have also sometimes, though not always, been treated as correlative terms: A universal is something that groups particulars into a class, and a particular is something that is grouped into a class by a universal but does not itself group things.

Some pairs of terms that initially look like correlative terms may turn out not to be. (For our purpose *husband* and *wife* are used as they were in the twentieth century.) It is tempting to argue that *husband* and *wife* are correlative terms on the grounds that each is definable in terms of the other:

A husband is a person who has a wife.
A wife is a person who has a husband.

However, while it is true that the concept of a husband is not more basic or primary than the concept of a wife and vice versa, this does not entail that they are correlative terms. Each is definable in terms of something common to both of them:

A husband is a male spouse.
A wife is a female spouse.

Exercises

1   Is the following analysis too strong, too weak, or adequate? If too strong or too weak, make the changes necessary to make it just right.

An object O increases in value at a time t iff people are willing to give more for it at t than at the immediately previous time.

2   Is the following analysis of *increase in value* for a particular person too strong, too weak, defective in some other way, or adequate? If it is defective in any way, make the changes needed to make it adequate.

An object O increases in value for a person P at a time t_1 iff P's desire for O is greater at t_1 than it was at the immediately preceding time.

3   It has been argued that the following analysis of the origin of property is too strong and too weak. Is there any other criticism that could be made against it?

An object O becomes the property of a person P if and only if P mixes P's labor with O.

4   Is the following analysis too strong or too weak? If it is defective in either way, change it so that the analysis becomes adequate.

An action A is merciful if and only if there is a person $P1$ and there is a person $P2$ such that in doing A, $P1$ gives $P2$ something good that $P1$ does not owe to $P2$.

5   Is the following analysis too strong or too weak? If it is defective in either way, change it so that the analysis becomes adequate.

A person P is perfectly merciful if and only if P does many merciful actions and no unmerciful actions.

6   Use your final analyses in (4) and (5) to give an analysis of these two analysanda:

An action A is just if and only if
A person P is perfectly just if and only if

7   In the following paragraph from Plato's *Gorgias,* what is Socrates saying the problem is with Gorgias' definition of rhetoric?

Socrates: Gorgias, what is your definition of rhetoric?

Gorgias: Speaking.
Socrates: How do you mean that, Gorgias? Do you mean rhetoric explains to sick people how they can get well?
Gorgias: No.
Socrates: Then, rhetoric is not concerned with all speech.
Gorgias: No. Of course not.

8   What is Locus implying is wrong with Hocus's analysis of a contract in this exchange?

Hocus: A contract is a promise between two people.
Locus: If Lee and Mee promise each other to meet at noon on the West Mall, have they made a contract?

9   What is Mar implying is wrong with Hob's analysis of social contract in this exchange?

Hob: To enter into a social contract it is sufficient if a person consents to a government.
Mar: If a person consents to letting a neighbor borrow a lawnmower, is there a contract?
Hob: No.

5.4   Dilemmas

In chapter 2, the valid inference forms of constructive and destructive dilemmas were explained. These may be called formal dilemmas because they do not say anything about the content of the premises or conclusions. In a more familiar sense, a dilemma always involves setting out alternatives that are somehow unacceptable. For example, consider this argument, which contains a dilemma:

If determinism is true, then humans are not responsible for their actions; and if indeterminism is true, then humans do not cause their own actions.

Either determinism is true or indeterminism is true.

Either humans are not responsible for their actions or humans do not cause their own actions.

The alternatives expressed in the conclusion are unacceptable because we want others to be responsible for their bad actions and we want to be the cause of our own actions.

Investigating unacceptable propositions is a common project because philosophers want to straighten out problematic beliefs. Many beliefs are either in tension with one another or inconsistent whether they are held unreflectively or reflectively. Often the tension or inconsistency is between the beliefs of two people, but sometimes they are in the same person. The analogous tension or inconsistency occurs in interpretation. Often two people have different interpretations of the same text. And sometimes a person thinks that the meaning of one part of a text is in tension with or inconsistent with another part. (Chapter 11 discusses this matter more extensively.)

The tension or inconsistency between texts or beliefs can be made explicit by formulating a dilemma. That dilemma can form the core of an essay. Often it requires no more than an introductory sentence or two and a relaxation of the ascetic style of formal logic. Consider this essay fragment that incorporates the example of constructive dilemma above:

> The nature of human actions is very important for understanding the nature of human beings. Yet, on the face of it, the nature of human action is perplexing and gives rise to the following dilemma. If determinism is true, then humans are not responsible for their actions; and if indeterminism is true, then humans do not cause their own actions. But either determinism is true or indeterminism is true. So, either humans are not responsible for their actions or humans do not cause their own actions. The purpose of this essay is to argue for a way out of this dilemma.

Although this fragment needs to be worked out in more detail – definitions need to be supplied, explanations as to why causality precludes responsibility, etc. – it is a start. Because material dilemmas conclude with unpleasant alternatives, philosophers try to resolve them, in a way that eliminates the unpleasantness. Since constructive and destructive dilemmas are formally valid, the only way to resolve them is to show that one of the premises is false. Since they have two premises, there are two standard ways of doing this: showing that the conjunctive premise, composed of two conditional propositions, is false, or showing that the disjunctive premise is false.

Showing that the disjunctive premise is false is called *going between the horns of the dilemma* because it shows that a person does not need to be gored by either horn. To show that the disjunctive premise is false is to show that both disjuncts are false and that there is some third possibility that is true. Consider this dilemma:

If Hobbes is right, then humans are nothing but machines; if Hume is right, humans have no substantial existence at all.

Either Hobbes is right or Hume is right.

Either humans are nothing but machines or humans have no substantial existence at all.

It is easy to see that this dilemma can be resolved by going between the horns. The second premise presents a false alternative. The philosophies of Hobbes and Hume are not the only choices. Good dilemmas are not so easy to defeat. They are usually formulated with a disjunctive premise that either does or at least seems to exhaust the alternatives as in the essay fragment above. The premise "Either determinism is true or indeterminism is true" *seems* to cover all the possibilities; there *seems* to be no other alternative.

Exercise

Are these really the only two possibilities? What is it about the disjunctive proposition that suggests that there are more than two possibilities?

The dilemma might, however, be susceptible to the other method of resolution. Showing that the conjunctive premise is false is called "grabbing the dilemma by the horns" because by grabbing both horns one avoids being gored by either one. Grabbing the horns consists of showing that at least one of the conjuncts is false. The dilemma in the essay fragment above may be susceptible to grabbing the dilemma by the horns, in this case, showing the conditional proposition on the left side is false. A philosophical author might argue that although determinism is true, humans are nonetheless responsible for their actions. Responsibility for an action attaches to a normal person who performs that action without coercion. If this tack were taken and incorporated into an essay, the result might look something like this:

The nature of human actions is very important to understand in order to understand the nature of human beings. Yet, on the face of it, the nature of human action is perplexing and gives rise to the following dilemma.

131

If determinism is true, then humans are not responsible for their actions; and if indeterminism is true, then humans do not cause their own actions. But either determinism is true or indeterminism is true. So, either humans are not responsible for their actions or humans do not cause their own actions. The purpose of this essay is to argue for a way out of this dilemma. I shall argue that the first premise is false because the first conjunct, "If determinism is true, then humans are not responsible for their actions," is false. For, even if determinism is true, normal humans are responsible for their actions, and are responsible for them because they are not coerced.

There is a third way of dealing with dilemmas: to produce a counter-dilemma. This typically consists of producing a dilemma that has the same disjunctive premise, and the same antecedent propositions in the conjunctive premise. But the consequents typically are contraries of the disjuncts of the conclusion of the original dilemma. The following essay fragment contains a dilemma and a counter-dilemma:

It might seem that human existence is absurd. This appearance of absurdity is tied to the issues of the existence of God, human freedom and salvation. The following dilemma suggests itself: If God exists, then humans are not free to determine their own destiny; and if God does not exist, then there is no hope for eternal salvation. God either exists or he doesn't. So, humans are either not free to determine their own destiny or there is no hope for eternal salvation.

However, this dilemma does not tell the whole story, as the following counter-dilemma shows: If God does exist, then there is hope for eternal salvation; and if God does not exist, then humans are free to determine their own destiny. Thus, either there is hope for eternal salvation or humans are free to determine their own destiny.

The dilemma may be represented as having this form:

$$\frac{(p \rightarrow \sim q)\,\&\,(\sim p \rightarrow \sim r)}{(p \vee \sim p)}$$
$$(\sim q \vee \sim r)$$

Relative to the dilemma, the counter-dilemma may be represented as having this form:

$$\frac{(\sim p \rightarrow q)\,\&\,(p \rightarrow r)}{(\sim p \vee p)}$$
$$(q \vee r)$$

These logical forms of the dilemma and counter-dilemma do not reveal the propositional content of the ps, qs, rs, and $s$es, and it's the propositional content that constitutes the meat of the dispute over freedom and salvation. Dilemmas and counter-dilemmas may also be represented as having these forms:

$$\text{Dilemma}$$
$$(p \rightarrow q) \& (r \rightarrow s)$$
$$\underline{(p \vee r)}$$
$$(q \vee s)$$

$$\text{Counter} - \text{dilemma}$$
$$(p \rightarrow \sim s) \& (r \rightarrow \sim q)$$
$$\underline{(p \vee r)}$$
$$(\sim s \vee \sim q)$$

(See also chapter 2, section 2.2)

Exercise

Write out the sentences from the essay-fragment above that correspond to p, q, r, and s in the forms of the dilemma and counter-dilemma in the passage about freedom and redemption.

Producing a counter-dilemma does not in itself refute a dilemma. It does not show that the original dilemma is unsound. However, counter-dilemmas do indicate that the corresponding dilemma is not cogent. One way of showing the lack of cogency is to indicate that the dilemma does not consider all the possibilities relevant to the debated issue. The above essay fragment makes it explicit that the dilemma does not consider all the issues relevant to whether human life is meaningful or not. The dilemma relates only to the downside of the existence or nonexistence of God. The counter-dilemma relates only to the upside of the existence or nonexistence of God.

Sometimes a dilemma and its counter-dilemma indicate that the circumstances of the debated issue produce a contradiction. A story is told of a sophist who agreed to teach a student to be a lawyer on the following condition: The pupil would not have to pay for the lessons unless he did not win his first case. When the student did not get any cases after his education had been completed, the sophist sued. The pupil defended himself by constructing a dilemma:

> If I win this case, then I do not have to pay my teacher (since the teacher will have lost his suit for payment), and if I lose this case, I do not have to pay my teacher (since, by our original contract, I do not have to pay him if I lose my first suit).
> Either I win this case or I lose this case.
> I do not have to pay my teacher.

The sophist rebutted the student with a counter-dilemma:

> If I (the teacher) win this case, then my student has to pay me, and if I lose this case, then my student has to pay me (since he has won his first case).
> Either I win this case or I lose it.
> My student has to pay me.

The fact that both the dilemma and the counter-dilemma are valid and their conclusions are contradictory suggests that some underlying contradiction is involved.

However, there is one more thing to notice about the student-teacher arguments. The conclusions are not disjunctive propositions. If these arguments were laid out more explicitly, the conclusion of the first would be, "Either I do not have to pay my teacher or I do not have to pay my teacher," and the conclusion of the second would be, "Either my student has to pay me or my student has to pay me." Since the second disjunct is redundant in each case, it is valid to delete it. This move is canonized in another rule of inference, which can be added to the rules of inference discussed in chapter 2:

Tautology

$$\frac{p \lor p}{p}$$

5.5 Scenarios

Philosophers often illustrate or prove a point by constructing a scenario. As its name suggests, a scenario is a detailed description of a situation that perspicuously establishes the intended point. Ludwig Wittgenstein's later philosophy was driven by his compelling scenarios. For example, near the beginning of the *Philosophical Investigations*, he in effect says this:

> Suppose that a group of builders has a language with only four words, "block," "pillar," "beam," and "slab." One worker calls out one of these four words and another worker brings him the appropriate item. This can be thought of as a complete primitive language.

The scenario shows that while this kind of behavior satisfies the standard account of what philosophers say a human language is like, this kind of behavior, as restricted as it is, does not give a fair description of genuine human languages. At best, it is a "complete primitive language." However, as philosophers and linguists understand natural languages, this primitive communicative practice is not rich enough to count as a language. That is, the standard philosophical picture of a language a century ago is inadequate. Wittgenstein goes on to develop a more adequate account. Powerful scenarios are vivid, lively, and sometimes wryly amusing, as Wittgenstein's is.

But scenarios can have pitfalls. There is a difference between being amusing and caricaturing. A caricature misrepresents. And a misrepresentation can never be used either to prove or refute a point. (To caricature a position and then to refute it is to commit the strawman fallacy. A strawman is something easily knocked down.)

Also the description of a scenario should not be tendentious or question-begging. An example was given in chapter 1.

> Suppose that Smith and Jones have their brains interchanged. Then Smith has Jones's brain, and Jones has Smith's brain.

Since it is disputable who is who when brains are interchanged, it is unfair for the author to identify one specific body as the person Smith and another specific body as the person Jones. That issue has to be discussed.

Another way in which a scenario can go wrong is to describe it in insufficient detail. (Because of issues of space, all the examples I give border on being insufficient.) When this happens, the author often draws an unwarranted conclusion on the basis of what she has described. The reader often does not notice the problem because he tends to cooperate with the author's thought. This cooperativeness is a background condition for understanding what the author means. Sometimes unreflectively following what the author says leads one astray. In these cases, I say that the author has committed the fallacy of the under-described scenario. Here's an example:

> A common view among philosophers is that the survival of human beings obviously requires that a large majority of their views are true. Otherwise,

their false beliefs would lead them to act in ways that would kill them off. But this common view is false. It is easy to describe possible communities that do quite well with (virtually) all false beliefs. Suppose there is a tribe that believes that everything is a witch. So they believe that some witches are good to eat; and some witches grow blueberries on their arms in the spring; and some witches bark; and some witches meow, and so on.

This scenario commits the fallacy of the under-described scenario, because the author is not considering that in addition to the false beliefs mentioned, the natives also have many true beliefs often related to the false ones, for example, this thing is good to eat, and that thing grows berries in the spring, and this other thing barks, and this other thing meows, and so on. (I pass over the likelihood that if the people in the scenario above believe that "witches" are good to eat, grow blueberries on their arms, and some are cats, they are not correctly described as believing that everything is a witch.)

It might be the case that the natives never utter sentences that directly express such beliefs or even consciously think of them, but that does not show that the natives do not have them. And the conclusive evidence that they do have them is their behavior.

Exercise

Is the following essay fragment an instance of the under-described scenario?

A common view among philosophers is that the survival of human beings obviously requires that a large majority of their views are true. Otherwise, their false beliefs would lead them to act in ways that would kill them off. But this common view is false. It is easy to describe communities that do quite well with (virtually) all false beliefs. Suppose that each person of the community believes that the qualitative features of things – how they look, smell, sound, taste, and feel to touch are the way that those things are in themselves, independently of being perceived.

5.6 Counterexamples

A counterexample, something that goes counter to some proposition or argument, is a powerful tool. People know how to use counterexamples by the age of five or six. A frustrated parent says to his child, "You never pick up the clothes in your room!" The child responds, "That's not true. Yesterday, I picked up my shoe and threw it at John." The parent is refuted. Some counterexamples induce laughter. A friend of mine had two precocious daughters. The older one once made some slight error, which the younger one pounced on unmercifully. In a desperate attempt to defend herself, the older child protested, "Nobody's perfect!" The younger smugly pointed her finger heavenward, indicating the Almighty. Thus was her sister refuted.

A counterexample may be a true statement that shows another statement to be false. In the universe of DC Comics, a counterexample to the statement, "No human being can fly," is "Superman can fly." A counterexample may also involve a scenario that shows that some statement or analysis is wrong. One of the most famous counterexamples of the twentieth century concerns a once-standard analysis of knowledge. According to that analysis, (propositional) knowledge is this:

S knows that p if and only if
(1) p is true;
(2) S believes that p; and
(3) S is justified in believing p.

To refute this analysis, Edmund Gettier constructed a couple of scenarios, each of which satisfied all three conditions in the analysans but which were not examples of knowledge. One of them went like this. Imagine that Smith is justified in believing the proposition "Jones owns a Ford." Smith has known Jones for many years; he has always owned a Ford; Smith saw Jones driving a Ford an hour ago, etc. Imagine further that Smith believes it. And finally imagine that Smith realizes that "Jones owns a Ford" entails "Jones owns a Ford or Brown is in Barcelona." But now imagine that Jones has sold his Ford, that he is driving a rented Toyota, and that Brown, coincidentally, is in Barcelona. Then the proposition "Jones owns a Ford or Brown is in Barcelona" is true; Smith believes it; and Smith is justified in believing it. Yet, Smith does not know it, because the grounds of his belief are coincidental to its truth.

Although this counterexample to the analysis of knowledge as justified true belief is relatively simple, even simpler ones can be constructed. Suppose Smith has known Jones for many years. He has met and talked with him often in a variety of places, and so on. Further suppose that he believes the proposition "Jones is walking across the West Mall" because he sees someone who looks exactly like Jones walking across the West Mall. And finally suppose that, although Jones is indeed walking across the West Mall, he is behind a wall and out of Smith's line of vision; that the person

Smith sees is not Jones but Jones's twin brother, dressed in Jones's clothes. Then all the conditions of the analysans are satisfied, yet Smith does not know "Jones is walking across the West Mall."

Exercises

1 If some scenarios are counterexamples, what does that show about the distinction between scenarios and counterexamples?

2 The Second Amendment to the US Constitution reads: A well-regulated Militia, being necessary to the security of a free State, the right of the people to keep and bear Arms, shall not be infringed. The following apparent counterexample, amendment 2.5, has been proposed: Well-regulated roads, being necessary to the security of a free State, the right of the people to drive shall not be infringed. (Suggested by a letter to the editor of the Austin *American-Statesman,* April 23, 2023.)

   By this amendment, state and federal governments and agencies may not require citizens to take drivers' tests or to possess drivers' licenses and must allow 18-wheel tractor trailers and Zamboni's to drive on neighborhood streets. But the absurdity of this proves that the interpretation of the second amendment by guns' rights supporters is mistaken.

   Is amendment 2.5 an actual counterexample to the interpretation that guns' rights supporters advocate? Why or why not.

One of the funniest counterexamples occurs in a work of literature. In chapter VII of *Alice's Adventures in Wonderland,* at the Mad Hatter's tea party, Alice claims that to mean what one says is the same as to say what one means. The Hatter counters that by saying, "Why, you might just as well say that 'I see what I eat' is the same thing as 'I eat what I see!'" (The Mad Hatter uses the same sentence-form as Alice, but substitutes "see" and "eat" for Alice's "say" and "mean," respectively.) The March Hare reinforces the Hatter's view by producing another counterexample when he says, "You might just as well say that 'I like what I get' is the same as 'I get what I like'."

It is crucial for the alleged counterexamples to be *obviously* false. If their falsity is not obvious, the person who made the original statement need not admit that she was wrong. For example, after the Mad Hatter's and the

March Hare's counterexamples, the narcoleptic Dormouse tries his own hand at producing a counterexample when he says, "You might just as well say that 'I breathe when I sleep' is the same thing as 'I sleep when I breathe'." The Mad Hatter counters with "It *is* the same thing with you." He implies that the Dormouse's alleged counterexample does not seem to be one.

Exercises

1   Is the Mad Hatter's statement a genuine counterexample to the Dormouse's statement?

2   Give an example that shows that saying and meaning are not always the same.

3   Allegedly but improbably, Plato defined a human being as a featherless biped; and Diogenes brought to the Academy a plucked chicken to serve as a counterexample. Revise Plato's definition to avoid the counterexample. (You must include "biped" or "featherless" in the revised definition.) Then think of a counterexample to the revised definition.

A counterexample may be given to an argument as simple as one with a single premise. Bertrand Russell asserted that "A genuine proper name must name something" entailed the proposition "Only a name that *must* name something is a proper name." Peter Geach called this "a howler in modal logic" ("The Perils of Pauline," in *Logic Matters*, Oxford: Basil Blackwell, 1972, p. 155). It is formally like arguing from the proposition "What you know must be so" to the proposition, "Only what *must* be so is really known." Geach's counterexample consists of a true proposition of the same form as Russell's premise and a false proposition of the same form as Russell's conclusion. Since a true premise cannot entail a false conclusion (see chapter 2), Geach showed that Russell's argument was invalid.

Here's another example of an argument being shown to be invalid by giving another argument of the same form that has a true premise and a false conclusion:

If Plato was an idealist, then Aristotle was a realist.
Aristotle was a realist.
_____

Plato was an idealist.

The premises and conclusion are both true, and its form of inference is superficially similar to the form of *modus ponens*. In fact, however, the argument is formally invalid, as indicated by this argument:

> If Plato is the author of *The Critique of Pure Reason*, then Plato is a great philosopher.
>
> Plato was a great philosopher.
> _____
> Plato wrote *The Critique of Pure Reason*.

Notice that the premises of the argument are true but the conclusion false. Thus, the argument must be invalid. It is an instance of what is known as the fallacy of affirming the consequent. In essay form, the original argument and its counterexample might be phrased in this way:

> It has sometimes been argued that Plato was an idealist. For, if Plato was an idealist, then Aristotle was a realist. Aristotle was a realist. However, this argument is unsound. One might just as well argue that Plato wrote *The Critique of Pure Reason*. For, if Plato wrote the *The Critique of Pure Reason*, then Plato was a great philosopher. And Plato was a great philosopher. Therefore, he wrote the *Critique*.

It is easy to think that apparent counterexamples are always genuine ones. But that is not true. Consider this apparent counterexample to the ontological argument for the existence of God by Anselm of Canterbury:

(1) God is the greatest conceivable being.
(2) Either the greatest conceivable being exists in the understanding only or it exists also in reality.
(3) If the greatest conceivable being exists in the understanding only, then it is not the greatest conceivable being.
_____
(4) God exists in reality also.

The monk Gaunilo advanced the following as a counterexample:

(G1) The Perfect Island is the greatest conceivable island.
(G2) Either the greatest conceivable island exists in the understanding only or it exists in reality also.
(G3) If the greatest conceivable island exists in the understanding only, then it is not the greatest conceivable island.
_____
(G4) The Perfect Island exists in reality also.

The falsity of the conclusion (G4) *seems* to show that something is wrong with the form of Anselm's argument. However, in this case, I think Gaunilo's alleged counterexample fails because (G1) is arguably false (does not express a proposition). So Gaunilo's argument does not consist of true premises. The description "The Perfect Island" does not genuinely refer to anything or express any concept. There are no answers to such questions as How big is the Perfect Island? What is its shape? What is the air temperature? Is it always sunny? What flora and fauna does it contain? In contrast, Anselm does have defensible answers to questions relevant to a perfect being. It knows everything that can be known; every action it performs is good; it is able to do everything that can be done; it is just; but it is not literally merciful. (The ontological argument is not cogent, but its failure lies elsewhere.) The point of the example of the ontological argument is that not every apparent counterexample is a genuine one.

Exercises

1 Does the essay fragment below present a genuine counterexample to an argument for abortion? Discuss.

> Some people think that abortion is justified because a woman has the right to do whatever she wants to with her own body; and having an abortion is doing something with her own body. The argument is unsound. One might just as well argue that punching a bystander in the nose is justified because a woman has the right to do whatever she wants to with her own body and punching a bystander in the nose is doing something with her own body.

2 Suppose for the sake of discussion that the apparent counterexample above is a genuine one. Does that show that abortion is unjustified?

The method of counterexample is often powerful because it allows for a kind of indirect attack on a proposition or argument that is not very persuasively attacked directly. It's unlikely that marshaling evidence against the proposition "A woman has the right to do whatever she wants to with her own body" would persuade many people who would otherwise believe it. The reason is commonplace; it's very widely accepted without argument. (Although it is commonplace, it is, I think, false. No one, male or female, has unlimited rights over the use of their own body.) The principle needs to be restricted in some way to be true. Human beings perhaps have the right to do whatever they want in connection with reproductive matters or privacy, or something similar, but not unlimited rights. It is possible that those who espouse the principle under discussion do not literally mean it, but mean something that is verbally similar to it such as, "A woman has the right to have anything done to her own body that she wants to." Yet even this principle is dubious since many states have laws against masochism, self-mutilation, and suicide. Thus, an indirect assault on the proposition has a much greater chance of success. That's what the method of counterexample provides.

Although a counterexample is a logically effective way of arguing against some position, often it may not be persuasive because the counterexample is not recognized as such. In these situations, more is required. The author must get the reader to recognize that the relevant proposition is false, perhaps by suggesting an explanation of why someone might think the proposition is true. Such an explanation is not proof that the proposition is false; rather, it psychologically prepares the reader for recognizing the proof. Some philosophers have borrowed the medical term "diagnosis" for preparing a reader for considering a certain line of argument. It is analogous to the preparatory procedure some psychotherapists use to get a patient to gain insight into the causes of his neurosis. Diagnoses can be quite controversial; they require a great deal of imagination and rarely, if ever, are definitive. Different people might believe the same false proposition for different reasons.

Some counterexamples simply refute a theory. If the theory is important, then the counterexample may be important. This is especially so when the counterexample attacks some central aspect of the theory, as Gettier's did. If the counterexample does not undermine a central aspect, it may simply point out that the theory needs fine-tuning and that it can be fixed by changing the wording. In such a case, the counterexample may be correct but not very important. The most important and powerful kind of counterexample is one that suggests some promising line of developing a different and more adequate theory. For example, recall the counterexample about Smith thinking that he saw Jones crossing the West Mall when in fact he saw only someone who looked like Jones. To many philosophers, the example seemed to indicate that knowledge requires a certain *causal* relation between the belief and the evidence and spurred interest in the "causal theory" of knowledge. One feature that made this counterexample important to many philosophers is that it seemed to show that there was something fundamentally wrong with the analysis of knowledge as justified true belief. That is, it seemed that the counterexample could not be avoided simply by fiddling a bit with the wording or by adding a more

142

precise phrase (other philosophers, however, did try, and still do try, to fix the original conditions). What also made the counterexample important is that it suggested a direction in which the correct analysis of knowledge might be found. The counterexample indicated that in order for something to count as knowledge, the right kind of causal relation has to hold between the belief and the thing believed.

Counterexamples are an important method in philosophical argumentation. Sometimes they can be short and to the point. A philosopher once said that the difference between human faces and animal faces is that animals can't change the expression on their faces (he was thinking of ants, aardvarks, and pigs). His colleague came back in a flash with "What about chimpanzees?" Other times, a counterexample takes a lot of time to develop. It needs a lot of stage setting and explanation to show that it really is a case of what it is supposed to be. I urge you to try to use them and label them as such in your essays.

There are no simple rules for thinking up counterexamples. One might say that one should run through a lot of examples in one's mind until one happens on a case that does not fit the proposition to be refuted, but it is fair to ask, "How do you do this?" or "How does one do this in such a way that one ends up with a counterexample and not just a lot of examples that confirm the proposition?" In other words, thinking up counterexamples ultimately depends upon imagination. Some people are talented in this regard and others not.

Exercises

1   Consider this brief essay:

> Some people think that abortion is justified because a woman has the right to do whatever she wants to do with her own body; and having an abortion is doing something with her own body. This argument for abortion is unsound. One might just as well argue that punching a bystander in the nose is justified because a woman has the right to do whatever she wants to with her own body and punching a bystander in the nose is doing something with her own body.

Make the premises and conclusion of the argument for abortion explicit. Do the same for the alleged counterexample. Explain why both arguments are valid arguments. Then attempt to either defend the original argument for abortion," or revise it in some way to avoid the counterexample.

143

2 Often famous counterexamples are more complicated than they need to be; and it is valuable to write an essay that simplifies or includes a simplification of such a counterexample. Select some elaborate counterexample that you have encountered. Try to construct a simpler one that has the same effect.

3 For an elaborate and influential counterexample, read Keith Donnellan, "Proper Names and Identifying Descriptions," in *Semantics of Natural Languages*, ed. Donald Davidson and Gilbert Harman, New York: Humanities Press, 1972, pp. 356–79.

4 Think of possible counterexamples to these propositions:
   (a) All humans are mortal.
   (b) All humans act out of their own self-interest.
   (c) Whatever promotes the greatest happiness for the greatest number of human is right.

5 Edmund Gettier's article, discussed above, generated a lot of interest soon after its publication. The following three articles concern additional counterexamples and various attempts to fix the analysis of knowledge. Read them for further specimens of counterexamples.
   (a) Michael Clark, "Knowledge and Grounds: A Comment on Mr. Gettier's Paper," *Analysis* 24 (1963).
   (b) Ernest Sosa, "The Analysis of 'Knowledge that P'," *Analysis* 25 (1964), 1–8.
   (c) John Turk Saunders and Narayan Champawat, "Mr. Clark's Definition of 'Knowledge'," *Analysis* 25 (1964), 8–9.

5.7   Reductio ad Absurdum

Reductio ad absurdum arguments are frequently used in ordinary argumentation with no difficulty. For example:

Many people believe the Enemy Principle, namely, that the enemy of my enemy is my friend, even though taken as a principle it is fairly obviously false. During the 1980s, both Iraq and Iran were our enemies. Further, Iran was the enemy of Iraq. So, by the Enemy Principle, Iran was our friend. But that is absurd. So the Enemy Principle is false.

Although this argument is easy to follow, people often have difficulty understanding why *reductio* arguments like this are valid and difficulty in understanding *reductio* arguments in philosophy when they are explicitly formulated.

Roughly, in a *reductio ad absurdum* argument, a person proves a proposition by assuming for the sake of argument the opposite of the proposition he wants to prove. The notion of a *reductio* argument exploits an aspect of the notion of entailment. Recall that entailment preserves truth. From a true proposition, only true propositions follow. This means that if a proposition entails something patently false, then that proposition must be false. Now, if that false proposition is the opposite of the proposition to be proved, then the one to be proved must be true. That is the strategy that *reductio* arguments exploit. In short, if some proposition entails a false proposition, then the first proposition must also be false, and its negation must be true.

As is obvious from this description of *reductio* arguments, it is crucial to show that the entailed proposition is false. There are two ways of doing this. The surer of the two ways is to derive a contradiction – any contradiction. For example, if you can prove that the opposite of your view of universals entails, say, that it is possible for an object to be in a certain place and not to be in that place at the same time, then it is clear that that view is false; thus yours must be true.

In formal logic, *reductio* arguments are always derivations of a contradiction. They can be represented in the following way, where $p_1, \ldots, p_n$ are premises, q is the desired conclusion, and r is any derived proposition:

p_1 $\mid q$

p_2

.

.

.

p_n _____

$\sim q$[Supposition of *reductio*]

.

.

.

$(r \;\&\; \sim r)$

Notice that the premises are listed in one column while the conclusion q is listed at the top right in a half box. The first line of the derivation $\sim q$ is the negation of the conclusion. The three vertical dots indicate whatever (valid) inferences are needed in order to derive some contradiction "$(r \& \sim r)$." (It should go without saying that the contradiction could be "$(q \& \sim q)$"). Since assuming $\sim q$ leads to a contradiction, it must be false. Consequently, q must be true.

Here is an example that is inspired by an argument of Avicenna, an eleventh-century Islamic philosopher:

There cannot be two Gods; that is, there cannot be two perfect beings. For suppose that there were two. Then one of them, call it G_1, would have a property P_1 that the other one did not have. (There must be such a property because if there are two things, there must be some property that distinguishes them.) P_1 either contributes to making G_1 perfect or it does not. If it does, then the other God G_2 would lack a property that makes a being perfect and hence would not be God. If it does not, then G_1 has a property that does not make it perfect, and in that case, G_1 has a property that is superfluous to being perfect and hence is not perfect.

This argument can be represented as follows:

(1) There are two Gods, G_1 and G_2. [Supposition of *Reductio*]
(2) Either P_1 contributes to making G_2 perfect or it does not. [Tautology]
(3) If P_1 contributes to making G_1 perfect, then G_2 is not God.
(4) If P_1 does not contribute to making G_1 perfect, then G_1 is not God.
(5) Either G_1 or G_2 is not God. (From 2, 3, and 4 by conjunction and constructive dilemma)
(6) There are two Gods, G_1 and G_2, and either G_1 or G_2 is not God. (This is a contradiction.)

(7) There are not two Gods.

The other, and less sure, way to show that the entailed proposition is false is to derive a blatantly false proposition. Hilary Putnam attempts to produce such a *reductio* as part of his defense that the meaning of a word, say, "water," is not determined by the psychological state of the speaker. For example, if there were a planet ("Twin Earth") exactly like our planet except that the mark "water" was used to refer to a substance that had all the phenomenal properties that water has on earth, but had a chemical composition different from H_2O, then the word "water" on Twin Earth would not mean the same as "water" on earth. Now, since some have doubted this, Putnam presented this *reductio* in defense of his view:

> Suppose "water" has the same meaning on Earth and on Twin Earth. [Supposition of the *reductio*.] Now, let the word "water" become phonemically different on Twin Earth – say it becomes "quaxel." Presumably, this is not a change in meaning *per se* on any view. So "water" and "quaxel" have the same meaning (although they refer to different liquids). But this is highly counter-intuitive. [Supposedly absurd conclusion.] Why not say, then, that "elm" in my idiolect has the same meaning as "beech" in your idiolect, although they refer to different trees? ("Meaning and Reference," in *The Philosophy of Language*, 4th edn, ed. A. P. Martinich, New York: Oxford University Press, 2001, p. 295, n. 2)

But is the conclusion absurd? At least one reputable philosopher was not persuaded (Jay David Atlas, *Philosophy Without Ambiguity*, Oxford: Clarendon Press, 1989, p. 136). So it is not as easy as you might think to produce a proposition that your audience will consider patently false and hence absurd. Consider the seemingly patently false propositions that some philosophers have held:

Nothing moves.
Only one thing exists.
All things are God.
Material substances do not exist.
"Sir Walter Scott" is not a proper name.
Humans do not act freely.

Indeed, inventing an ingenious argument for a blatantly false proposition is the shortest route into the history of philosophy. Consider trying to prove the proposition "Some human actions are free" by a *reductio*. One might argue:

> Suppose that no human actions are free. [Supposition of the *reductio*.] Then no human beings are responsible for their actions. But this is absurd. Therefore, some human actions are free.

The problem with this argument is that many philosophers will maintain that it is not absurd to hold that human beings are not responsible for their actions. They may offer their own *reductio* argument that no human actions are free:

> Suppose that some human actions are free. Then some events, namely, human actions, have no cause. But this is absurd, since all events have causes. Therefore, no human actions are free.

What is a person to do? Know what the standard of success is. In philosophy, there seem to be two competing standards, though in some cases they may not be mutually exclusive.

One standard is that a philosophical conclusion should not, if reasonably possible, contradict common sense, that is, the generally shared beliefs of non-philosophers. This standard is motivated by the position that the job of a philosopher is to justify or explain ordinary beliefs, not to change them. This is what Wittgenstein meant when he said, "Philosophy leaves everything as it is." Philosophers who adopt this standard have been called *descriptive philosophers*. Of course, it is not always possible to justify all of our ordinary beliefs. Also, there may well be no one set of nontrivial basic beliefs that all people have. Thus, the aim here is an ideal that cannot always be achieved. In the above example, "Some human actions are free" would fit the commonsense view.

The other standard is that a philosophical conclusion should not contradict basic theoretical propositions. This standard is motivated by the view that the job of philosophy is to produce the neatest and intellectually most satisfying explanation of reality. While philosophers in this tradition often disagree about what the best explanation is, just as descriptive philosophers disagree about what the content of common sense is, they agree that one should choose one's philosophical principles first and then use them to determine what reality is like. Such philosophers have been called *speculative philosophers*. A special form of *reductio* argumentation has been called the *mirabilis consequentia*. It consists of showing that a proposition "not-p" entails the proposition p. An elegant case of this is an argument by Bertrand Russell against common sense:

> Common sense leads to science. Science says that common sense is false; therefore, common sense is false.

We can bring out the *reductio* structure more clearly if we formulate the argument in this way:

> Proof:
> (1) Suppose common sense is not false. [Supposition of the *reductio*]
> (2) If common sense is not false, then science is true. [Premise]
> (3) If science is true, then common sense is false. [Premise]
> _____
> (4) Common sense is false. [From 1, 2, and 3 by modus ponens.]

In an essay, this argument might be expressed in the following way:

> Common sense must be false. For, suppose that it is not false. If common sense is not false, then science is true, for common sense gave rise to science.

148

And, if science is true, then common sense is false, for science says that the commonsense view of reality is false. Therefore, common sense is false.

Students often find *reductio* arguments disorienting for a couple of related reasons. First, you may wonder how a philosopher can use some premise and then discard it. How can Russell prove that common sense is false when he begins by asserting that common sense is true? The source of this disorientation is the erroneous assumption that the author of any *reductio* argument in any way asserts or subscribes to the supposition of the *reductio*. Russell, for example, does not assert that common sense is true; he merely supposes or pretends for the sake of the argument that common sense is true. So he never commits himself to its truth. He exploits or uses to his own advantage the proposition that common sense is true, without subscribing to it. He offers the proposition for consideration of its consequences, and when he shows that it has absurd consequences, he shows that it is false and consequently that his own view is true.

Second, a *reductio* argument can be disorienting if you think that the author subscribes to the contradiction that he derives. What you must realize is that the contradiction is not something that the author endorses or is otherwise committed to. She is reporting the contradiction that follows if you reject his position. Consider the following *reductio*, again inspired by Russell:

Descriptions are not names. For suppose they were. Then a name could be substituted for a description if the name and description referred to the same object. Now, since "Scott" and "the author of *Waverley*" refer to the same object and since George IV wanted to know whether Scott was the author of *Waverley*, it follows that George IV wanted to know whether Scott was Scott.

Russell did not believe that George IV wanted to know whether Scott was Scott. He was pointing out that absurdity follows if one accepts his opponent's view that names are descriptions.

One final example will illustrate how *reductio* arguments often introduce a proposition to which the author does not subscribe and which is actually the opposite of the conclusion he desires. For example, one might argue that definite descriptions have no meaning in this way:

[1]Suppose that definite descriptions have meaning. [2]Then "the author of *Waverley*" means Scott (since Scott is the person who authored *Waverley*). [3]Further, if "the author of *Waverley*" means Scott, then the sentence "Scott is the author of *Waverley*" is a tautology. [4]But this is absurd. [5]Therefore, definite descriptions have no meaning.

Notice that the supposition, expressed in [1], is the contradictory of the conclusion [5]. [1] is used as a premise; it is merely supposed for the sake of argument. The author is not asserting or committing himself to [1]. He uses [1] to show ultimately that [1] is false and that the contradictory of [1], namely [5], is true. [3] is absurd. Since [3] supposedly follows from [1], [1] must be false. Thus, the contradictory of [1], namely [5], must be true.

5.8   Dialectical Reasoning

Dialectic has many meanings. It is sometimes used as a term of praise and sometimes pejoratively. In either case, *dialectic* refers to a kind of reasoning. In this section, it will be applied neutrally either for the process or product of deriving a new or revised thesis through a sequence of preliminary propositions. Thus, a philosopher may consider the truth of a proposition. That proposition is shown to be false. Another proposition, more or less closely related to the false one, is considered for its truth; that proposition too is shown to be false or otherwise inadequate. As systematized by Hegelian philosophers, the dialectical process begins with some proposition, say, "Humans have free will"; after it has been criticized, its contradictory may be considered, "Humans do not have free will," and then the next thesis is some more precise statement of the original proposition, which avoids the original criticisms, say, "Some human actions are caused by free will." Textbook writers describe this consideration of three propositions, thesis, antithesis, and synthesis. Actual dialectical arguments are rarely so tidy. I'll summarize this general procedure as follows:

(a)   It is reasoning that proceeds by considering a series of topically related propositions.
(b)   Each succeeding proposition usually comes out of or is inspired by prior propositions.
(c)   Each succeeding proposition is supposed to be closer to the truth than any earlier one.

These three aspects of dialectic call for some brief comment. Concerning (a), the semantic relation between the two propositions is paradigmatically that of negation. G. F.W. Hegel, with whose name dialectics is most closely tied, preferred one dialectical proposition to be the negation of the other. However, it is prudent not to take this feature too seriously. Often, one dialectical proposition is merely the contrary of another. (Two propositions are contrary just in case they cannot both be true, but both may be false.) For example, one might move from the proposition that *humans have a natural tendency to do evil* to the proposition that *humans have a natural tendency to do good* and, after examining the deficiencies in both, eventually conclude that *humans have some tendencies to do evil and some tendencies to do good.*

Concerning (b), one proposition comes out of the prior proposition by considering its logical consequences and in that way discovering the limitations of the concepts expressed in it. Succeeding propositions usually arise from one or more of the following types of revision:

(1)   negation
(2)   expansion
(3)   hedging

Negation is the classic Hegelian type of revision. A philosopher might begin with the thesis "Universals exist" and then negate this, in the face of objections, to "Universals do not exist."

Expansion is making something fuller or more explicit. A philosopher who begins with the proposition "All humans are free" may explain this by expanding it as "All humans are born free although some are made slaves by law." There are many forms of expansion. Qualifying a proposition is one type. Jean-Jacques Rousseau says, "Man is born free; yet everywhere he is in chains." The claim is pithy, but not literally true, even without cavils about his use of metaphor. In the course of his exposition, it becomes clear that what he means is "Man, considered as a creature in the state of nature, that is, not restricted by civilization, is born free; yet in civil society he is always in chains or unlikely to be happy." Qualifying a thesis in this way is sometimes called "nuancing."

Hedging is weakening a proposition. A philosopher who changes "Humans are necessarily two-footed" to "Humans are normally two-footed" or changes "All human actions are free" to "Some human actions are free" is hedging his proposition.

Concerning (c) above, dialectic has a pedagogical motivation. The systematic treatment of the succession of propositions is supposed to be an easy way of leading a person to the truth. The successive consideration of a series of propositions shows why other possibilities are not correct. This is especially helpful when the correct view is very complicated. A dialectical treatment of a view should reveal why the complicated view is unavoidable. For example, H. P. Grice in his article "Meaning" considers one after the other the following three propositions:

(1)   By an utterance x, a person S means that p if and only if S intends an audience A to believe that p in virtue of x.
(2)   By an utterance x, a person S means that p if and only if S intends an audience A to recognize that S intends A to believe that p in virtue of x.

(3)   By an utterance *x*, a person *S* means that *p* if and only if *S* intends an audience *A* to come to believe that *p* at least in part because *A* recognizes that by uttering *x*, *S* intends *A* to come to believe that *p*.

It would be difficult to get a reader to believe (3) much less to understand it, if she had not seen why Grice found it necessary to reject (1) and (2) as too simple.

In a dialectical treatment of an issue, the later propositions are supposed to be more certain and better grounded than the earlier ones. They are more certain and better grounded because the dialectical development has allowed the arguments for a thesis to be presented, the objections to it to be aired, and either refuted or used to improve upon the original thesis. Various sorts of vagueness and inaccuracy of the sort discussed in chapter 6 have been eliminated.

Dialectical reasoning need not consist simply of a series of assertions and refutations. Here is an example of dialectical reasoning in an essay, in which the focus is on the meaning of a question.

ON THE REASON TO BE MORAL

People sometimes ask, "Why should I be moral?" and cannot seem to find a satisfactory answer. Perhaps it is because the answer is trivial or tautological. To be moral is to do what should be done. So the question in effect asks, "Why should I do what I should do?" the answer to this question is tautologous, "I should do what I should do."

Unfortunately, it is just as plausible that the question, far from having a self-evident answer, involves a contradiction. Someone who asks this question is wondering why he or she should act morally when it is against his or her self-interest to do so. The questioner is in fact asking, "Why is it in my self-interest to act morally when it is against my self-interest?" One wants an answer that says, "It is in one's self-interest to act morally when it is against one's self-interest to act morally." and that answer is contradictory. Since people think it is dangerous to think or to teach that people should not act against their self-interest, it is obvious why the question is problematic.

Now it seems that both explications of the question are defective. The second explication mistakenly assumes that one should always act in one's self-interest; and that is not true. People often have an obligation to act against their self-interest. So taking self-interest into account, the question should be framed like this: "Why should I be moral when it is against my self-interest to do so." the first explication is defective in a similar way. It mistakenly assumes that self-interest plays no role in the question. Taking the force of self-interest into account, the question might be framed, "When it is against my self-interest, why should I be moral." the only difference between the forms of the two questions is their focus or emphasis, one trying to motivate moral behavior when the psychological force of self-interest is great, the other trying to defeat that psychological force when morality is called for.

In one form of dialectical reasoning, an author might combine dialectical reasoning with a *reductio*. Consider this essay fragment:

One might think that *the only things that are real are things that exist.* a moment's reflection, however, will show that this cannot be so. For, if it were, then nothing would be able to change. For everything that changes changes from something that exists at a certain time to something that does not exist at that time. Since what does not exist is not real, by our original principle, change would be impossible. This is obviously absurd.

Thus, it seems that *the things that are real are things that exist and things that do not exist.* Yet this position seems impossible as well. For it likewise does not explain how change is possible: Whatever changes exists. If what changes becomes what does not exist, then it becomes nothing; for what does not exist is nothing. But this is impossible. Thus, something like our original proposition is true. Yet, it must be modified to take the fact of change into account: *the only things that are real are things that exist at some time.* Thus, everything that changes changes from something that exists at one time, say t_1, to something that exists at another time, say t_2.

In this passage, there was a dialectical development that crucially involved the three italicized propositions:

(1) The only things that are real are things that exist.
(2) The things that are real are things that exist and things that do not exist.
(3) The only things that are real are things that exist at some time.

The move from proposition (1) to proposition (2) was motivated by a *reductio* argument, as was the move from (2) to (3). (2) also seems to contradict (1) and to incorporate that contradiction, although in fact the two apparent conjuncts of (2) are not contradictory. (It is perhaps this sort of appearance that led Hegel to claim that reality is contradictory.) Concerning (3), notice that it is superficially closer to (1) than (2). It seems to be a "return" to (1) – with a difference. (3) is more complex and precise than (1). In short, there is a sense in which (3) supersedes (1) and (2), and a sense in which (2) is the opposite of (1).

Here's another example of an essay that incorporates a dialectical method:

---

[1]All human actions are egoistic. [2]Everyone is motivated by his own narrow self-interest. [3]No one acts in a way that he thinks will be harmful to himself. [4]The current hedonism is evidence of this.

[5]One might object that egoism cannot be true. [6] People who give to charity, parents who sacrifice for their children, and soldiers who give their lives for their country, might seem to prove that egoism is false.

[7]Yet, this is not sufficient to refute egoism. [8] People always act out of their own self-interest, even though that self-interest is not immediately accessible. [9]People give to charity to avoid feeling guilty; parents sacrifice for their children for the vicarious pleasure they receive from their later success; and soldiers give up their lives, not for their country, but to avoid the shame of cowardice and the inevitable execution for desertion if they don't. (This passage is inspired by Charles Landesman, *Philosophy: an Introduction to the Central Issues*, new York: holt, Rinehart and Winston, 1985, p. 24.)

There are four propositions that are important for understanding the dialectical structure of this passage. Sentence [1] states the thesis. Sentence [5] tentatively denies [1] in the form of an objection. Sentence [7] reaffirms the thesis in a general way and prepares the reader for sentence [8], which is a more precise reformulation of the thesis, which is made possible in virtue of [5].

The purpose of dialectical reasoning should be rhetorical or pedagogical. Leading the reader through a number of plausible alternatives on some problem is supposed to make the understanding of the true proposition simpler. The point is to instruct, not to dazzle.

As you become familiar with the writing styles of major philosophers, you may notice that the dialogue form seems to lend itself to dialectical reasoning. The give and take of discourse invites the assertion of a proposition; its refutation; its replacement by another proposition that takes account of the refutation by one speaker; and its opposite by another. Each speaker can refute the proposition of the other and thereby lead each speaker to revise his thesis successively. Nonetheless, not all dialogues exhibit this kind of dialectical reasoning. Often the dialogue form is used merely to develop at great length a thesis stated at the beginning and never revised.

A caution should be aired here. Although setting out one's reasoning dialectically is a good way to develop an argument, be careful about trying to use the dialogue form to express a dialectical progression in your own essay. It is a much more difficult form to write in than it might appear. Only the best philosophers and philosophical stylists, such as Plato, Berkeley, and Hume, for example, have succeeded with it. One pitfall is cuteness. Do not substitute cleverness or humor for thought and substance. Another pitfall is digression. A dialogue must be controlled. Although interesting asides and philosophical subplots might be introduced, it is important not to let the dialogue meander or get off course, like the beginning of *Tristram Shandy*.

Dialectical reasoning is helpful for essay writing because it often provides an easy method of organization. In the course of thinking about your essay before you write, or in the course of taking notes before drafting, people often fall into this pattern of thinking:

On the one hand, X
On the other hand, not-X, because of P
Then again, X because of Q
On the other hand, not-X because of R

Students often find this kind of see-sawing frustrating, and they come to think that they don't know what they think or what they ought to think. And this tends to cause writer's block. One way out of this problem is to use the see-sawing thinking to your own advantage. Don't think of it as wavering or uncertain; think of it as dialectical! Use it as the basic structure of the middle part of your essay.

Exercises

1 Construct short dialectical passage in which these sets of propositions play the key role:
   (a) No human actions are free.
   (b) Some human actions are free.
   (c) All human actions are caused; but some human actions are not coerced.

2 Write a 300–500-word essay in which the following dialectic is played out:

   The Correct Criterion of Moral Behavior:

   (a) The Golden Rule: Do unto others as you would have them do unto you.
   Objection: Different people want to be "done unto" in different ways. You may want a designer purse for a present, but the potential recipient has no interest in designer fashion.
   (b) The Platinum Rule: Do unto others as they would have you do unto them.
   Objection: Some people desire the wrong things. A person may want you to supply them with a harmful drug.
   (c) The Depleted Uranium Rule: Do unto others as they ought to be done unto.
   Objection: The goal was to get a criterion, that is, an operational test for moral behavior. The Depleted Uranium Rule is unhelpful.
   (d) [Supply your own conclusion.]

The most famous practitioner of dialectical argumentation was Plato, and according to one interpretation, he thought that the process never reaches a satisfying stopping point because there are no final answers in philosophy. Whether that is true or not, the dialectical process in a good student essay will not exceed the word-limit set for it.

6
Some Constraints on Content

In chapter 2, we discovered that validity and truth work together to produce sound arguments and that to be persuasive a sound argument must be cogent as well, that is, recognizably sound. Why are most valid philosophical arguments and many sound philosophical arguments not cogent? The answer is that the evidence presented for their premises is either not of the right sort for their audience or not presented in such a way that the audience recognizes its evidential force. If a person cannot see that each individual premise in an argument is true, she will not be moved to accept its conclusion. If she cannot follow the reasoning, she will not accept the conclusion.

It would be wonderful if there were some easy way of explaining what constituted good evidence for a philosophical premise or how one could go about finding it. Unfortunately, there isn't. Philosophers often use the techniques described in the last chapter – *reductio ad absurdum* and other forms of reasoning – but the correct approach for showing a specific audience the solution to a specific problem cannot be described in general because of the diversity of experiences and values of audiences. When people do philosophy themselves, their attention is directed to these matters and style is not supposed to interfere with understanding that substance.

With that disclaimer out of the way, I want to say something about three issues that relate to evidence: the pursuit of truth, the use of authority, and the burden of proof.

6.1   The Pursuit of Truth

As much as possible, you should try to ensure that what you say is true. Do not strain to say something "deep" or say something merely because you think it sounds deep. Anyone who can write 1,000 words on a

Philosophical Writing: An Introduction, Fifth Edition. A. P. Martinich.
© 2025 John Wiley & Sons, Inc. Published 2025 by John Wiley & Sons, Inc.
Companion website: www.wiley.com/go/Martinich5e

philosophical topic, without saying anything false, much less outrageously false, has achieved something quite significant. Depth will take care of itself.

You will not always succeed. Sometimes you will make honest mistakes. This is something to guard against, but not to be paralyzed by. Worry about the dishonest mistakes. I have already mentioned the temptation to write something false because it *sounds* deep. Other temptations include the desire to write something false because you believe your professor believes it. In the long run, it is better to be committed to the truth than to what you think your superiors believe is the truth. It is also often better in the short run; saying something you do not believe often rings hollow and can be detected by a sensitive reader.

In recent decades, some intellectuals and students have come to say that there is no such thing as truth or the truth. (I think they believe this when they are doing philosophy or literary theory, but I don't think they believe it during the ordinary course of their life.) The belief that nothing is true has the problematic consequence of being committed to a truth, namely, nothing is true. And that supposed truth is self-refuting.

Sometimes intellectuals claim only to reject Truth, with a capital "T," but I find their explanations of the difference between truth and Truth either inadequate or nonexistent. Denying the existence of truth is one of those things that strikes some people as sounding deep. I think it is dangerous.

6.2   The Use of Authority

People rely upon authorities for many of the beliefs they have and the decisions they make, and often rightly so. It is legitimate to rely upon the predictions of weathermen about the weather – sorry, bad example – upon the judgments of physicians about one's health, upon the judgments of physicists about the nature of the universe, and so on. Yet, what makes this kind of reliance on authority justifiable is the fact that the authorities have good reasons for their views, reasons that do not depend upon authority. Ultimately, the evidential value of any authority is founded upon the quality of the evidence he provides. It is a mistake to substitute an appeal to some philosopher's authority for his evidence. For example, consider this essay fragment, which includes a misuse of authority:

Universals are general objects that cause individual objects to exist. Universals either exist in objects or apart from objects. But, since Plato, the greatest or at least one of the greatest philosophers of all times, held that universals exist apart from objects, this must be true and they cannot exist in objects.

This fragment misuses Plato's authority because his greatness as a philosopher is irrelevant to the nature of universals. Other great philosophers, e.g. Aristotle, held that universals exist in objects, and others, e.g. that they do not exist at all, e.g. William of Ockham. Their beliefs are equally indifferent to the issue. What is relevant is the argumentation that either establishes or refutes the view that universals exist in things; and of course, an author may quote passages from any of these authors, in order to give credit where credit is due, as part of her argument whether for or against universals. In textbooks on informal logic, an illegitimate appeal to authority is called "the fallacy of authority."

There are also legitimate appeals to authority, as just suggested. It is impossible to prove everything in an essay or even a book. Some propositions have to be assumed or presupposed (1) in order to begin her reasoning from a proposition that someone else has (allegedly) established or (2) to use some premise that she cannot prove herself but which has been proven by someone whom the author can expect the audience to accept as an authority. Here is an example of (1):

Descartes argues that his existence follows from his thinking. He pursues the same general line of argument to prove that God exists, that he is not identical with his body, and many other things. For the purposes of this essay, let's assume that Descartes is correct. I want to argue that his position can provide a rational foundation for individualism and a democratic form of government.

In this fragment, the author uses the authority of Descartes to provide the assumption she needs to develop the main point of her essay.

Concerning (2), citing the results of an authority can save you the time and effort of providing what requires a proof but is not central to your own project. This use of authority motivates the use of such phrases as, "As Gödel has shown ...." This use of authority is effective, however, only if what your authority has supposedly shown is both known to and accepted by your audience. Referring to an obscure or widely doubted argument is unacceptable, such as saying to a group of political or economic conservatives, "As Karl Marx has shown ...."

Also, when you refer to an author's argument approvingly, you are not completely relieving yourself of some burden of proof and putting it all on authority. Rather, you are taking the burden of that argument on yourself even though you do not present all its parts. If your authority's argument is defective, then your argument is defective. (If the authority's argument is good, she of course gets the credit since she devised it.)

While referring to an authority in order to use her argument for yourself is a way of abbreviating the argument and avoiding quotation, sometimes quotation is desirable. An authority can be quoted either to express an argument to which the author of an essay subscribes or to express an argument the author intends to attack. Authorities can be friends or foes. A favored authority should be quoted only if the author cannot express the thought more clearly or briefly than the authority has already done. For if the author can present it better in her own words, she should. Resorting to quotation in such a case is in effect admitting some degree of failure. An authority can also be quoted if her words have compelling eloquence. Everyone who discusses Hobbes's views about the nature of man in the state of nature feels compelled to quote him: "and the state of man is solitary, poor, nasty, brutish and short." A quotation might be compelling yet tautologous: "Everything is what it is, and not another thing" (Bishop Butler) or silencing, "Whereof we cannot speak, thereof we must be silent" (Wittgenstein).

A disfavored authority should be quoted if it is necessary to prove that you have presented her position fairly and accurately. In describing the authority's position, it is very important to include an interpretation in a way that seems to be most defensible, even though you think it ultimately cannot withstand the assault of your objections. To state an opponent's position unfairly is to set up a *straw man*. To then knock it down is to knock down a straw man, not a great achievement.

Students are especially susceptible to misusing authority because most of their essays require extensive use of authorities, usually some distinguished and very dead philosophers – Plato, Descartes, Hume, Kant, Elizabeth Anscombe, and Philippa Foot – and they do not know what it is about an authority that is important. What is important is not their fame, nor their admirable character, nor their possibly exciting lives, but their arguments. As I have indicated above, in most philosophy the Argument [Reasoning] is all. And this explains why philosophical authorities play such a large role in most philosophical essays, those of professional philosophers as much as those of students: Great philosophers have constructed great philosophical arguments that should first be mastered, then criticized, revised, and extended. The great philosophers of the past set the terms of philosophical debate, not because philosophers have an inordinate respect for tradition, but because the tradition consists of the arguments that philosophers, made great by their arguments, have devised. As the distinguished historian of medieval and modern philosophy Etienne Gilson once said, "The only thing that belongs in the history of philosophy is philosophy."

In addition to their use of the works of great philosophers, students often have to research the *secondary literature*, that is, the books and articles that have been written by scholars about the great philosophers. Sometimes students are expected to report what these scholars have said, sometimes also to evaluate it. In either case, what is important is the evidence or reasons they give for their views. The secondary literature should be investigated in order to discover whether it throws any light on the primary topic.

6.3 The Burden of Proof

Connected to the issue of evidence and authority is the issue of who bears the burden of proof in an argument. Roughly, the person who asserts or otherwise relies upon the truth of a proposition for the cogency of her position bears the burden. Recall, however, that it is impossible to prove every proposition. In every science, some propositions are taken as basic and ground level. They are simply assumed without proof. In geometry, these principles are axioms, which traditionally were considered self-evident. Further, there are many propositions, which, although they are not self-evident, need not be proven every time they are used, since the evidence for them is very familiar. For example, it needn't be proven that the world is round and very old, that humans use languages to communicate, and so on. However, in most contexts you should not simply assume that only one object exists or that nonhuman animals use languages to communicate. These are controversial views and need support. There are some propositions, however, that are neither self-evident nor supported by evidence presented in the essay itself that might still be used. Sometimes propositions are used conditionally or as suppositions. That is, someone might try to prove that there is empirical knowledge on the assumption that there is mathematical knowledge. In this case, the person would be proving the existence of empirical knowledge conditionally. He assumes *for the sake of the argument* that there is mathematical knowledge in order to draw a consequence of that assumption. Such conditional use of a proposition is legitimate unless the inferred proposition is philosophically outrageous. (If the proposition is philosophically outrageous, then the truth of the assumption or the inference from the assumption should be checked.)

161

In one of its forms, philosophical skepticism tries to exploit the requirement about the burden of proof. This brand of skepticism purports to assert nothing. Rather than trying to assert or prove that no one knows anything, the philosophical skeptic merely raises problems for any claim that is made, often in the form of a question. If someone says that an object looks red, the skeptic asks whether it is possible that the person has a defective vision that makes white things look red. If someone says that a tower viewed in the distance is round, the skeptic asks whether it might actually be rectangular. The skeptic in effect maintains that while every philosophical doctrine is indefensible because it cannot satisfy the burden of proof, skepticism itself is irrefutable because, by asserting nothing, it has no burden. In writing an essay or engaging in any discourse, an author forgoes skepticism, because she expects her audience to understand what she is saying and presupposes that her words have meaning and that she knows what they mean.

One implication of these facts is that an author should write in such a way that she can legitimately expect her audience to understand what she means. Ordinarily words should be used in their usual senses, and technical terms should be explained in terms that the audience can be expected to understand.

Exercise

Does a skeptic have no burden of proof? Does she not have the burden of assuming that she knows what her skeptical words mean?

Of course, while an author always must presuppose some knowledge on the part of her audience, the trick is to be able to figure out what can be presupposed and what needs to be supported by proof or evidence. There is no rule of thumb about how to figure this out other than by paying attention to what your professor says in class in order to determine what he will and will not allow you to assume. You may need to ask explicitly about whether certain things can be assumed.

You should think about whether your argument needs some proposition that is evident or merely supportable by evidence. In order to refute skepticism, for example, must there be a proposition that is evident, or is it sufficient that there be a true proposition beyond reasonable doubt? In ethics, is anything evident? Do any substantive moral principles, such as "It is always wrong intentionally to say what is false" or "It is always wrong to appropriate the property of another person," need to be evident, or is it sufficient that they be more reasonable than any competing principle? These continue to be controversial philosophical questions, and how you answer them will largely determine the type of argument you will need to construct in order to support the thesis of your essay.

7

Some Goals of Form

Essays ought to be intelligible to the reader. A great argument that is unintelligible to a reader is a failure. Three of the most important ways a philosophical author can make her essay intelligible are to make it clear, concise, and coherent. Philosophers also strive for what they call "rigor." These four qualities are the topics of this chapter.

7.1   Coherence

One of the most serious failings in an essay is incoherence. As I am using the word, incoherence is different from nonsense or meaningless-ness. Meaninglessness applies to individual sentences, "Twas brillig, and the slithy toves did gyre and gimble in the wabe." A meaningless sentence can rarely be made meaningful by changing its position in a text (cf. John Hollander's poem, "Coiled Alizarine" in *The Night Mirror* (1971)). Sometimes an incoherent group of sentences can be made coherent simply by giving them a fuller context. These two incoherent sentences

Chalk is a white soft limestone. Cheese is a dairy product.

become coherent in a larger context:

Chalk is a white soft limestone. Cheese is a dairy product. Brits use them to vividly mark a difference, as in "Kee and Lee are chalk and cheese."

Philosophical Writing: An Introduction, Fifth Edition. A. P. Martinich.
© 2025 John Wiley & Sons, Inc. Published 2025 by John Wiley & Sons, Inc.
Companion website: www.wiley.com/go/Martinich5e

In philosophical essays, incoherent sentences often can be made coherent with some rearrangement, plus some stylistic adjustment. Consider this fragment:

Some people are dangerous. It is necessary to fear everyone. The desire to live is the dominant human desire. A person never knows who is dangerous.

Although the words *person* and *danger* occur in the first and fourth sentences, their connection with each other is not made clear by the middle two sentences. But with some rearrangement and stylistic touches, the line of reasoning becomes coherent (added words are in boldface).

Some people are dangerous **to others**. A person never knows who **these** dangerous **people are**. The desire to live is the dominant human desire. **Therefore,** it is necessary to fear everyone.

Exercise

The words, *therefore, but,* and *finally,* are words that help sentences cohere. Think of ten other words that do the same.

Sometimes incoherence results from putting more than one important thought into a single sentence. Breaking sentences down into simpler sentences and then trying various rearrangements of the parts may get one to see how the thoughts cohere.

Achieving coherence in philosophy is not a trivial accomplishment because a philosopher is usually dealing with a problem that involves conceptual confusion. Consider this example, which occurs in a chapter about the philosophy of Niccolò Machiavelli:

Now although the revolution effected by Hobbes was decisively prepared by Machiavelli, Hobbes does not refer to Machiavelli. This fact requires further examination.

Hobbes is in a way a teacher of Spinoza. Nevertheless, Spinoza opens his *Political Treatise* with an attack on the philosophers. The philosophers, he says, treat the passions as vices. By ridiculing or deploring the passions, they praise and evince their belief in a nonexistent human nature; they conceive of men not as they are but as they would wish them to be. Hence their political teaching is wholly useless. Quite different is the case of the *politici*…. The greatest of these *politici* is the most penetrating Florentine, Machiavelli. It is Machiavelli's more subdued attack on traditional philosophy that Spinoza takes over bodily and translates into the less reserved language of Hobbes. (Leo Strauss, "Machiavelli," in Leo Strauss and Joseph Cropsey, eds., *The History of Political Philosophy*, 3rd edn, Chicago: University of Chicago Press, 1987, pp. 298–9.)

From the first two sentences of the passage just quoted, the reader gets the idea that the author will examine the fact that "Hobbes does not refer to Machiavelli" since that fact is expressed by the main clause of the first sentence. But the author's discussion in the full paragraph suggests that he intended to discuss something like what he indicates in the subordinate clause of the first sentence ("Although the revolution … prepared by Machiavelli."). Unfortunately, his discussion is roundabout. All he needed to say was that Spinoza used Machiavelli's arguments but expressed them in Hobbes's vocabulary.

Coherence has a close connection with continuity, the way an idea in one sentence moves to the idea in the next sentence on its way to the end. An essay that meanders, seemingly not directed to any particular destination, is usually defective even if each sentence is charged with great rhetorical energy. (Literary essays, some of which are also philosophical, like those by Michel de Montaigne, are prized for their imaginative meandering because they exhibit the process of discovering new conceptual connections, to coin a phrase, *philosophical stream-of-consciousness.*)

Coherence is achieved in various ways. Sometimes one part of an essay coheres with another because they share a subject matter, as in this essay fragment:

> Plato holds that universals really exist. Universals then are part of the ultimate furniture of the world. If there were no universals then nothing else could exist.

Each sentence in this fragment is held together by its shared subject matter: universals.

Other essays hang together by the use of stock phrases that mark the boundaries of large parts of the essay: the beginning, the middle, and the end. Consider these:

> I begin/To begin
> I shall now argue/Consider the argument
> I conclude/To conclude/In conclusion

Even if these phrases are not elegant, they effectively inform the reader of where he is in the essay, and all three together tie the large structural units of the essay into a whole.

Other linguistic devices connect smaller portions of essays, one paragraph to another, one sentence to another, and even one part of a sentence to another part of the same sentence. Such devices are often called *transitional phrases*. Their effect is much more local than phrases like, "I begin," "In conclusion," and "I shall argue," which control relatively large portions of text. Most of the linguistic devices available for tying essay parts together occur in the middle of an essay, where most of the twists and turns of the argument occur. The author needs to supply her reader with road signs marking where the subarguments are introduced and objections are raised and answered. One good place for these road signs is at the beginning of paragraphs. For example, consider the opening phrases of six successive paragraphs from Charles Landesman's *Philosophy: An Introduction to the Central Issues*:

> An argument against hedonism was developed by G. E. Moore…
> The hedonist has two responses to Moore. First, … Second, …
> Another argument against hedonism …
> The hedonist replies …
> Thus hedonism is not refuted …

At the very beginning, Landesman makes clear what the main topic of each of these paragraphs is. The reader should be grateful to the author for keeping him informed of where he is in the essay. Your professor will be similarly grateful – and may well express his gratitude in the way you like best – if you use similar types of transitional phrases.

Here is another example of transitional phrases at the beginning of successive paragraphs:

> We shall begin our consideration of empiricism by turning to Locke.
> One might object to Locke's empiricism by pointing out that …
> There is a twofold reply to this objection.
> The objector, however, might not accept this reply on the grounds that …

In addition to transitional devices that begin paragraphs, there are also transitional words and phrases that are useful within paragraphs. The words *therefore* and *consequently* indicate the conclusion of an argument, often wholly within a paragraph. The words *further, furthermore, moreover,* and *in addition* indicate that additional evidence or information about some matter will be provided.

Pronouns and nominalizations can also be used to effect coherence. Compare these two sequences:

Plato argues that the nature of justice is more easily observed in the state than it is in the individual. Plato uses the premise that what is larger is more easily observed.

Plato argues that the nature of justice is more easily observed in the state than it is in the individual. His argument uses the premise that what is larger is more easily observed.

Both passages express the same information. Yet the second coheres in a way that the first does not. The coherence is achieved by the use of two words: *his* and *argument*. The pronoun *his* requires the reader to find its antecedent, which is in the prior sentence. Similarly, the abstract noun "argument," formed from the verb "argue," requires the reader to find its antecedent, which is also in the preceding sentence. So, although abstract words should not be used for their own sake, there are reasons for using them and one of them is coherence. Here are three more examples of having one sentence cohere better with another by changing a verb from one sentence into an abstract noun and using it in the following sentence:

Thrasymachus proposes that justice is what serves the strong. His proposition is refuted by Socrates.

Camus recommends that we choose our values. His recommendation is a good one.

Heidegger challenges contemporary philosophers to return to the roots of philosophy. His challenge has been met in unexpected ways by Derrida.

Virtually all the principles and devices for achieving coherence in an essay that I have mentioned should be familiar to you from courses in composition. What I have tried to do is to make you aware that those general principles and devices apply to philosophy as well and to try to move you to use the available devices in your own philosophical prose.

Exercise

Write out three successive paragraphs from some philosophical book or article that contain explicit transitional phrases in each paragraph.

7.2 Clarity

It is quite possible for an essay to be coherent but not clear. Each sentence might be obviously tied to every other without any of the sentences conveying the author's thought:

> Art challenges the prevailing principle of reason: in representing the order of sensuousness, it invokes a tabooed logic – the logic of gratification as against that of repression. Behind the sublimated aesthetic form, the unsublimated content shows forth: the commitment of art to the pleasure principle. The investigation of the erotic roots of art plays a large role in psychoanalysis. (Herbert Marcuse, *Eros and Civilization*, New York: Vintage Books, 1955, pp. 168–9).

There is coherence here, but not, I think, clarity. Marcuse could have made roughly the same claims in this way:

> Art is as important to life as reason although philosophers have often overlooked this fact. Art is primarily concerned with the satisfactions of sensuous experience. Even when constrained by specific artistic forms, the sensuousness of art can still be perceived. A large part of psychoanalysis has been devoted to investigating the sensuous satisfactions that come from art.

It is slightly embarrassing for a philosopher to preach about clarity, because so much philosophical writing lacks that quality. Nonetheless, clarity remains an ideal. Wittgenstein wrote, "Whatever can be said can be said clearly" (*Tractatus Logico-Philosophicus*). Schopenhauer wrote, "The real philosopher will always look for clearness and distinctness; he will invariably try to resemble not a turbid, impetuous torrent, but rather a Swiss lake which by its calm combines great depth with great clearness, the depth revealing itself precisely through its clearness" (quoted by Peter A. French, "Toward the Headwaters of Philosophy: Curriculum Revision at Trinity University," in *Proceedings and Addresses of the American Philosophical Association* 58 (1985), p. 615). Joseph Butler wrote, "Confusion and Perplexity in Writing is indeed without excuse, because anyone may, if he pleases, know whether he understands and sees through what he is about" (Joseph Butler, *Five Sermons*, Indianapolis: Hackett, 1983, p. 12). Butler may have overstated the truth; perhaps an author does not *always* know that his writing is confusing, especially when he understands his material thoroughly. Nonetheless, what Butler meant is true in very many cases. Further, just because it is likely that an author might not know that his writing is confused unless he thinks about that very possibility with some care, it is all the more important that he do so. For what Butler says immediately after the passage above is right: "and it is unpardonable for a man to lay his thought before others when he is conscious that he himself does not know whereabouts he is, or how the matter before him stands" (Butler, *Five Sermons*, p. 12). There is no excuse for a person who intentionally writes in a confused way. Authors have an obligation to be clear.

Clarity is relative to an audience. What is clear to one person at one time in one situation might not be clear to another person at another time in another situation. What counts as a clear exposition of Gödel's incompleteness theorem for a Harvard logician might not count as a clear exposition for a person taking his first course in philosophy. Whether writing is clear or not depends in part upon what facts or beliefs the author can rightfully presuppose that his audience possesses.

How many times have you heard people say in frustration, "Well, you know what I mean," when they have repeatedly failed to say what they mean about the most ordinary sorts of things? Think about how much more difficult it is to say something *exactly* right about the most central, important, and elusive of our concepts when no one has previously said it exactly right. In philosophy, after failing to say something correctly, it is never acceptable to fall back on the phrase, "Well, you know what I mean."

If the audience knows what the author means without him saying it correctly, then it is trivial, and if it is not trivial, the audience cannot be sure of what the author means.

It is easy to say, "Be clear," and difficult to say what clarity is. In the broad sense in which I am using the term, clarity is a complex concept with many dimensions. In philosophy, the dimension that stands out most of all is precision. Precision avoids three things: ambiguity, vagueness, and indeterminateness.

An ambiguous word, phrase, or sentence is one that has two or more meanings. The sentence "Mary went to the bank" is ambiguous between "Mary went to the financial institution" and "Mary went to the river's edge." Although it is highly unlikely that the sentence just considered would cause any philosophical confusion, there are ambiguous sentences that have, and calling attention to the ambiguities involved in them constitutes philosophical progress. Psychological egoism holds to this proposition: Every person acts only to satisfy his own desires. This sentence seems at once both obviously true and outrageous. How is this possible? It is possible because it is ambiguous. In one sense, it means, "Everything a person does is something that he wants to do." In order to act, a person must be moved to act by something, and this thing that moves a person is called a *want* or a *desire*. This is true and not very exciting; many would consider it trivial. In another sense, the thesis of psychological egoism means, "Every person acts only to satisfy his own desires and no one else's." This makes psychological egoism outrageous and false. Gandhi, Martin Luther King, Jr, and Mother Theresa are three indubitable examples of people who, although they did what they wanted to do, were also moved to do things to satisfy the desires of other people and only for the good of those other people. That is what they desired. When the trivially true sense of the thesis of psychological egoism is conflated with the outrageous and false sense, the thesis seems compelling and profound. Psychological egoism trades on this ambiguity. (See Hastings Rashdall, *Theory of Good and Evil*, Oxford: Clarendon Press, 1907.) Once the ambiguity of the thesis is pointed out, psychological egoism is not persuasive.

Ambiguity should not be conflated with vagueness:

Parent: Where are you going?
Teenager: Out.
Parent: What are you going to do?
Teenager: This and that.

The teenager's answers are vague, not ambiguous. They lack specificity. Writers are often vague when they do not know how to formulate their thought precisely although there is a precise formulation of it. Vagueness should ultimately be eliminated in these cases. What this means is that you should work to eliminate unnecessarily vague words and sentences. This is not to say that vagueness should not occur in the early drafts of your essay. On the contrary, this is a good place for it. When you are first working out your thoughts, write down whatever comes to mind. Many of these things will be vague. That is okay. After you have written your initial thoughts, revise. Eliminate the vagueness by reflecting more carefully on the issue; also use a dictionary and thesaurus to help you find the precise word that you want. (A dictionary and a thesaurus serve different purposes. A dictionary defines a word; it should be used to verify that the word you use has the meaning you think it has. A thesaurus gives clusters of words that are related in meaning; it is helpful when you are trying to identify the exact word you need and can only think of a related word.)

So far, I have been talking about avoidable vagueness. Some vagueness is unavoidable. Some phenomena lack sharp boundaries by their very nature, and they would be misrepresented if overly specific language were used to describe them. One importantly vague concept may be the ordinary concept of a person. Suppose that two people, Sharp and Blunt, are operated on and their brains interchanged. After the operation, which person is Sharp and which is Blunt? If you think that the obvious answer to this question is that Mr. Blunt is the object consisting of Blunt's brain in Sharp's body and Mr. Sharp is the object consisting of Sharp's brain in Blunt's body (on the grounds that whoever has a person's brain is that person), then consider a related, though different, situation. Suppose that Sharp and Blunt are operated on; their brains are interchanged. However, in the course of the interchange, all the brain states of each brain are also interchanged. That is, all the original states of Sharp's brain are now encoded in Blunt's brain, and all the original states of Blunt's brain are now encoded in Sharp's brain. In this situation, Sharp's body has Blunt's brain but Sharp's brain states, and Blunt's body has Sharp's brain but has Blunt's brain states. Now which object is Sharp and which Blunt? People might well argue about which is the right answer. Another way to handle the question, however, is to claim that there is no *right* answer, because the concept of a person is not so definite as to allow an answer to this question. The situation is so bizarre that a solution to it has never been built into the ordinary concept of a person. Now nothing prevents us from adding to that original concept something that does determine the answer. Only be aware that in adding to that concept, we are thereby changing it, and, more precisely, are admitting that the original concept had some degree of vagueness.

The point of all this is that some vagueness is built into some concepts and that it is not a defect when your writing reflects this vagueness. However, it is important to be aware of this vagueness. As Aristotle said, "It is the mark of an educated person not to require more precision than the subject allows." (See Wittgenstein, *Philosophical Investigations*, for more about precision and exactness.)

In addition to the avoidable vagueness that is objectionable in philosophy, and the unavoidable vagueness that is to be recommended, there is a third category, that of avoidable vagueness that is to be recommended. This is a kind of vagueness that is put to work in the service of style. Often, especially when a topic is difficult or when what is to be said about the topic is quite original, a precise formulation of one's views, though intelligible in itself, might be relatively unintelligible to an unprepared reader. In such cases, it is often rhetorically advisable to begin with a vague statement of one's position and use it as the occasion to invite a more precise formulation of it. For example, John Searle had astonishingly original things to say about intentionality in his book *Intentionality*, most of which, when formulated precisely, were unavoidably couched in technical terms. Such terms would have been unintelligible to his readers early in the book. Thus, as a first shot at explaining his views, Searle writes:

> All of these … connections between Intentional states and speech acts naturally suggest a certain picture of Intentionality: every Intentional state consists of a representative content in a certain psychological mode. Intentional states represent objects and states of affairs. . .. Just as my statement that it is raining is a representation of a certain state of affairs, so my belief that it is raining is a representation of the same state of affairs. Just as my order to Sam to leave the room is about Sam and represents a certain action on his part, so my desire that Sam should leave the room is about Sam and represents a certain action on his part. (*Intentionality*, Cambridge: Cambridge University Press, 1983, p. 11.)

Searle's use of "represent" and "representation" helps establish a context that is familiar to philosophers. Yet philosophers have rarely, if ever, spelled out what a representation is. Searle is aware of this vagueness and is exploiting it. He goes on to say, "The notion of representation is conveniently vague." He admits to "Exploiting this vagueness" and acknowledges that the notion "will require some further clarification." He is in effect inviting the clarification, which shortly after he provides at some length. After providing the clarification, he points out that his use of "represent" and "representation" could be eliminated in favor of the technical explanations he provided in the clarification. Yet it is convenient not to replace them because those vague terms are shorthand for complex syntactic constructions. Notice, then, how vague language can be rhetorically effective: It gives a reader an intelligible entrance to an essay; it moves the essay forward by inviting further clarification and encouraging brevity.

Indeterminateness is still different from ambiguity and vagueness. Indeterminateness is a kind of incompleteness. It is symptomatic of the lazy and half-formed thought. Consider the sentence "Humans are selfish." This sentence is indeterminate, because it does not specify whether all or only some humans are being referred to, nor whether they are always or only sometimes so. There are important differences in the truth-conditions of these propositions:

All humans are always selfish.
All humans are sometimes selfish.
Some humans are always selfish.
Some humans are sometimes selfish.

There are all sorts of ways in which a proposition might be indeterminate, and it is impossible to enumerate them here. So one must always be on guard against indeterminateness. Indeterminateness is also one reason why the passive voice is often offensive. Some philosophers assert, "The world is constituted," as if this expressed a complete thought. But what we want to know is who or what constitutes it, not to mention what "constitute" means in this case. The sentence "The world is constituted" would be less misleadingly written, "The world is constituted by____." This sentence schema would at least make clear that something is missing. It is not sufficient to complete the sentence in this way: "The world is constituted by consciousness," because even this sentence does not make specific what consciousness is involved. There are at least three obvious possibilities:

The world is constituted by God's consciousness.
The world is constituted by each human consciousness.
The world is constituted by human consciousness collectively.

Which way is the original statement to be taken?

It is tempting to write indeterminate sentences. They are often pithy, intriguing, and epigrammatic. They give the appearance of depth, yet they are shallow. They lack the depth that comes from hard thinking. And they unjustifiably spare the author the effort of thinking an issue through completely. Don't spare the effort.

After writing a draft of your paper, it is a good thing to go over your draft and look up key terms in either a dictionary or thesaurus to see whether there isn't a more precise word for what you mean. Often the more precise word is a bigger or an unusual one. If that is so, then use it. But do not use the bigger word simply because it has more syllables. (More precise words are often longer than related words because it is part of the economy of language to use the shortest words for the most common purposes, and the precision required for philosophy is uncommon. Philosophers often need to use unusual words because their thoughts are unusual.)

There are many other quirks of a person's style that may inhibit clarity or require the reader to spend a fraction of a second longer in order to understand. Some of these are explained in other parts of this book. I'll end with one that is too common and easy to correct. Avoid outdated words, such as aforementioned, thereof, whilst, and whomsoever.

7.3 Conciseness

Conciseness combines brevity and content. A sentence or group of them conveys a lot of information in a brief space. Brevity, perhaps, does not call for much comment. It is desirable because it typically makes fewer demands on the reader's attention and understanding. An author should realize that she is costing her audience the time it takes to read her writing. A student's professor is a captive audience; don't also torture him.

Although brevity is a good policy, it admits of exceptions. Sometimes the rhythm of language recommends a wordier sentence. Also, sometimes brevity approaches turgidity. That is, it is sometimes necessary to use more, rather than fewer, words in order to stretch out the content of a sentence and thereby make it more intelligible to your reader. Short sentences, dense in content, are often less intelligible to a specific audience than longer sentences with the same content.

Further, brevity does not guarantee efficiency; it concerns only *how* something is said and not at all what is said. In determining the efficiency or economy of a sentence or essay, one must consider content in addition to brevity. A brief but vacuous sentence does not communicate more efficiently than a prolix but informative one. Thus, it is not in itself desirable to sacrifice content for the sake of brevity, although this might be desirable for some other reason: to vary sentence length or to prepare the reader for some complicated explanation. Thus, brevity and content must be balanced. That is the force of the admonition to be concise.

While a short sentence sometimes conveys more than a long sentence, sometimes a long sentence is indispensable. Most concise sentences can be viewed as expressing what many short sentences might have conveyed. For example, the sentence

Descartes has radical doubts about the ability of humans to know anything

can be viewed as conveying the same information as these three:

Descartes has doubts.
The doubts are radical.
The doubts are about the ability of humans to know anything.

A large part of conciseness consists of just this kind of economy of expression. But there is more to it than that. Sentence-combining allows the author to express her thoughts in an organized way. The syntactic structure of the concise sentence about Descartes's doubts makes clear that the basic idea is that *Descartes has doubts.* The other two ideas expressed in the sentence are subordinate. The idea that *the doubts are radical* modifies the first, and the idea that *the doubts are about the ability of humans to know anything* is a specification of Descartes's doubt.

There are all sorts of devices for organizing and subordinating in natural languages. We have already seen that adjectival and clausal modification can be used for this purpose. Sentence connectives are another such device. Think about the difference between

> Descartes begins by doubting the existence of everything, and he concludes that he exists.
>
> Descartes begins by doubting the existence of everything but he concludes that he exists.
>
> Although Descartes begins by doubting the existence of everything, he concludes that he exists.

In the first sentence, the word "and" expresses that the ideas expressed in each clause receive equal emphasis. In the second sentence, the ideas are contrasted and there is more emphasis on the second than on the first in virtue of the meaning of "but." In the third sentence, the idea expressed in the first clause is conceded by the author and the idea expressed in the second clause is emphasized in virtue of the meaning of "although."

The nuances expressed by "and," "but," and "although," and many other sentence connectives, e.g. "because," are important. Abuses of them are obvious. For example, contrast this passage:

> Although Proclus is the second greatest Neoplatonist, Plotinus is the greatest. Proclus was born about ad410, but he died in 485. Plotinus's philosophy was organized by Proclus into a series of triadic emanations.

with this one:

> Although Plotinus is the greatest Neoplatonist, Proclus is the second greatest. He was born about A.D. 410 and died in 485. He organized Plotinus's philosophy into a series of triadic emanations.

You should be able to figure out why the second passage is stylistically superior to the first. Although I can't explain all the different sorts of sentence-combining techniques, you should pay attention to the syntactic structures of your sentences to make sure that they are emphasizing what you want to emphasize and subordinating what you want to subordinate. You should experiment with different clausal arrangements to see which one best conveys your thought.

One way to enhance conciseness is to rephrase some prepositional phrases as gerund phrases. For example, rephrase

The recognition of the existence of universals solves many problems.

as

Recognizing that universals exist solves many problems.

And rephrase,

The restatement of the argument of Descartes ...

as

Restating Descartes's argument ...

Exercise

1   Combine the following sets of sentences into one sentence that expresses the same thought. You may add connectives, delete words, and change the syntactic structure as you please.

(a)   Utilitarianism is a theory.
The theory concerns ethics.
The theory has a principle.
The principle is that one should act to ensure the greatest good for the greatest number. J. S. Mill is the author of the principle.

(b)   Plato is an author.
Plato wrote the *Phaedo*.
The *Phaedo* concerns the soul.
Plato argues that the soul is immortal.

(c)   Sartre is an existentialist.
Camus is an existentialist.
Marcel is an existentialist.
Marcel is a Christian.

7.4 **Rigor**

Philosophers often espouse rigor, which they often explain to be clarity (in some narrow sense), precision, and explicitness. Clarity, especially as it relates to precision, has already been discussed. What about explicitness?

Logicians are perhaps the greatest proponents of explicitness. Yet even logicians retreat from the ideal when they introduce various abbreviations, e.g. the iota operator, and conventions for dispensing with symbols, such as omitting final parentheses from formulas of logic.

Communication in natural languages, much more than in artificial ones, gets along quite well with much less than total explicitness. Total explicitness is inadvisable for a number of reasons. First, it would take up an unreasonable amount of physical space. Second, totally explicit language is more difficult to process mentally than much inexplicit language. (Human comprehension is better when the human has to make some inferences about the material than when everything is explicit.) Third, the author may not be able to say explicitly what he means. One skill needed for effective writing is knowing what should and what should not be explicit. There are then two parts to what a speaker or writer communicates: what he expresses and what he implies. What he expresses is what is explicit in the words he uses. What he implies is what he communicated in virtue of various features of the context of his utterance. For example, consider this essay fragment:

> Immanuel Kant is the author of several, long, classic works in philosophy, including his *Critique of Pure Reason* and *Critique of Practical Reason*. His distinction between noumena and phenomena and his views about the contribution that the mind makes to structuring reality have had a great influence on many distinguished philosophers for the last one hundred and fifty years.

Although the author does *not say* that Kant is a good philosopher, he surely *implies* this in the essay fragment. He also does not say that many philosophers have read Kant's work, but this is implied by the context. It is highly unlikely that what the author says of Kant could be true unless many philosophers had read Kant.

Although our ability to imply much of what we mean is a virtue of natural language communication, it does cause problems. It is often difficult for an author to know what she can assume her audience believes and also difficult to know when she has said enough to allow the audience to draw the correct implications from what has been said. In ordinary contexts, people rarely have any trouble deciding this issue. It's different with philosophy. Philosophy is so general that often what one philosopher takes for granted another philosopher finds absurd. Compare the beliefs of idealists with those of realists, for example, or materialists with dualists. The student has another problem. How can a student know what to make explicit and what to leave implicit when her audience, the professor, probably already knows everything true that the student has to say? (For the answer to this question, see chapter 1, section 1.1, "The Professor as Audience.")

Being too explicit can result in clumsy writing. Consider this passage from G. E. Moore, who has just finished discussing the differences between such assertions as "I am standing up," "I have clothes on," and "I am speaking in a fairly loud voice":

> But in spite of these, and other, differences between those seven or eight different assertions, there are several important respects in which they are all alike.
>
> (1) In the first place: All of those seven or eight different assertions, which I made at the beginning of this lecture, were alike in this respect, namely, that every one of them was an assertion, which, though it wasn't in fact false, yet *might have been false*. For instance, consider the time at which I asserted that I was standing up. It is certainly true that at that very time I *might* have been sitting down, though in fact, I wasn't; and if I *had* been sitting down at that time, then my assertion that I was standing up would have been false. Since, therefore, I might have been sitting down at that time, it follows that my assertion that I was standing up was an assertion which *might have been false*, though it wasn't. And the same is obviously true of all the other assertions I made. At the time when I said I was in a room, I might have been in the open air; at the time when I said I had clothes on, I might have been naked; and so on, in all the other cases. (From G. E. Moore, "Certainty," *Philosophical Papers*, New York: Collier Books, 1966, pp. 225–6.)

In short, what should be explicit is what is most important. What should be implied is what can reasonably be assumed either as background information shared by both author and reader or as obviously following from what is explicit in the text.

Exercises

(1) The passage above from G. E. Moore contains more than 200 words. Rewrite in fewer than 150 words.

(2) Make the following sentences more concise:
- (a) "The first point is a point which embraces many other points" (from G. E. Moore, "A Defence of Common Sense," in *Philosophical Papers*, New York: 1959, p. 32).
- (b) By using the recognition of the fact that Descartes in no way refutes the philosophical view of skepticism, we can get a better handle on the proper conditions underlying the concept of knowledge.

8
Problems with Introductions

Well begun is half-done.

(Ancient Greek Adage)

Often the hardest part of writing an essay is its introduction. When students and other authors try to begin writing the introduction first, they often find themselves unable to write at all. Writer's block.

One way to prevent writer's block is to write the introduction last. Recall that earlier I said that writing the introduction last is often a good idea because often you discover that your essay ended up saying something different from what you originally intended. At the end of the process, you can say what you will do in the essay because you can see what you have done. In any case, at some time you will have to write the introduction.

Some correct ways of beginning an essay were discussed in earlier chapters. In this chapter, I discuss three ways of *not* beginning the essay. Section 8.1 is about how authors sometimes slip away from their topics. Section 8.2 is about how authors sometimes hide the significance of their argument by describing it as providing the solution to a relatively minor problem. Section 8.3 is about how authors sometimes begin their essays with a running start instead of starting right in.

8.1   Slip Sliding Away

One of the more important articles on the philosophy of language is Keith Donnellan's "Reference and Definite Descriptions." Although this article was influential and exhibits substantial philosophical ability, it is, I think, a mix of good and bad philosophical writing. Here is the first paragraph of that article in full.

Philosophical Writing: An Introduction, Fifth Edition. A. P. Martinich.
© 2025 John Wiley & Sons, Inc. Published 2025 by John Wiley & Sons, Inc.
Companion website: www.wiley.com/go/Martinich5e

Reference and Definite Descriptions
Definite descriptions, I shall argue, have two possible functions. They are used to refer to what a speaker wishes to talk about, but they are also used quite differently. Moreover, a definite description occurring in one and the same sentence may, on different occasions of its use, function in either way. The failure to deal with this duality of function obscures the genuine referring use of definite descriptions. The best known theories of definite descriptions, those of Russell and Strawson, I shall suggest, are both guilty of this. Before discussing this distinction in use, I will mention some features of these theories to which it is especially relevant. (Keith Donnellan, "Reference and Definite Descriptions," in *The Philosophy of Language*, 6th edn, ed. A. P. Martinich and David Sosa, New York: Oxford University Press, 2013, p. 140.)

Consider the first sentence:

Definite descriptions, I shall argue, have two possible functions.

It is an excellent beginning. It states simply and clearly what Donnellan intends to do in his article. He says that definite descriptions have "two possible functions." He does not name those functions or define them. But he does not need to. Not too much information should be packed into a sentence, and the broad details of the two uses he mentions can be unfolded step by step. The first sentence should orient the reader. An overly specific introduction would not succeed in orienting readers but in confusing or daunting them. Like an aggressive glad-hander, an overly specific or complicated introduction would be off-putting. The vagueness of Donnellan's first sentence is inviting. The first sentence inclines readers to want to know something about the two functions. Donnellan does that in the second sentence:

They are used to refer to what a speaker wishes to talk about, but they are also used quite differently.

The phrase, "used to refer," alludes to "the referential use of definite descriptions," which is a familiar philosophical topic, one that Donnellan has every right to expect his audience of professional philosophers to understand. By mentioning the referential use of definite descriptions, he is further putting the reader at ease. The reader is becoming oriented to the topic because referring is a familiar topic. The second clause of the sentence, however, introduces something substantial and not familiar, "they [definite descriptions] are also used quite differently." How are they used differently? What is the name of this different use? Is it like referring, and if not, how is it different? These are natural questions for the reader to ask, and they motivate readers to move forward.

The reader has a right to have these questions answered immediately. Unfortunately, the answers are not immediately provided. Although Donnellan eventually gets around to answering these questions, it comes much later in the article. Instead of either naming or describing the second of the "two possible functions" of definite descriptions, Donnellan changes the direction and focus of the article. He says something that is true of both uses of definite descriptions:

> Moreover, a definite description occurring in one and the same sentence may, on different occasions of its use, function in either way.

While this third sentence provides some additional information about both uses, namely, that both may occur in the same sentence, the information does not help to advance the article at this stage. Donnellan has identified one of the two uses of definite descriptions, the familiar referential use, but not the other, which presumably is unfamiliar. In the third sentence, he says something that applies to both of them. Since we don't know anything about the alleged second use other than that it is not identical to the first, it is not informative to read that a definite description might function in either way in one and the same sentence. We still have no idea about what the second function of definite descriptions is.

The third sentence could be justified if Donnellan returned to the main focus of his article and answered the two questions he raised in the reader's mind earlier: What is the name of the other use? How does it function differently from the referential use? Unfortunately, the next sentence does not answer either question but slides further away from both of them:

> The failure to deal with this duality of function obscures the genuine referring use of definite descriptions.

This is an assertion on Donnellan's part. Presumably, he will substantiate it somewhere later in his article. But readers have no indication of where; no indication of how; and no indication of how the failure to be clear about the second use or function obscures the referring use of definite descriptions. The phrase, "obscures the genuine referring use," suggests that Donnellan's main interest concerns reference and not the unnamed, undescribed, and still mysterious other function. (I do not believe that readers in 1967, when the article first appeared, could have known this, but

Donnellan was indeed primarily interested in the function of referring and not in the other.)

An ideal reader should have the sense that this article is starting to slip away; he has to continue to play the game of reading and comprehending this article without really knowing what he is committing himself to. That is, Donnellan is now talking about "this duality of function" as if the reader knew what both are, even though he has not given the audience any good reason for thinking that the second function exists.

The mystery of the second use continues with the next sentence:

The best known theories of definite descriptions, those of Russell and Strawson, I shall suggest, are both guilty of this.

Both Bertrand Russell and P. F. Strawson were famous in large part for their work on referring. In his article, "On Referring," Strawson criticized Russell's views as presented in the article "On Denoting." The principal difference between the words "denoting" and "referring" is historical. In 1905, when Russell wrote, "denoting" was the current philosophical term for what Strawson called "referring" in 1950. Again the author continues to discuss referring without any mention or knowledge of "the other use" of definite descriptions. The second use of definite descriptions hovers over the discussion like a specter. (One final point about this sentence is that its last word, "this," is too far away from its antecedent, which is the first phrase of the preceding sentence.)

The contrast between the two possible functions of definite descriptions completely disappears in the next and final sentence of the paragraph:

Before discussing this distinction in use, I will mention some features of these theories to which it is especially relevant.

The focus of the article is now on the theories of Russell and Strawson. The distinction between two possible functions of definite descriptions is now in the background. The phrase, "Before discussing this distinction in use," is a promissory note to bring the discussion back to the purported central topic of the article at some unspecified later point. (This turns out to be the beginning of the third section of the article.)

There is one further item to glean from this last sentence of the paragraph. Donnellan's use of the phrase "this distinction in use" instead of "distinction in function" suggests that he is using "function," and "use" synonymously.

There are probably two reasons why Donnellan slides into the discussion of Russell and Strawson. First, the views of Russell and Strawson on referring were two of the most important ones; no discussion of referring could very well ignore their work. Second, Donnellan was arguing for a view of referring that was completely new. He claimed to see two uses of definite descriptions where previous philosophers had seen only one. He was perhaps concerned that beginning with the stark assertion that there were two uses would be unsympathetically received or that the reader would immediately demand to know how his views tied into Russell's and Strawson's. For this reason also, he may have rushed to discuss Russell and Strawson.

Since I have criticized Donnellan's opening paragraph rather severely, it is legitimate to demand that I suggest an alternative:

> Definite descriptions, I shall argue, have two possible functions. They are used to refer to what a speaker wishes to talk about, but they are used quite differently. *They are used to express a unique property that an object has.* I shall call these two uses the referential and the attributive uses, respectively. Neither one of these uses is more familiar than the other. Rather, the two uses have been conflated under the single idea of denoting or referring. Both the theories of Russell and Strawson involve this conflation and I hope to show that each of their theories describes different aspects of the two uses; this helps to account for the apparently extreme disagreements between them. I should say that in fact they are often speaking past each other, one about the referential use, the other about the attributive use.

The italicized sentence above is intended to repair what I have argued is an egregious omission in Donnellan's original paragraph. It is supposed to capture what he means by the attributive use, which he gets around to explaining in the third section of his article, where he recovers from the slide begun in the first paragraph of the article:

> I will call the two uses of definite descriptions I have in mind the attributive use and the referential use. A speaker who uses a definite description attributively in an assertion states something about whoever or whatever is the so-and-so.

A speaker who uses a definite description referentially in an assertion, on the other hand, uses the description to enable his audience to pick out whom or what he is talking about and states something about that person or thing.

The first sentence names a distinction that Donnellan wants to establish. The second and third sentences constitute a first shot at characterizing each term of that distinction. That is just how an author should proceed. There are, however, some problems with sentences two and three. Although these problems are primarily philosophical, they show up as stylistic problems too. One of the philosophical problems is that sentences two and three are overly specific. Donnellan intends those sentences to characterize his distinction. But they are too specific to count as an adequate characterization. Since definite descriptions can occur in sentences used to make promises, statements, oaths, threats, apologies, and so on, Donnellan cannot legitimately explain their function by talking only about assertions. A second philosophical problem is that both characterizations rely upon the word "about." This is a problem because philosophers have traditionally used the notion of aboutness to distinguish the referential use from other grammatical functions. So Donnellan's characterization of the distinction between the referential and attributive uses of definite descriptions is not adequate at this point.

8.2   The Tail Wagging the Dog

One of the greatest articles of the twentieth century is H. P. Grice's "Logic and Conversation." It is great because of its novel and powerful theory of linguistic communication, not because of its literary structure, which, I think, is defective. His article begins with a description of a relatively narrow problem in the philosophy of logic and two attitudes that philosophers of different ideologies have taken toward it. The article then proceeds to its main work, the construction of a general theory of conversation, which supposedly has within it the resources to solve the problem. What is wrong with this structure from a rhetorical point of view is that such a narrow and abstruse problem is not sufficient to justify the construction of a theory as complicated and wide-ranging as Grice's. This rhetorical problem is a consequence of a substantive philosophical point: a narrow problem cannot justify the construction of an elaborate and general theory. Metaphorically, Grice appears to be using a cannon to kill a fly. Since the introduction of Grice's article is too long to be reproduced here, I have devised an essay fragment that suffers from the same defect:

LOGIC AND CONVERSATION

It is well known in philosophical logic that the logical constants, that is

&, v, ~, ⊃, ↔, ∃

do not appear to correspond in meaning with their standard English translations,

and, or, not, if ..., then, if and only if, there exists

Philosophers have typically taken one of two attitudes towards this lack of correspondence. The Formalists think that this is one indication of the inexactness of natural language and say, "so much the worse for natural language." The Informalists think that this is one indication of the narrowness of formal languages and say, "so much the worse for artificial languages." Both groups agree in assuming that there actually is a divergence in meaning between the logical constants and their natural language translations. I shall argue that this common assumption is false. I shall do this by developing a theory of linguistic communication that applies to the use of language in general.

Since it is the theory of linguistic communication that ought to be and in fact is the focus of this essay, that should be the focus of the article from the very beginning. The problem in philosophical logic and its solution in terms of the theory of communication could be brought in at the end of the article as evidence of the theory's power.

With these considerations in mind, the following would have been a better way to begin the essay:

LOGIC AND CONVERSATION

The goal of this essay is to develop a general theory of linguistic communication. In addition to its inherent interest, such a theory can be used to solve a large number of philosophical problems. One of these is a problem in philosophical logic, which I shall solve after presenting my theory. This solution is just one of many possible illustrations of the theory's power.

This way of structuring the essay puts the solution to the logical problem at the end. It is ironic that although Grice motivates his article by proposing to solve a problem, he never does get around to explaining how his theory solves it. However, anyone who knows the problem and understands Grice's theory can figure out the solution for himself.

There is nothing wrong with writing an essay on a narrow topic. What is wrong is leading the reader to believe that the narrow topic is the focus of the essay and not some broader one. It looks like the rhetorical tail is wagging the rhetorical dog. When I first read Grice's article, I was dubious. His theory struck me as unacceptably complex because I thought it was designed to solve only one problem in philosophical logic. Once I realized the power of his theory, I was awed by its elegance.

One reason Grice's article begins badly is that it was excerpted from a much longer work, his William James Lectures at Harvard in 1962. To mention this is partially to explain why the essay is structured as it is and partially to excuse it, but it does not justify it.

8.3 The Running Start

Consider this essay fragment:

THE PRINCIPLES OF DESCARTES'S PHILOSOPHY

[1]The history of philosophy is long and difficult. [2]It consists of many periods – ancient Greek and Roman, medieval, Renaissance, and modern – and many schools

---

of thought – realism and idealism, monism and dualism, atomism and materialism. [3]Is it possible to write a general history of philosophy? [4]Is it possible for any one scholar to read and understand all the work of all the historical figures he needs to, in order to write a general history?

[5]The purpose of this essay is modest. [6]It is an attempt to state the general principles of Descartes's philosophy.

This is an example of "the running start." Instead of jumping right into his topic, the author warms up by talking in the most general terms about the history of philosophy. The thesis of the essay is stated clearly and succinctly, but too late, in the second paragraph. The first paragraph is no more relevant to the stated thesis than it is to any essay in the history of philosophy. So it does not really introduce this particular essay. It should be eliminated. The essay does not suffer from lopping off the first paragraph. On the contrary, it is strengthened by it.

One teacher of writing advised deleting the first two paragraphs of the penultimate draft of the essay. This advice is hyperbolic. What is strictly true is that the author should recheck the first paragraph or two to see whether all or parts of them can be eliminated.

Do not try too hard to avoid ruminations early in drafting your essay. Many people need a running start in order to get up to speed. Feel free to include superfluous material in your drafts if that gets you going. A running start is better than no start at all. But the superfluous material should be deleted in the final draft.

I have explained that the first paragraph of an essay may be a running start because it no more introduces the topic of that essay than it does any other essay. Some more specific remarks are in order. Sentence [1] is trivial. Who would doubt that the *history* of philosophy is long? Who would doubt that it is difficult? Trivial first sentences do not orient readers. The title of the essay is more informative than [1].

Sentence [2] is not trivial, but it is also largely irrelevant. Little of the detail it provides is necessary for understanding the principles of Descartes's philosophy. The partial catalog of epochs and schools of philosophy, none of which will be mentioned again in the essay, is irrelevant to its main topic. The questions in [3] and [4] are red herrings. Even though they are not rhetorical questions, the author has no intention of answering them. One can imagine the stream-of-consciousness that

189

accompanied the writing of sentences [1]–[4]: "Darn, I have to write an essay on the history of philosophy.... What the hell do I know about philosophy? ... what topic can I choose from 2,500 years of heavy-duty thinking? ... I can't read all the relevant works ... I haven't read anything except Descartes's *Meditations*. Ahhh! that's it!"

This brings us to [5] and [6], two clear, precise, and fully justified sentences, the two sentences that express the thought that should have begun the essay.

Here's another example of "The Running Start," committed by a famous historian of political philosophy:

> Men often speak of virtue without using the word but saying instead "the quality of life" or "the great society." But do we know what virtue is? Socrates arrived at the conclusion that it is the greatest good for a human being to make everyday speeches about virtue ... When the prophet Isaiah received his vocation, he was overpowered by the sense of his unworthiness ... Who is right, the Greeks or the Jews? Athens or Jerusalem? Perhaps it is this conflict which is at the bottom of a kind of thought which is philosophic indeed but no longer Greek: modern philosophy. It is in trying to understand modern philosophy that we come across Machiavelli. (Leo Strauss, "Machiavelli," in Leo Strauss and Joseph Cropsey, eds., *The History of Political Philosophy*, 3rd edn, Chicago: University of Chicago Press, 1987, pp. 296–7.)

As the dots of ellipsis indicate, this opening paragraph about Machiavelli's political philosophy goes on at greater length. The reader really does not need to know about the discordant attitudes of ancient Rome and Israel to understand Machiavelli's project of describing how to run a government effectively without appealing to Christian principles. Strauss then spends two pages discussing Hobbes and Spinoza before he begins his protracted treatment of Machiavelli. (Strauss's opening passage is an even more egregious instance of the Running Start, because it begins on page 296 of the book he edited with another scholar. He had ample opportunity in the Introduction or in an earlier chapter to vet the two options in ancient thought.)

Exercises

1   Rewrite the following passage in such a way that it avoids the pitfalls discussed in this chapter.

Promises, Obligations, and Abilities

One of the great areas of philosophy is ethics. Philosophers have often worried about what is right and what is wrong. One of the central concepts of ethics is obligation, and we should ask what the relation is between obligation and ability. The issue here can be illustrated by considering a paradox of promising.

(1) Whenever a person makes a promise to do x, he thereby puts himself under an obligation to do x.

(2) If someone is obligated to do x, then he can do x ("ought" implies "can").

(3) Some people sometimes make promises they cannot keep.

Each of propositions (1)–(3) is well supported. Proposition (1) is analytic; it is part of the concept of promising that, if one has promised to do something, then one is obliged to do it.

The distinction between analytic and synthetic propositions is most closely associated with the name of Immanuel Kant and he used the distinction to separate the realm of logic from the realm of fact. Humans have no access to unadorned reality, according to Kant, rather all human knowledge is filtered through and conditioned by such concepts as causality, substance, and temporality.

2 Which beginning of an essay is better, A or B? Why?

A. [1] The three versions [2] of Hobbes's theory of the way sovereignty by institution arises may [3] on the surface seem different enough to be claimed as having discrepancies, yet [4] after careful examination, these versions complement each other. [5] Their retellings [6] offer details supporting Hobbes's attempt to refute the English Civil War.

B. There are three versions of Hobbes's theory of sovereignty by institution. On the surface, they may seem different enough to indicate that they are inconsistent with each other. However, a careful examination of these versions shows that they complement each other. Each version adds details supporting Hobbes's attempt to show that civil war is unjustified.

Don't read on until you have answered the question above. Here are some comments that explain why B is better.

[1] The essay may start too quickly. Should you assume that the reader knows that there are three versions of Hobbes's theory?

[2] You don't need both "may" and "seem". Choose just one of them.

[3] A complete thought has already been expressed. Replace the comma with a semicolon; the "yet"-clause expresses a complete thought.

[4] The first sentence contains too much: an allusion to three versions of a theory; one interpretation; and an alternative interpretation.

[5] "Retellings" is a clumsy word.

[6] Hobbes did not refute the English Civil War. Wars are not things that can be refuted. He tried to show that civil war (not just the English Civil War) was unjustified.

3 Which beginning is better? Why?

> *Original:* Thomas Hobbes was a seventeenth century philosopher who wrote several texts on government. In his treatise *Leviathan*, Hobbes examines the purpose and nature of government.
> *Revision:* In his treatise *Leviathan*, Thomas Hobbes (1588–1679) examines the purpose and nature of government.

4 The following passage is an example of an essay that begins well. For each sentence, specify its function. Use the section numbers or descriptive titles from "An Outline of the Structure of an Essay" as much as possible. Some sentences of the passage announce things that will be done later in the paper; express these facts in specifying the function of the sentence. For example, if some sentence says that objections will be answered at a certain place, say that the function of the sentence relates to "Objections."

[1]In this paper I offer an interpretation of the argument at the beginning of *Republic* 10 (597c1–d3). [2]The argument – sometimes called the Third Bed Argument (TBA) – shows that the Form of bed is unique. [3]The argument is interesting because it uses the One Over Many principle (OM), which justifies positing Forms. [4]But unlike the use of OM in the first Third Man Argument (TMA) of *Parmenides* (131a1–b2), the use of the OM in TBA does not produce an argument which is liable to becoming an infinite regress. [5]Since the TBA is in every other respect a classic statement of the theory of Forms usually associated with the middle dialogues, we can conclude that this theory is

not metaphysically bankrupt, as is sometimes claimed. [6]Whatever the problems with the TMA, they do not infect the whole theory of Forms in the middle dialogues because there is at least one instance of a clear enunciation of the theory which does not fall prey to the infinite regress of the TMA.

[7]In section 1 of this paper, we analyze the TBA and add three assumptions necessary to make it valid. [8] As well, we explain these assumptions and offer textual evidence for them. [9]In section 2, we survey recent commentaries on the TBA and defend our interpretation against these commentaries. [10]In particular we show that under our interpretation, the TBA is not liable to being turned into an infinite regress of Forms of bed. [11]In section 3, we see what implications this latter fact has for a theory of Forms which holds that the Form of f is, in some way, itself f. [12]We show in what way this central doctrine of the middle dialogues theory of Forms can be held without threat of inconsistency or infinite regress. [13]In section 4, we apply our interpretation of the TBA to the TMA, showing that the fallacious step of the TMA can be brought to light by considering the important differences between the two arguments. (Richard D. Parry, "The Uniqueness Proof for Forms in *Republic* 10," *Journal of the History of Philosophy* 23 (1985) pp. 133–4.)

9

How to Read a Philosophical Work

Every philosophical author, at least since Plato, was a reader first. And one way to improve your writing is by paying attention to how a good author writes. How does she structure a sentence? How do individual sentences cohere in a paragraph? How do the paragraphs cohere? Does she use, abstract or concrete words, precise ones or imprecise?

I shall focus on reading article-length philosophical texts because their length is substantial but not overwhelming.

9.1 Find the Thesis Sentence

The best place to put a thesis statement, one that states what the author wants to show or prove, is at the beginning of the article. Since the thesis statement should be the organizing principle for the article, it is important to identify it. To do this, read the article through fairly quickly. Look for words that announce that the thesis is about to be stated. This includes such phrases as

> In this article, I shall argue that …
> The aim of this article is …
> My thesis is …
> I want to prove …

While a thesis statement should be near the beginning of the article, it may not occur in the first sentence. Background information may be given first. In W. V. Quine's classic article, "Two Dogmas of Empiricism," background information is given in the first three sentences, followed by the thesis statement at the end of the first paragraph.

Philosophical Writing: An Introduction, Fifth Edition. A. P. Martinich.
© 2025 John Wiley & Sons, Inc. Published 2025 by John Wiley & Sons, Inc.
Companion website: www.wiley.com/go/Martinich5e

[a]Modern empiricism has been conditioned in large part by two dogmas. [b]One is a belief in some fundamental cleavage between truths which are *analytic*, [c]or grounded in meanings independently of matters of fact, and [d]truths which are *synthetic*, or [e]grounded in fact. [f]The other dogma is reductionism: the belief that each meaningful statement is equivalent to some logical construct upon terms which refer to immediate experiences. [g]Both dogmas, I shall argue, are ill-founded.

[a] locates the article within the area of empiricism; [b] and [f] state those dogmas. They contain technical terms, which Quine briefly explains in [c] and [e]. The paragraph ends with [g], which announces Quine's project. This opening is a masterpiece of clarity and conciseness.

Here's another example from a classic article:

This paper consists of two parts: the first has an expository character, and the second is rather polemical.

In the first part I want to summarize in an informal way the main results of my investigations concerning the definition of truth ... [The rest of this paragraph and the beginning of the next paragraph have been deleted.]

In the second part of the paper I should like to express my views concerning these objections.[1]

Exercise

Identify the main thesis in the passage below, selected from the article "Meaning," by H. P. Grice. State the main thesis in 25 words or fewer. Then state the main thesis in 35–75 words.

[Consider the following sentences:]

"Those spots mean (meant) measles"
"Those spots didn't mean anything to me, but to the doctor they meant measles."
"The recent budget means that we shall have a hard year."

(1) I cannot say, "Those spots meant measles, but he hadn't got measles," and I cannot say, "The recent budget means that we shall

---

[1] Alfred Tarski, "The Semantic Conception of Truth and the Foundations of Semantics," *Philosophy and Phenomenological Research* 4 (1944); reprinted in A. P. Martinich, ed., *The Philosophy of Language*, 5th edition (New York: Oxford University Press), p. 69.

have a hard year, but we shan't have." That is to say, in cases like the above, *x meant that p* and *x means that p* entail *p*.

(2) I cannot argue from "Those spots mean (meant) measles" to any conclusion about "What is (was) meant by those spots"; for example, I am not entitled to say, "What was meant by those spots was that he had measles." Equally I cannot draw from the statement about the recent budget the conclusion "What is meant by the recent budget is that we shall have a hard year."

...

Now contrast the above sentences with the following:

"Those three rings on the bell (of the bus) mean that the bus is full."
"That remark, 'Smith couldn't get on without his trouble and strife,' meant that Smith found his wife indispensable."

(1) I can use the first of these and go on to say, "But it isn't in fact full – the conductor has made a mistake"; and I can use the second and go on, "But in fact Smith deserted her seven years ago." That is to say, here *x means that p* and *x meant that p* do not entail *p*.

(2) I can argue from the first to some statement about "what is (was) meant" by the rings on the bell and from the second to some statement about "what is (was) meant" by the quoted remark.

...

When the expressions "means," "means something," "means that," are used in the kind of way in which they are used in the first set of sentences, I shall speak of the sense, or senses, in which they are used, as the *natural* sense, or senses, of the expressions in question. When the expressions are used in the second set of sentences, I shall speak of the sense, or senses, in which they are used, as the *nonnatural* sense, or senses, of the expressions in question. I shall use the abbreviation "means$_{NN}$" to distinguish the nonnatural sense or senses.

...

I do not want to maintain that *all* our uses of "mean" fall easily, obviously, and tidily into one of the two groups I have distinguished; but I think that in most cases we should be at least fairly strongly inclined to assimilate a use of "mean" to one group rather than to the other. The question now arises is this: "What more can be said about the distinction between the cases where we should say that the word is applied in a natural sense and the cases where we should say that the word is applied in a nonnatural sense?"

...

I want first to consider briefly, and reject, what I might term a causal type of answer to the question, "What is meaning$_{NN}$?" We might try to say, for instance, more or less with C. L. Stevenson,[2] that for x to mean$_{NN}$ something, x must have (roughly) a tendency to produce in an audience some attitude (cognitive or otherwise) and a tendency, in the case of a speaker, to *be* produced *by* that attitude, these tendencies being dependent on "an elaborate process of conditioning attending the use of the sign in communication."[3] This clearly will not do.

... [Several pages of criticism are omitted.]

I will now try a different and, I hope, more promising line. If we can elucidate the meaning of

"x meant$_{NN}$ something (on a particular occasion)" and
"x meant$_{NN}$ that so-and-so (on a particular occasion)"
... this might reasonably be expected to help us with
"x means$_{NN}$ (timeless) something (that so-and-so),"
"A means$_{NN}$ (timeless) by x something (that so-and-so),"

and with the explication of "means the same as," "understands," "entails," and so on.

A first shot would be to suggest that "x meant$_{NN}$ something" would be true if x was intended by its utterer to induce a belief in some "audience" and that to say what the belief was would be to say what x meant$_{NN}$. This will not do.

... [Several pages of criticism and revised analyses are omitted.]

Perhaps then we may make the following generalizations:

(1) "A meant$_{NN}$ something by x" is (roughly) equivalent to "A intended the utterance of x to produce some effect in an audience by means of the recognition of this intention ...

(2) ... x means$_{NN}$ (timeless) something (that so-and-so)," might as a first shot be equated with some statement or disjunction of statements about what "people" (vague) intend (with qualifications about "recognition") to effect by x. ...

---

[2] *Ethics and Language* (New Haven: 1944), ch. 3.
[3] Ibid., p. 57.

Not every philosophical article has the proof of a substantive thesis as its goal. Some are expository; they are written to clarify issues without proving which of several competing views are correct. In these cases, the main topic of the article may be formulated as a question or set of questions early in the article such as this:

> What is meaning? What is the meaning of a word? How do people mean things with words? Are meanings objects or actions?

Authors sometimes summarize their results around the middle of the essay. They might use expressions like this:

> My aim so far has been to show …
> So far, I have shown how …

The most common place for philosophers to state their thesis is in the final section or paragraph of the article. I think this is a bad practice, but you need to know what philosophers commonly do to help you find their theses.

With the thesis statement identified, you should look for the principle propositions that the author used to support it; then objections to the propositions asserted; and finally the author's reply to the objections. You are in effect looking for the outline that the author had in mind or should have.

9.2   Precision of Words, Phrases, and Sentences

To understand what an author is saying, it is necessary to distinguish between (1) what the author is asserting or affirming in her own right to be true and (2) what she is asserting or affirming to *seem* or *appear* to be true. Very often, the very things that the author says *seem* or *appear* to be true are things that the reader will believe to be true. So the reader may be inclined to think that when the author is asserting that p, in sentences that begin like these:

> It seems to be the case that p
> It appears that p

In fact, the author is not asserting that p, but is calling attention to the appearance that it is true that p in order to go on to show that really it is *not* the case that p.

> It seems/appears that the sun moves around the earth. The evidence for this are our own senses and the testimony of how things appear to everyone we know ... However, ... Copernicus ...

Notice that somewhere following the assertion of what seems or appears to be the case, there will be some word or phrase ("However," or "This appearance is false" or "This evidence is inconclusive") that indicates that what seems or appears to be the case is not.

We should not forget, however, that sometimes what appears to be the case actually is the case. "This meat seems to be rancid" and "The patient appears to be recovering" are sentences that express something that is consistent with the meat being rancid and the patient actually recovering.

While "apparently *p*" and "it is apparent that *p*" look like they may be reporting something that is false, they often are expressing what the author believes is true: "Kant walked around his block every evening after supper; but apparently he sometimes went to Agatha's house." In reading, it is important to ask yourself what makes the most sense of passage.

In order to distinguish between the cases of false or misleading appearance from the other cases of appearance, some authors will combine the verb "seem" or "appear" with the subjunctive mood:

> It *may/might seem/appear* that the sun moves around the earth.

In these cases, it is highly likely that the author rejects the propositional content of the sentence. But not always. If the verbs "appear" or "seem" occur along with some reference to the first person, as in "it appears/seems to me that," then the import of the verb phrase is quite different.

Suppose that the author is trying to throw some proposition into doubt, say, the proposition, "A person can pretend to do something purely by imagining that she is doing something." Since the burden of proof always rests on the person who is asserting a proposition, the author, who merely finds the proposition of doubtful truth, does not have to prove the contradictory of it. To cast doubt on a proposition, it is enough for the author to prove, "It seems/appears to me that it is not the case that a person can pretend to do something purely by imagining that she is doing something."

9.3 Proving the Case

After identifying the main thesis of the article, the reader should try to figure out how the author proves his case. Philosophers often give the impression that their primary modes of reasoning are analysis and deductive argumentation. But there are other modes that are probably equally important. We will consider two of them in this section.

The first is "insight." Plato, Thomas Hobbes, Søren Kierkegaard, and Friedrich Nietzsche are four philosophers who are often insightful. An insight is an observation that is easy to understand when it is pointed out, but it is something that people tend not to guide their decisions in appropriate circumstances. Here are four examples. (1) Plato wrote that it is better to suffer an injustice than to do an injustice. Why? Because it is unjust to do an injustice. Think about the many people who act unjustly to prevent what they think is an impending injustice against them. Similarly, as Paul of Tarsus wrote, a person may not do evil so that good may come of it (because it is evil to do evil). (2) Thomas Hobbes wrote that to say that the claim that God appeared to me in a dream is the same as the claim that I dreamed that God appeared to me. Just as the latter has no evidential value, neither does the former. (3) Kierkegaard wrote that people are condemned to live their life forward but to understand it backward. What people do is influenced by what they think is the significance of past events. But the actual significance of what they will do is a function of future events, about which we will know only after we act. People sometimes believe they can be immunized against responsibility for future consequences by not deciding what they should do. But, as Jean-Paul Sartre quipped, "No decision is a decision." (4) Friedrich Nietzsche said that to declare that this world is a vale of tears and that there is another better world than this one is to slander this world.

When a philosopher is trying to write something insightful, you need to consider whether what she is saying is universally true, true in only some or many cases, or false. In addition to being a great poet, John Milton was a philosopher. In *Paradise Lost*, Satan said, "It is better to reign in hell than to serve in heaven." Is that true? Would it be better to be the leader of Al-Qaida than to be an employee of a human rights group?

Exercise

Satan also said, "The mind is its own place, and in itself can make a heaven of hell, a hell of heaven." Is that true, always, sometimes? Is what Satan said true? Are there confirming examples? What does that show? Are their disconfirming examples? What does that show?

The second mode of reasoning that is important to philosophy is inference to the best explanation, that is, giving the best explanation one can for some phenomenon. Here is a seemingly trivial example. On Monday, you go into a classroom and see some students who look very much like students you saw in that classroom the previous week. Are the Monday students the same ones you saw last week in that classroom? It is possible that each of last week's students has a twin who is attending class today in clothes that look just like the clothes worn by students last week. Possible, but ordinarily a poor explanation of the similarity. The best explanation is that the students seen on Monday are the same students seen last week. You may be able to see how pervasive and important these judgments are if you consider that you also have to decide whether the classroom is the same, the streets you walked on are the same. If the author is claiming to be making an inference to the best explanation, ask yourself whether there are other explanations that are just as good or better.

Think about a philosophical passage or article that claims to contain an argument. Can you find one? If so, then the author must be expressing her premises somewhere. These may be indicated by words and phrases such as "I need the premise" and "My first premise is." But a premise may not be introduced so explicitly. Too often authors claim to argue for something, without actually giving an argument. They are supporting their position in some other way, say, by giving examples or giving counterexamples. Here's an example of appealing to someone's authority. Suppose an author arguing for mind/body dualism writes "Plato, the first defender of mind/body dualism, argued that the soul is a substance because it is simple." The author may want the reader to accept the proposition that the soul is simple because Plato held it. But that is not a good reason. What the author ought to do is present Plato's reasoning, indicate her agreement, and then introduce it, "The soul is simple," as a premise. One source of thinking that citing the view of an authority is an argument is the phrase, "argument from authority." "Argument" is being used more broadly than the one we discussed in chapter 2. In this broad sense, an argument does not require premises and evidence.

Not every reference to an authority is an argument from authority. A reader may describe some position that a well-known philosopher held, without thereby committing herself to it. In such cases, the careful reader will be on the lookout for a sentence like "But the concept of substance-simplicity has unsolvable problems." As indicated in section 9.2, author may use the subjunctive mood or "seems" – "One may think (or: it seems) that the existence of the mind can be proved by noticing that a human being is conscious of itself" – in order to introduce a possibility that will later be rejected: "*However*, self-consciousness does not … ." And there are other cases in which the author comes to endorse the premise that was introduced with the subjunctive mood or "it seems": "Self-consciousness is indeed the premise that proves that the mind is independent of the body." The best advice is to read slowly and carefully.

Similar to the distinction between (1) what the author is asserting or affirming in her own right to be true and (2) what she is asserting or affirming to *seem* or *appear* to be true is the distinction between

(a)   what the author is asserting or affirming in her own right to be true and

(b)   what she is representing as the view of her opponent.

One article begins as follows:

> W. V. Quine is a realist. He believes that substances that exist independently of perception exist.

This gives the impression that the author believes these propositions. She does not. Her next sentence is:

> I shall argue against this position.

The indicative mood, "is" and "does not believe," is used by the author for rhetorical effect. The two introductory sentences are designed to set up the audience for a striking reversal: The author disagrees. A problem with the sentence, "I shall argue against this position," is that it is not clear whether the author does not believe that Quine is a realist or that she does not believe that realism is true. Further sentences should resolve the lack of clarity.

10

Reading, Writing, and Networks of Belief

10.1 Understanding and Interpretation

The hardest topics to explain and hardest for you to understand in this book are those in this section, namely, *understanding* and *interpreting* the *meaning* of texts in the semi-technical senses to be explained. Let's begin with the word *meaning*. Of its many senses, we are primarily interested in one, the meaning of the words in texts made at a particular time or what an author (or speaker) meant in using those words. The senses are obviously connected. Authors typically use words that have certain meaning in order to mean something. Here I am ignoring the differences between what and how words mean from what and how authors mean. The meaning of the words, "I apologize for misrepresenting your position," do not apologize, but an author can use those words to apologize. So, although the words' meaning and author's meaning are not identical, they are related. Something they have in common is that what the speaker means and what her words mean are fixed at the time they are used. The meaning of many words changes over time, but in the sense I am using "mean," the meaning does not change. When Paine wrote in *The American Crisis*,

> These are the times that try men's souls. The summer soldier and the sunshine patriot will, in this crisis, shrink from the service of their country; but he that stands by it now, deserves the love and thanks of man and woman,

the meaning of those words or what he meant in writing them is the same now as it was in 1776, roughly, that genuine patriots need to take action to defend their cause. This sense of *meaning* is different from the sense in

Philosophical Writing: An Introduction, Fifth Edition. A. P. Martinich.
© 2025 John Wiley & Sons, Inc. Published 2025 by John Wiley & Sons, Inc.
Companion website: www.wiley.com/go/Martinich5e

which "mean" indicates the significance or importance that the text has over time and for different people. That meaning, meaning as importance, does change. In the eighteenth century, the importance of the text for many readers was that they were moved to oppose the British rule by force. In the twenty-first century, readers marvel at the rhetorical skill exhibited in the text or how terrible the suffering of the rebels would be at Valley Forge and other places in the late 1770s.[1]

Let's suppose now that the author has written a text and that the meaning of its words is fixed. Further suppose that a student has read the text, has an *understanding* of it, and intends to write an interpretation for other readers. So we now have the original text, *The American Crisis*, a reader, her understanding of it, and an *interpretation* that she needs to write. One source of possible confusion is that a student-author A is also a reader and will shortly become an interpreter. These ideas of author, reader, and interpreter signify roles that people play, and the same person can be an author, reader, and interpreter of different texts, each of which has other readers, interpreters, and authors. I am going to try hard to be clear about who is playing each role and when they are playing it. Explaining this material and understanding it the first time it is read is difficult. Coming to understand it requires close attention and probably re-reading.

Implicit in the preceding paragraph is the fact that I am using *understanding* and *interpretation* in technical senses for two different things. An understanding of a text is the cognitive grasp of the meaning of the words of the text or of what the author tried to communicate by those words. Usually, a reader correctly understands the text. When the text is philosophical (or legal or literary or religious), the reader sometimes misunderstands it. For our purposes, misunderstanding will be treated as a kind of understanding, just as giving bad advice is a kind of advice. For our purposes, the interpretation comes later in time than the understanding. In practice, understanding and interpretation often proceed together. In short, a person's understanding of a text is *for herself*; a person's interpretation of that understanding is *for others* (for her readers).

---

[1] There are other senses of *meaning* that should also not be confused with our sense of linguistic meaning, as indicated by these examples, "By 'The author of *The American Crisis*', the student meant [was referring to] Thomas Paine," and "Thomas Paine meant [intended] to write *The American Crisis*" a year before he actually did.

The skills of reading and writing (understanding and interpreting) are equally important for students.[2] *Understanding* a text, as I will use the term, is grasping the mental or cognitive content of the text. *Interpreting* a text will be used to express that understanding in a way that the interpreter thinks will enable her readers to understand or (when the author is a student and the reader is her professor) will enable her readers to understand that she knows her subject.[3] Her essay, the written expression of the student's understanding of the text, is her *interpretation* of the text.

A standard piece of advice is "Know your audience." The audience or reader will understand what the lecturer says if the lecturer uses words the audience knows and draws upon experiences the audience has had.[4] Not knowing what language is being used and not drawing on the audience's experience is a recipe for incomprehension and boredom. Fortunately for the purposes of this chapter, the structure of many beliefs of the speaker and her audience are similar. So, a description of that structure will help the student understand her own situation as an author and reader, and the professor's situation as a reader of the student's essay.

All linguistic communication requires numerous beliefs. Let's concentrate on the statement, "The Spanish oaks are turning red." The reader needs to know that oaks are trees, that the leaves of several kinds of trees turn color in autumn, and that October is one of the months of autumn in the northern hemisphere. These necessary beliefs are prejudgments in the sense of having them before the reading begins. But they are not prejudices as long as the person acquired them by reasonable processes and is willing to reconsider them in light of new evidence. Coming to understand the text involves adding new beliefs to her preexisting network of beliefs. This process may involve deleting some of the prejudgments in order to add others that yield a plausible understanding. But most of the network, most of the prejudgments, do not change.

When the reader who understands the text prepares to express her understanding in an essay, she begins formulating an interpretation for an

---

[2] Different thinkers want to hold that readers aim at understanding what the author wanted to communicate or that readers are or ought to be interested in their response to the text, or something else. For our purposes, the classical idea of understanding the meaning of the text is the most helpful.

[3] I recommend writing for one's classmate, roommate, friend, or parent for practice.

[4] To put this point in terms of speaker and audience, the speaker needs to know the language that the audience understands; it is not necessary for the audience to be able to speak the speaker's language.

audience. Part of her understanding may be conceived with words that she thinks will be understood by her reader; other parts of her understanding may need different words or a different ordering of the words. A simple example is an author's understanding that a text says that Kee is an ophthalmologist. If she is writing for an audience of eight-year-old children, the author should write, "Kee is an eye-doctor" rather than "Kee is an ophthalmologist." A more pertinent example: Suppose she is writing about Thomas Hobbes's metaphysics. If she writes, "Hobbes was a mechanistic materialist," and does not think about the reader's beliefs or knowledge, her attempt to communicate may fail because *mechanism* and *materialism* are technical terms. She may also fail to convince her professor that she knows what she is saying because the student's job is to get her professor to know that she understands what she is talking about, as was explained in chapter 1, section 1.1. So the student's first sentence about Hobbes, mechanism, and materialism is fine if it is followed up with definitions of mechanism and materialism. The student's essay then may begin like this:

HOBBES'S PHYSICS OR METAPHYSICS

Thomas Hobbes is a mechanistic materialist. *Mechanism* is the view that all change occurs when one moving body makes contact with another moving body. *Materialism* is the view that only bodies, things extended in space, exist. The evidence that Hobbes is a mechanist and materialist is found in ...

If the student uses the method of successive elaboration (see chapter 4), then her second draft may be something like this:

HOBBES'S PHYSICS OR METAPHYSICS

Hobbes is a mechanistic materialist. *Mechanism* is the view that all change occurs by the contract of one moving body against another. *Materialism* is the view that only bodies, things extended in space, exist. That mechanism and materialism are not the same view, one may consider that a scientist may hold that everything

---

is a body and that the motions of some bodies cause an effect at a distance. (As a matter of fact, many quantum physicists believe that entangled pairs of photons have this property.) The evidence that Hobbes is a mechanist and materialist is found in *De corpore* (*On Body*).

Exercise

In the essay fragment above, is the student-author acting prudently in adding the sentence in parentheses? Think.

So far, my description of the process of moving from understanding to interpretation may seem to suggest that going from reading to understanding to interpretation is a simple operation. It rarely is. Understanding a philosophical text usually comes in fits and starts, alternating with bits of interpretation that may be revised by further reading and reflection. Sometimes people think they understand something until they try to write out that understanding; when nothing coherent is forthcoming, they prudently reread the text. I am not saying that understanding always requires the ability to express their understanding in words. A person may learn how to solve some mathematical problems and then go on to do new ones without being able to explain how to do it to someone else. It's the difference between being a good mathematics teacher and a mathematician in a classroom. A workman's practical skills of fixing motors, plumbing, and electronics sometimes cannot be adequately explained to another person: "You take the thingamabob and attach it to the whatchamacallit."

The difference between one's understanding of a text and one's interpretation of it may be conveyed by saying that one's understanding is *for oneself*, and one's interpretation is for *one's reader*. Unfortunately, great philosophers too often seem to write for themselves, that is, to present a solution to a philosophical problem in terms that they understand but that their readers do not. This is especially true of highly original philosophers, who are great because they have created or arranged beliefs that readers don't have. So, readers have a difficult time converting the philosopher's beliefs into their own networks.

Sometimes an author's verbalization of her own understanding improves her understanding of the text. Upon writing out her understanding (her interpretation), she sees how she can improve and make the text more intelligible to her readers. She distances herself from her understanding and acquires a kind of third-person or objective view of her understanding, and that may trigger a better understanding. Sometimes reading her (partial) interpretation allows her to see that she has made a mistake or that another wording would improve the understanding. This objectification of one's own understanding helps because new beliefs may not be transparent to oneself. New beliefs involving unfamiliar concepts are especially difficult to integrate into one's other beliefs. Reading and writing, understanding and interpretation, often proceed, to change the metaphor, as alternating steps, and sometimes lead one to retracing those steps and going off in a different, better direction.

Sometimes understanding and interpretation are effectively simultaneous. But for almost all philosophical texts, understanding and interpretation are discriminable. (See the process of drafting your essay in chapter 4. Recall in that chapter that the best way is the one that works for you.)

Exercises

1 In the text below which sentence, A or B, better explains its main point? If you think some combination of the two may be the best, write it down.

(A) Most philosophical texts, like literary, historical, and religious ones, are subject to more than one interpretation. Two or more intelligent people with substantial background knowledge may reasonably disagree about the precise meaning of a text. Some of the reasons for these disagreements are commonplace: the words have more than one meaning; different authors begin with beliefs different from their readers; and different readers have different beliefs from each other. Other causes do not need to be discussed here.

(B) Most important philosophical texts are subject to more than one interpretation because interpreting a text requires at least believing that the words have a particular meaning and knowing what thought the philosopher wanted to communicate with those words with that meaning. Other causes for multiple interpretations do not need to be discussed here.

2 State another reason or cause why two people may have different interpretations of a text.

3 Extra credit. Give still another cause for different interpretations.

Since most words have more than one meaning, the reader is constantly guessing or inferring (using those words broadly) the right meaning. How does one determine which meaning is the right one on an occasion? The general and minimally helpful answer is that it is the most likely meaning that the philosopher would have intended to communicate; the reader weighs the linguistic and nonlinguistic context. The linguistic context may be the sentences surrounding the passage to be interpreted or texts from other philosophers. The nonlinguistic context may be the socio-politico-economic context. Were changes in trade, technology, wealth disparity, military victory, or loss creating or inviting new philosophical theories? Were new scientific theories, for example, those of Copernicus, Galileo, Newton, Darwin, or Freud, inviting or inviting new philosophical theories? The difficulty of identifying the exact meaning of a philosopher's words is illustrated by the possibility that the philosopher might mean that everything is water (Thales) or fire (Heraclitus) or minds and ideas (Berkeley). Also, a philosopher may use a familiar word (even a technical word in philosophy) in a different way to create a new theory.

10.2   Networks of Belief

W. V. Quine and J. S. Ullian referred to the normal structure of beliefs, as "the web of belief"[5] because of all the connections among the beliefs. Although I took the concept from them, I use a different term, *the network of belief*, and have a different conception.

There are two common, but sometimes misleading, ideas about belief. First, *a belief* is often thought of as something that is unique to one person. One might say that Kee's belief that Biden won the 2020 election is not identical with Lee's belief that Biden won the 2020 election on the grounds that Kee's belief has to be in his mind or brain, and none of Kee's mental or brain states are in Lee's mind or brain. Alternatively, their beliefs are different in that the brain states correlated with their separate beliefs are numerically different.

However, there's another way of counting beliefs such that Kee and Lee have the very same belief, namely, that Biden won the 2020 election. At least 100,000,000 Americans have that same belief. It is this way of counting beliefs that is important for understanding the structure of networks of

---

[5] *The Web of Belief*, 2nd edition (New York: Random House, 1978). For the sake of simplicity, only normal networks in the descriptive sense of *usual* or *standard* will be discussed.

belief.[6] In normal communication, each person tries to get the other person to have the same beliefs relevant to their purposes.

Exercise

Suppose Kee believes that he feels a pain in the big toe of his left foot. Can anyone else have exactly this belief? (Think.) Give a reason for your answer.

Suppose that Kee believes that snow is white and coal is black. In addition to calling them beliefs, we can call them propositions: Kee believes the proposition that snow is white and coal is black but not the proposition that snow is black.

Propositions are or represent the content of a person's beliefs, and a person's beliefs are or are represented by propositions. Recall from chapter 2 that propositions have truth-values. I will use the verb *know* when it is more idiomatic than *believe*.[7] Some properties of the network of beliefs will be described now. Some of these properties operate in the background of writing. The others are in the forefront of writing.

10.3   Numerosity, Connectedness, and Unity

Networks have to have many beliefs, just as a fishing net is held together by many knots connecting many strings. A person cannot have the belief that it is raining without also having such beliefs as that rain is water, that it falls from the sky, that it comes from clouds, and that it is usually safe to drink. Further, each of these beliefs involves other beliefs such as that the sky is above the earth, that air seems to be drier on days with cloudless skies, that drinking is taking water into the mouth and swallowing it, and that being safe to drink means that it will not cause pain, illness, or death.

---

[6] We have to talk about the sense in which multiple people can have the same belief because communication is partly getting one person, the author, to get the reader to have the same belief as the author. In other words, if an author and reader could never have the same belief, communication would be impossible.

[7] Philosophers think people don't know as much as they think they do.

The description of the numerosity just given implicitly contains the idea that the beliefs are connected, some immediately to another belief and some mediately:

(1)   Thomas Hobbes was a seventeenth-century philosopher.
(2)   Hobbes wrote *Leviathan*.
(3)   It is unknown whether John Locke read *Leviathan*.
(4)   Hobbes and Locke were English.
(5)   The English and the French were often enemies in the seventeenth century.
(6)   The French live on a different continent from the Chinese.
(7)   China's great leader in the twentieth century was Mao Zedong.

Each of these seven beliefs is immediately connected to at least one other belief. Most are mediately connected to more than one. (A connection between two things A and B is mediate just in case there is a third thing C that connects them.)

The connections among beliefs are of various sorts. Some beliefs (as propositions) entail other beliefs (see chapter 2). Some beliefs are causally related to others, as when the belief that it is raining caused the belief that the ground is wet. Some beliefs are connected by probability, for example, the belief that Kee drank a liter of vodka and the belief that Kee is drunk. Some beliefs are connected to others by inference to the best explanation. Lee sees a tall man in a yellow hat walking with a chimpanzee at 10:00 AM on Monday and sees a tall man in a yellow hat walking with a chimpanzee at 10:00 AM on Tuesday. Lee believes that the man and the chimpanzee seen on Monday are the same man and chimpanzee seen on Tuesday by inference.

The network of beliefs would not be numerous or connected unless they were united in some way. All the knots and strings in a net constitute one net; the numerous, connected beliefs are united and form one network. Does there have to be something that connects them? For millennia, Western philosophers thought there was something, a mind or a soul that held all the beliefs (and other mental states and objects) together. In the late eighteenth century, David Hume criticized that view. He claimed that he did not find anything except impressions and ideas *when he looked inside himself.* This wording is paradoxical. The friends of minds would say that by looking inside himself, Hume undermined his no-mind view. Reflecting on beliefs supposedly never involves the perception of a soul or mind. Immanuel Kant improved Hume's language by saying that the unity of consciousness is not an object of experience but is presupposed by experience. To say that the unity of appearance is not an appearance of unity is an epigram.

Exercise

Friedrich Nietzsche sardonically wrote, "if you gaze for long into an abyss, the abyss gazes also into you" (*Beyond Good and Evil*, chapter 4). Was David Hume right to think that when he looked into himself, nothing was looking back at him?

Not all beliefs in a network must always be accessible. But each must be able to be accessed at some time. Kee does not remember right now how many children were invited to his sixth birthday party. But if he tries to recall it, he will remember that six children were invited. If he cannot access it, then he must have forgotten it, and it is no longer a belief.

Application to Writing: You want to convince your reader that your interpretation of a text is correct. You may know which belief the reader has that you think is incorrect. Suppose you are a materialist and believe that everything can be reduced to the motion of bodies, and your reader has the belief that everything is conscious (panpsychism). You may need to know that the reader's belief is closely connected to an understanding of the two-slit experiment in quantum physics (even though that experiment does not entail panpsychism). To convince your reader, you would need to include a criticism that he might accept. If you cannot do this, your interpretation can do no more than show the reader that your view has some merit.

Exercise

Other than the seven numbered propositions above, (1) give an example of two beliefs that are immediately connected; then (2) give an example of a third proposition indirectly connected to the two in (1).

10.4   Generality

A fourth property of networks is generality. Quantifiers like *all, most, some,* and *few*, as well as quantifying adverbs like *always, everywhere, sometimes,* and *somewhere*, indicate different levels of generality (in addition to helping connect one belief to another). To give a familiar example, the belief that all humans are mortal is connected to the belief that Socrates is mortal.

Application to Writing: Be sure to make clear to your reader whether you are relying on a proposition that is true of everything (relevant to the topic), everything in normal conditions, almost all things ("Birds fly"), most things, some things, or one thing. The proposition, *self-preservation is the strongest human desire,* can be used to express a proposition with various degrees of generality, depending on the circumstances envisioned.

Exercise

1   Is the belief that no human being has feathers connected with the belief that Socrates does not have feathers?

2   Is the belief that some human beings are mortal connected with Socrates is mortal? Give a reason for your answer.

10.5   Accommodation

Beliefs are continuously being added and subtracted from the network. They are added when they are needed such as when one is adding beliefs to help negotiate the terrain; they are subtracted when they are no longer needed, as when the belief that a rock on a path needs to be avoided is forgotten once it has been passed. Forgetting is a brilliant tool for eliminating unnecessary beliefs. Beliefs that are regularly useful have a long life. Beliefs usually are added and subtracted in clusters because they are connected. Suppose that Lee's marriage has ended. When a friend Mee hears of the divorce, she adds that belief to her network, but also these:

Lee is deeply sad.
Lee will need emotional support from me (Mee).
I (Mee) need to be with Lee tomorrow.

Accommodation is the best word I could think of for this property because it suggests fitting one or more things into something already existing. Regarding changes in the network, it is supposed to capture the relevant aspects of a dynamic system, one that regularly changes or is updated.

10.6   Tenacity and Certainty

Tenacity and certainty are different properties but are treated together because it is easy to confuse them. I will begin with two scenarios in which the difference between them is marked. Kee and Lee enter a well-lit room and see a four-foot square painting twenty feet away. Kee asks what color it is. Lee says "Purple." Kee asks whether Lee is sure it is purple. Lee replies, "I'm certain." Kee asks Lee to inspect the painting from a few inches away. Doing this, Lee sees that it consists of tiny red and blue squares. As a result, Lee easily gives up his belief that the painting is solid purple. Lee's belief was certain but not tenacious. The other scenario concerns the beliefs of many contemporary theists. For at least several decades, many theists have claimed that they would never give up their faith or belief that God exists but that they have moments of doubt about its truth. For some of them, this belief could not be a matter of faith if it were not occasionally subject to doubt. This is a case of a belief being tenacious but not certain or not always certain. A belief may be tenacious because of overwhelming evidence, because of its great explanatory power, or because of its emotional value. Let's now describe these two properties in some detail, beginning with tenacity.

Tenacity can be attributed to beliefs in two ways, comparatively and non-comparatively. Non-comparative beliefs are judged individually and not in relation to other beliefs; they are strongly held and consequently not easily given up. Highly tenacious beliefs are held so securely that they are given up only reluctantly and some may not be able to be given up at all no matter how much evidence against them is presented. Religious beliefs are tenacious for some people, while beliefs about political parties and ideologies such as communism, liberalism, democracy, and capitalism are for others. Tenacious beliefs usually have broad explanatory value ("Every event has a cause") or ethical value ("It is wrong to cause unnecessary pain to an innocent person").

Let's now turn to beliefs that are relatively or comparably more tenacious than others. Kee tenaciously believes that the US Senate has 100 senators and that the House of Representatives has 435 members, and he believes the former more tenaciously than the latter. The comparative use of tenacity is such that it is possible that one or both beliefs that are compared are not tenacious non-comparatively; for example, Kee believes that Joe Biden will be reelected president in 2024 more tenaciously than he believes that Donald Trump will be the Republican nominee. In fact, Kee could give up each belief in the face of substantial evidence. (This is written in 2023; so one or both beliefs may turn out to be false.)

People who hold beliefs tenaciously tend to look for additional evidence that confirms their beliefs, a phenomenon called *confirmation bias*. The selective search for evidence often leads to harmful consequences. The belief that the possible side effects of childhood vaccines outweigh the risk of the diseases themselves makes children unnecessarily vulnerable to illness and keeps the diseases in circulation. During the COVID-19 pandemic of 2020–2022, some people refused to believe that the virus was life threatening or refused medical treatment for it. One patient dying for weeks in a hospital begged her nurse to tell her what disease she had up to her last conscious moment. She did not believe that she had COVID.

Probably the most famous Western philosopher to explicitly search for and specify a proposition that was absolutely tenacious was Rene Descartes in both *Discourse on the Method of Conducting the Mind* and *Meditations on First Philosophy*. He maintained that it is impossible for anyone who thinks about anything not to believe that he, the thinking thing, exists. In the twentieth century, G. E. Moore and Ludwig Wittgenstein thought that the class of certain things was much broader than Descartes's initial claim. Wittgenstein in effect discussed tenacious beliefs under the rubric of things that "stand fast" for people. He thought these things were so fundamental to human life that they are not genuinely beliefs but make belief possible. The earth is old and people have existed for hundreds of years may be examples of things that stand fast.

In summary, a tenacious belief is one that is firmly held. Some beliefs are comparative; one is more tenacious than another.

Application to Writing: Evidence, reasoning, or argumentation that such and such is true may not be able to convince a person who tenaciously believes that such and such is not true. Too many Americans tenaciously believe that human actions do not contribute to global warming, the evidence be damned. To paraphrase the last proposition of Wittgenstein's *Tractatus Logico-Philosophicus*, "Whereof we cannot rationally convince, thereof we may reasonably remain silent." And to paraphrase the serenity prayer: Let us convince others of the true propositions that we can; not try to convince them of the true propositions we can't; and have the wisdom to know the difference.

Exercise

Write down two additional tenacious beliefs, ones that you think your friends also have.

Certainty, like tenacity, has both an absolute and comparative use. Kee is certain that the US House of Representatives has 435 members but more certain that the Senate has 100 members. (Yes, this example is like the one used about tenacity. Usually, the tenacity and certainty of a belief are approximately the same.)

Tenacity may be said to be subjective in that its strength depends on the mind of the person who has it; there is no objective sense of tenacity. In contrast, certainty can be subjective or objective. Subjective certainty refers to the psychological attitude of a person: Kee's belief about the Senate and House of Representatives is an example. A belief is objectively certain if the proposition is self-evident, as these examples:

Every white horse is white.
If it is raining, then it is raining.
Either snow is white or snow is not white.

In short, subjective certainty is a property of a person's mind; objective certainty is a property of a proposition.

Application of Certainty to Writing: In chapter 2, I recommended using the logically weakest propositions you can in order to increase the likelihood that your reader will accept that your thesis is true. Suppose your essay is a refutation of skepticism. You might rely on the proposition that people who are in pain are certain that they are in pain. But your reader may not accept that every feeling of pain is certain, for example, they may think that there are experiences that may be discomforts that are not pain, and consequently that they are not certain that some pain is a pain. And they may think that some anticipations of pain are judged to be painful when, upon reflection, they judge that they were not in pain. One way to avoid the borderline cases is to describe a related experience and make a weak claim about it. For example, while a person may not be certain about whether some experiences are pain, a person experiencing intense pain is certain that he is in pain.

Application of Tenacity to Writing: If you want to prove that *p* to your reader, but he holds not-*p* tenaciously, try to use a reductio ad absurdum argument. That is, assume *not-p* is true and then show that it entails a contradiction. If you can get your reader to see that his belief that *not-p* involves a contradiction, his belief that it is true may end.

Exercise

In chapter 2, the concepts of logically stronger and logically weaker propositions were distinguished. Explain how experiencing an intense pain can be shown to be logically stronger than feeling a weak pain.

10.7 Blocks

Every reasonable person, that is, every person who is not dogmatically certain that he has never had a mistaken belief, is logically committed to having a network of beliefs that is inconsistent. Some beliefs contradict others. The proof is simple. Consider Bo who writes down as many of his beliefs as he can think of. Now form the conjunction of Bo's beliefs, which conjunction he is logically committed to:

$$(B_1 \ \& \ B_2, \ ..., \ B_n)$$

Bo, who is reasonable, also believes that at least one of his beliefs is mistaken, even though he does not know which of his beliefs is mistaken. If he knew that, he would drop that belief from his network to make it consistent. The best that Bo can do is to believe that at least one of his beliefs is false. That is tantamount to believing this:

$$\sim(B_1 \ \& \ B_2, \ ..., \ B_n).$$

Conjoining the two beliefs above, Bo is logically committed to the contradiction

$$((B_1 \ \& \ B_2, ..., \ B_n) \ \& \sim (B_1 \ \& \ B_2, ..., \ B_n))$$

Now within a logical system (closed under deduction) having a contradictory proposition is disastrous because it entails every proposition. I mentioned this in chapter 2, when I said that every argument with contradictory premises is valid.

217

Do not be hard on Bo. Because he is reasonable and intellectually honest, he would never use the contradictory proposition above to prove an ordinary proposition. (He might use it to prove that his network is inconsistent.)

Occasionally, people suspect that some subset of their beliefs is false and realize that if they used all those beliefs, they might prove some proposition that they know is false or at least do not want to believe is true. In this kind of case, a fallible and honest person like Bo *blocks* the inference that would take them from some of their beliefs to the conclusion that they know or believe is false. A familiar case of this relates to the signers of the Declaration of Independence, which begins, "All men are created equal." Some of these signers also believed that some people (not themselves) are created inferior to others and are legitimately enslaved, but they knew they could not say this without being exposed as inconsistent and worse. Another example, again from the Declaration of Independence, concerns those who believe everything in the Declaration, which includes the proposition that the right to life is "unalienable [sic]," yet also believe in capital punishment. These proponents of capital punishment block the inference to the proposition that the right to life is alienable and that proposition contradicts the proposition that life is unalienable. (If this example is difficult to understand, it may be because people are pretty good at masking their contradictions.) Psychologists call holding such discrepant beliefs *cognitive dissonance.*

High IQs do not immunize people from believing inconsistent propositions. For example, take any one of the conservative justices of the Supreme Court of the United States who are *originalists;* they believe that the relevant meaning of the Constitution is the meaning that it had when it was ratified in the eighteenth century. In 2022, the Court argued that facts about eighteenth-century Americans have the consequence that having personal privacy or access to abortion could not have been a protected constitutional right at that time and therefore is not one now. Justice Clarence Thomas observed that the same reasoning meant that there is no right to use contraception, or to have sex with a consenting adult partner, or to marry someone of the same sex. However, other justices, who "joined Thomas in the majority insisted that their decision did not place these other rights in peril," did not explain "how these rights are different from abortion."[8] They blocked the inference to the proposition that there is no right to contraception, sex, or marriage between people of the same gender. Thomas was consistent; the other justices were not.

---

[8] David Cole, "Originalism's Charade," *New York Review of Books* November 24 (2022), p. 19.

Exercise

In chapter 2, I said that one person's modus ponens is another person's modus tollens. What are the plausible modus ponens and modus tollens arguments for the right to birth control (or homosexual conduct or same sex marriage) relevant to the belief that abortion is or is not a protected right; and which groups (prolife or prochoice) are committed to those arguments?

A relatively benign use of blocks involves beliefs that are not strictly true, but which people subscribe to for the sake of simplicity. Almost everyone believes that all birds fly. But they also believe that penguins do not fly. With another of their beliefs made explicit, that penguins are birds, their beliefs can be shown to be formally contradictory, but they block the inference whenever appropriate. Of course, a person could revise her belief about birds to *almost all birds fly, but penguins are birds and do not fly*. But an easier route is to keep her false belief and not apply it when penguins are the topic of conversation. A related reason for keeping the false belief is that they may not know whether turkeys and peacocks count as flying or not. A similar case involves bigots who think that people with racial or ethnic property *P* are unworthy to be friends but in fact have friends who have *P*.

Application to Writing: If you know that your reader blocks certain inferences that follow from some tenacious belief, you need to think about ways in which you can reduce the tenacity. Your reader may believe that all people of race (ethnicity and sexual orientation) *P* have the property *X*. If the reader has a friend Lee who is *P*, one might point out without rancor that the reader's general belief is undermined by fact that Lee is *P* but not *X*. If your reader weakens his belief to "Almost all *P*s are *X*" or "A disproportionate number of *P*s are *X*," you have more work to do.

Exercise

Can you think of a reason for holding that the supposedly benign use of blocks may not be benign?

10.8   Porosity

Networks are incomplete in more than one way.[9] We will focus on one particular type, *porosity*. As many beliefs as people have, they could have many more. Suppose Lee walks out of her apartment and arrives at a party two miles away. She acquired short-term beliefs that helped her navigate the distance. At the party, she forgets most of those beliefs because they have no lasting value. Let's consider two beliefs that she retains:

Ba. I walked out of my apartment.
Bb. I walked into the party location.

Earlier, she had or could have had many more beliefs such as Bc–Bg:

Bc. I turned the door handle of my apartment door.
Bd. I pulled the door open.
Be. I went into the hall.
Bf. I got into a taxi.
Bg. I got out of the taxi a mile from the party and walked the rest of the way.

Our supposition is that during the party only Ba and Bb were still in her network. But now further suppose that a partygoer asks how she got out of her apartment. Lee does not specifically remember how but she believes that she usually turns the door handle and walks out into the hall and has no reason to think that she did anything else earlier that evening. So she has filled the gap between Ba and Bb with Bc–Be. The partygoer notes Lee's wet shoes and asks whether she walked the entire way. Using reasoning like the one that yielded Bc-Be, she constructs Bf and Bg, which further fill the gap between Ba and Bb. Someone may prefer to say that Lee did not construct Bc–Bg but retrieved them from latent memory.[10] Our focus here is on the porosity of networks, as the idea of a network

---

[9] One kind of incompleteness may be called *indeterminateness*. If Ms. Bo believes that Mr. Chou walked across the South Mall, she may have no belief about whether he was walking quickly or slowly. But if asked about which, she may make her belief more determinate because she tends to notice people who walk slowly, and she does not recollect that Lee was walking slowly. Her new, more determinate belief is that Lee was not walking slowly. Indeterminateness will tacitly be used in the discussion of porosity.

[10] Someone may argue that constructed beliefs are not genuine memories. Maybe not, but they are beliefs that people often use.

suggests, not the nature of beliefs.[11] One good reason for a porous network is that it saves space in the brain for other beliefs.

The porosity of networks is related to the porosity of texts. Gaps among beliefs cause gaps in texts and consequently cause differences in interpretation. Below is a short passage from Hobbes's *Leviathan* about "laws of nature," that is, precepts that establish or maintain peace, not laws of physics.

> These dictates of reason men use to call by the name of laws, but improperly; for they are but conclusions or theorems concerning what conduces to the conservation and defense of themselves; whereas law, properly, is the word of him that by right hath command over others. But yet if we consider the same theorems as delivered in the word of God that by right commands all things, then are they properly called *laws*.

One interpretation attributes theistic belief to Hobbes; the other does not. (Each interpretation is about Hobbes's beliefs about laws of nature,[12] not about the interpreter's belief about divinity.) Nontheist interpretation:

N1. In the first sentence of the paragraph, Hobbes refers to the laws of nature when he says that the theorems of reason are not laws.
N2. The first sentence of a paragraph is stylistically the strongest position.
N3. The theorems of reason are the laws of nature, as indicated by the titles of chapters 14 and 15.
N4. The word "law" is improperly applied to the laws of nature because no one commands the laws of nature.
N5. The phrase "laws of nature" should be taken as an idiom like "left in the lurch" and "kicked the bucket." No actual lurch or bucket is referred to by those idioms.

---

[11] It is worth mentioning the difference between remembering an experience – Lee remembers walking out the door – and remembering a proposition – Lee remembers that she walked out the door.

[12] For Hobbes, laws of nature relate to behavior among people that establish and maintain peace, not laws of physics.

The nontheist interpretation in effect supplements the passage from *Leviathan* with gap fillers provided in **boldface**.

> These dictates of reason men use to call by the name of laws, but improperly; **by "dictates of reason" I mean the laws of nature properly**; they are but conclusions or theorems concerning what conduces to the conservation and defense of themselves; whereas law, properly, is the word of him that by right hath command over others. **And since no one commands the laws of nature since the state of nature is a condition in which no one has political authority**. But yet if we consider the same theorems as delivered in the word of God that by right commands all things, then are they properly called *laws*. **But God plays no part in the science of politics because God is not an object about which humans can reason. He is incomprehensible**.

Let's now consider a theist's interpretation of the same passage from interpretation:

Theist (interpretation):

T1. Genuine laws have two elements, a proposition that expresses what is to be done or not done, and a force that indicates how the proposition is to be taken.

T2. When there is a chance of misunderstanding, one should use an "as"-expression.

T3. Because only propositions can be proved by reason – not sentences that begin with a phrase that indicates the force of the proposition such as "I command" or "I counsel" – propositions proved by reason are theorems, and as propositions, they are not laws.

T4. The word "law" is improperly applied to laws of nature when they are considered as theorems.

T5. In chapter 25, Hobbes says that the same proposition may be either commanded or advised.

T6. In chapter 31, Hobbes says that God speaks to human beings through reason.

T7. In chapter 32, Hobbes says that the laws of nature are the undoubted laws of God.

T8. The last sentence in a paragraph is stylistically as strong as the first sentence.

Notice the similarities and differences between the theist and nontheist interpretations.

Exercise

Fill in the supposed gaps in Hobbes's text to support the theist interpretation:

> These dictates of reason men use to call by the name of laws, but improperly; they are but conclusions or theorems concerning what conduces to the conservation and defense of themselves; whereas law, properly, is the word of him that by right hath command over others. If we consider the same theorems as delivered in the word of God that by right commands all things, then are they properly called *laws*.

Considering two incompatible interpretations leads us to ask, which one is good, and which is bad, or are both good but one better than the other? There are properties of good interpretations, which are the subject of chapter 11.

11

Virtues of Good Interpretations

11.1   Good Interpretations and Correct Ones

Some interpretations are good and some bad. Some interpretations are good, but others are better. Occasionally, the best interpretations enjoy as much consensus among experts as the best theories of global warming. Although there are educated dissenters among interpreters and scientists, dissent itself does not show that the disagreements are merely matters of opinion. The disagreements may arise from differences in their networks of belief or from undetected fallacious reasoning, as discussed in chapter 10.

Believing that an interpretation is good does not simply result from a gut feeling. Good interpretations have good-making properties. Those properties or virtues are the topic of this chapter. Notice that the topic is *good* interpretations, not correct ones. Of course, readers want interpretations to be correct, but interpretations do not wear their correctness on their sleeves. Good interpretations are valuable because they tend to be correct.

My claim that in most cases it is easier to perceive goodness than correctness may seem odd, possibly because of the philosophical tradition that goodness is simple and directly intuited. But that is not how goodness operates in most spheres. Goodness comes from having good-making properties. This is easiest to see for things that have functions. A good knife is sharp, easily handled, and durable. A good odometer is one that accurately measures distance, usually in miles or tenths of miles, is easy to read, and durable. Goodness comes from something having the virtues appropriate to it. So reflecting on the virtues of good interpretations points us toward the correct ones.

Philosophical Writing: An Introduction, Fifth Edition. A. P. Martinich.
© 2025 John Wiley & Sons, Inc. Published 2025 by John Wiley & Sons, Inc.
Companion website: www.wiley.com/go/Martinich5e

It is fair to wonder why there is any gap between some good interpretations and correct ones. The brief answer is that interpreters are not in an ideal situation with respect to the text. I have already mentioned the danger posed by an interpreter's false beliefs and the danger of defectively applying a belief to a text. Another factor is that complex interpretations have many dimensions, and these dimensions have various properties in different degrees. Suppose one interpretation has virtues A, B, and C and defects d and e while another interpretation of the same text has virtues D and E and defects a, b, and c. Further suppose that each interpretation gives different weights to the various virtues and defects. There are typically no agreed-upon numerical values for the virtues, defects, and weights mentioned. So, no numerical calculation can settle the matter. This abstract description of the complexity of interpretation will be made concrete in examples provided throughout this chapter.

One last preliminary point. Some properties have both comparative and noncomparative uses. Some things are red and do not need to be compared with anything else that has a color. But one thing may be redder than other red things. So being redder is comparative. Several interpretations can be good with one being better than another and one being the best of all. This is true of the individual virtues of interpretation discussed in the rest of the chapter. For the most part, people rely on their experience and rules of thumb to judge what has more of one property than another. Ajax and Odysseus are worthy of Achilles' armor, but who is worthier? Ajax is braver and stronger than Odysseus, but Odysseus is wily and imaginative. (If you think the answer is easy, see Paul Woodruff, *The Ajax Dilemma* (Oxford University Press, 2014). I disagree with his judgment.)

Let's now look at the eight virtues of interpretations.

11.2 Simplicity

The first virtue of interpretation is simplicity, which roughly means *the fewest number of entities*.[1] Let's begin with an example from outside philosophy. In Alexandre Dumas's *The Count of Monte Christo*, the eponymous count sets out to punish several people who framed him for a crime. Well into the novel, a seemingly new character appears with the same project as the count. But that seemingly new character shortly disappears from the novel, and the count reappears. Although Dumas does not say that the new

---

[1] In a comparative sense, a simpler theory is one that uses fewer entities than the thing to which it is being compared. *Entity* is used in its broadest sense.

character is the count in disguise, that interpretation is simpler and hence better.[2] (It contributes to another virtue, coherence, discussed shortly.)

Simplicity operates in many situations. Human beings use simplicity when they judge someone they see today as identical with the person they saw the day before. Detectives judge that the same person burgled three different houses in one neighborhood if the *modus operandi* (MO) was the same in each burglary, unless they get substantial evidence that more than one person was involved.

In philosophy, monism is better than dualism if it succeeds in explaining reality in terms of one kind of thing instead of two or more. The long popularity of dualism was the apparent inability of monism to explain material and mental phenomena as aspects of one thing. Recently, monism has been reinvigorated by making a psychic property fundamental of reality. (See https://plato.stanford.edu/entries/panpsychism/.)

Simplicity is also operating when the same configuration of letters or indistinguishable sounds are taken to mean the same one thing. An interpretation that attaches the same meaning to each occurrence is simpler and hence better than one that attached different meanings to the same visual or aural forms. However, so many words are homonyms or have multiple meanings, that it is often reasonable to interpret a word as having one meaning in one place and a different meaning in another, for example, "The matter to be discussed in this essay is matter." Sometimes the author of a text is mistaken about her own use of words. She may think that she is talking about one thing instead of two. For example, "statement" is ambiguous between the action of writing certain words and the proposition that is stated in virtue of writing those words. The latter has a truth-value and is not an object in time; the former takes time and has no truth-value.

Sometimes an interpreter will say that two different words have the same meaning. This is an attractive tactic when it would make an otherwise puzzling passage plausible or at least less puzzling.

Exercise

Simplicity in the number of individual entities involved is only one kind of simplicity. Name and briefly describe two others. (There are more than two.)

---

[2] Interpretation is an instance of inference to the best explanation, that is, an attempt to make the best sense of the world. Judgments about simplicity and other properties are also inferences to the best explanation.

Let's now consider an example in which what appears to be good is incorrect, due to a mistaken belief. Traditional biblical interpretation contains several such mistakes. One was the interpretation that the unnamed serpent in Genesis was identical with Satan (more precisely: the satan) in the book of Job, with Lucifer in the book of Isaiah, and with the tempter in the Gospel of Luke. Four possibly different entities were reduced to one. But in the nineteenth century, scholars knew that the serpent, the satan, Lucifer, and the tempter were not identical. Each of them originated at different times in different places with different characteristics. The serpent originated in Canaan; the satan was a state official in Persia or Babylon; and so on for Lucifer and the tempter. In other words, the correct interpretation recognizes four entities, not one.[3] Why did the conventional interpretation last so long? Because a tenacious belief in the networks of scholars over many centuries was mistaken, namely, the belief that one reliable author was relatively directly involved in the origin of all the stories.

Incorrect judgments about simplicity do not occur only in textual interpretations. The theory that claimed that all chemicals consist of atoms was a great advance over the theory that had taken the dozens of chemical elements to be the basic kinds of things. Later, the discovery that atoms consist of subatomic particles was a further advance in natural science.

11.3   Coherence

As mentioned above, sometimes an interpretation high in simplicity contributes to another virtue, such as coherence. Chapter 7, section 7.1 discussed coherence as related to the form or structure of your essay, which may be an interpretation of someone else's text. The present section discusses coherence as it exists in the text you are interpreting. Suppose you are interpreting the first sentence, slightly edited, of the Introduction of Thomas Hobbes's *Leviathan*:

> Nature, by which God made and governs the world, is imitated by human beings, who make an artificial nature, namely, a sovereign, to govern themselves.

---

[3] Eusebius claims that the divine being who views the corruption of Sodom in Genesis, the word sent out by God in Psalm 107, a military leader in the book of Joshua, and the divine being that appears to Moses in the burning bush are all identical with the Son of God (See Eusebius, *The History of the Church*, ed. Andrew Louth (London: Penguin Books, 1989), p. 5) But the verse from the Psalm is about thanking God for saving Israelites.

The text coheres:

> Hobbes connects God's creation of nature with the human creation of a sovereign by imitating God. Just as God created nature and governs it, human beings created a sovereign who governs them.

The passage coheres through the repetition of the same or cognate words, *nature, make,* and *govern*. Natural languages have various ways to indicate coherence. One is the repetition of topic-specific words.

> *Governments* that have one human being as their leader can be divided into two types: **monarchies** and tyrannies. **Monarchies** are *governments* led by one good person. Tyrannies are governments led by one bad person.

Authors sometimes intentionally interrupt the coherence of a text. Natural language has resources for these interruptions: "I will now turn to a different topic."

The desire to find coherence is strong. Often it correctly leads you to interpret the author's meaning as the opposite of the literal meaning of the words used. Consider this text:

> [1] The USA is the wealthiest country in the world but has many poor people who could be helped by substantially increasing the tax rate on the 5% richest people. [2] Yet this is not done because politicians are bought off by the richest people, and most people think the poor deserve their situation. [3] This is a fine country.

The plausible interpretation of sentences [1] and [2] is that the United States is not a fine country. So the author's apparent positive evaluation of the United States in sentence [3] does not cohere with [1] and [2] unless it is taken sarcastically. The coherent interpretation is that sentence [3] is sarcastic, and the author meant that the United States is not fine.

Exercises

1   What is it about the three sentences about wealth in the USA that makes it plausible that sentences [1] and [2] are to be taken straightforwardly and sentence [3] is to be taken sarcastically?

2   The two-sentence text, "Descartes thought that dualism had to be true. Hobbes was a materialist," does not cohere. Rewrite the sentences to make them cohere.

11.4 Consistency

Chapter 2 provided one reason for being consistent. If we call that kind of consistency *internal consistency* (the consistency of the interpreter's network of belief), another kind is aptly called *external consistency,* that is, consistency attributed to the author of the text being interpreted. Many philosophers think that attributing consistency to the author is required by fairness (aka is called *the principle of charity*). If the principle is right, then faced with a choice between two interpretations, one of which makes the text contradictory and one that does not, the interpreter should choose the latter, ceteris paribus. The phrase, "ceteris paribus" (that is, in normal circumstances), is important because philosophers have contradicted themselves. Consistency should not be attributed to a text if it requires extravagant and implausible judgments about what the author or her text means.

Better than the principle of charity is the *principle of "most likely to be meant"*: Attribute to an author the position that she most likely was advocating, given her likely beliefs and intentions and the words of the text.

Exercise

Consider a sentence from the Declaration of Independence, "All men are created equal." This sentence was drafted by eighteenth-century white, American colonists. Given their beliefs, what is the most likely interpretation of that sentence: (1) that the author or authors meant that all white male human beings are created equal or (2) that all human beings are equal? Is the belief that *all human beings are created equal* inconsistent with the beliefs of the male colonists? If so, how should the sentence be interpreted?

Here is an example of an apparently inconsistent text. In chapter 14 of *Leviathan,* Hobbes says that liberty (freedom) is the absence of external impediments; he repeats that view at the beginning of chapter 21, "Of the Liberty of Subject." Later in that chapter he says that when subjects create their sovereign there is "no restriction at all of his own former natural liberty." His point seems to be that creating a sovereign does not create an *external* impediment. However, later in chapter 21, he indicates that civil laws are impediments, that the swords in the hands of sovereigns to enforce those laws are impediments, and that the only liberty left to a subject are the actions the sovereign has not forbidden. How should this apparent contradiction be treated?

Usually, interpreters can plausibly argue that an apparent inconsistency by an author is not a genuine one in one of these ways:

(a) The author changed his mind. This is especially plausible when the contradictory positions are in works written years or decades apart and when there are numerous apparent contradictions.
(b) Another way is to say that the author meant a word, phrase, or sentence in one way in some places and in another way in other places. Conceivably, an author could use say "laws of nature" to refer to physical laws in one place and the same phrase to refer to laws of human behavior that do not depend on governments.
(c) The interpreter could say that the author means a word, phrase, or sentence literally in one place and figuratively in another.
(d) About apparently contradictory sentences,
    (i) the interpreter could say that the author was not herself asserting one of the contradictory propositions, but expressing an opponent's view, or
    (ii) that she was using one of the contradictory propositions in a *reductio ad absurdum* proof, or
    (iii) that she intended the reader to insert a word or phrase that would restrict the scope of the apparently contradictory proposition. (An example of iii: When Hobbes said that civil laws are impediments, he meant that civil laws are impediments insofar as the threat of the sovereign's punishment prevents most people from disobeying them.)

Exercise

1 Another example of an apparent contradiction in Hobbes's philosophy concerns his conception of the state of nature, that is, the human condition before a government is formed. He says that there are no laws in the state of nature; at another point, he says that people in the state of nature rely on the use of the laws of nature to form a government. It seems contradictory to assert that there are no laws in the state of nature and that there are laws in the state of nature that people use to get out of that state. (Read chapter 14 of *Leviathan* for more information about the context.) How can Hobbes's statements be made to be consistent? (Hint: what role might gaps in the text provide what is needed to make the statements consistent? See chapter 10.)

> 2   A good interpretation needs to be *internally* consistent with the interpreter's network of beliefs. Why is this a requirement of rationality? Is it relatively easy to achieve in interpretations? Why?

11.5   Defensibility

The next virtue is *defensibility*. In addition to giving positive reasons and evidence for your position, you need to defend your position against criticisms that are intended to refute it. The adversarial setup of criminal and civil trials in the United States and other governments applies this idea. Both prosecutors and defendants, plaintiffs and respondents, have the opportunity to plead their cases. The need to consider both the positive and negative evidence is illustrated by this obviously defective reasoning for the proposition that *all human beings are male*: Adam was male, Abel was male, ..., Socrates was male, Plato was male, ..., and so on. Unless more of the relevant evidence is considered, no evidence falsifies the proposition. Of course, more relevant evidence needs to be considered: Eve was female, ..., Xantippe was female, ..., Indira Gandhi was female, and so on. The falsity of "All humans are male" is demonstrated.

The pro and con structure of reasoning is required by the principle that all the relevant evidence and reasoning must be considered. However, taking the phrase, "all the relevant evidence and reasoning" strictly can rarely be achieved. What gets closer to the truth is the principle that as much relevant evidence as is reasonable must be considered. Included in this principle is the evidence that the interpreter's opponent has presented.

The need to consider all the evidence is illustrated by two interpretations of Rene Descartes's best-known doctrine, namely, that he exists or that it is impossible for a thinking being to doubt that he exists. Before giving the interpretations, I will give a summary, suited to our purposes, of Rene Descartes's Second Meditation of his *Meditations on First Philosophy*.

THE SECOND MEDITATION

Yesterday I [Descartes] thought of reasons to doubt every belief I've ever had, and right now I see no way of justifiably eliminating my doubts. Consequently, I will set

---

aside anything that is the least bit doubtful and treat it as though I had found it to be outright false; and I will carry on like that until I find something certain, just one thing that is solid and certain. I will suppose, then, that everything I see is false. I will believe that my memory tells me nothing but lies. I have no senses and so on.

But isn't there a God who gives me the thoughts I am now having? But maybe I'm the author of these thoughts. If I am, then doesn't it follow that I am *something*? ... Now that I have convinced myself that there is nothing in the world – no sky, no earth, no minds, no bodies – does it follow that I don't exist either? No; I have determined that this proposition, *I am, I exist,* is true.

The first interpretation of this passage will be called "The Argument Interpretation," according to which, "I exist" is the conclusion of an argument.

THE ARGUMENT INTERPRETATION OF DESCARTES'S COGITO

The first constructive result of Descartes's *Meditations* is his argument that he exists from the premise that he was thinking. To be more explicit, the premise of his argument is "I think [or: doubt]." His conclusion is "I exist." He knows that the premise is true because in thinking he sees with his mind's eye that it is true. Given the truth of the premise, the conclusion must be true because a necessary condition for the truth of "I think" is the existence of the thing that "I" refers to. That is, the conclusion "I exist" must be true because the premise is true. In short, speaking in his own name, "I, Descartes, exist." So Descartes's argument is sound.

In addition to being valid, Descartes's argument is also cogent for anyone who follows his reasoning in her own case. Use "I" to refer to yourself.

I am thinking.
Therefore, I exist.
Q.E.D.

The Argument Interpretation is brief but good as far as it goes. It seems to have the virtue of *consistency* because nothing in it suggests that Descartes's doctrine is inconsistent. It also has the virtue of *coherence*; it shows how Descartes's text sticks or hangs together. A third virtue is *palpability*. It gives a plausible interpretation of Descartes's position; it does not attribute to Descartes anything unlikely such as relying on divine revelation or reading tea leaves. But this interpretation does not have the virtue of *defensibility* because no possible objection is considered along with a good answer to it.

Let's now consider the second interpretation, "The Intuition Interpretation":

THE INTUITION INTERPRETATION OF THE CARTESIAN EGO

The most famous doctrine in Descartes's philosophy is "I think; therefore, I am." However, these five words – three in the Latin version, *cogito; ergo, sum* – are misleading. The word *ergo* suggests that Descartes is presenting an argument. If this were true, then he would be presupposing that his reasoning is reliable; but that presupposition has been shown to be doubtful in the First Meditation. A person may think his reasoning is reliable when it is fallacious.

Descartes was looking for something that was evidently true and did not depend on anything else for its truth. One might say that he is looking for something both subjectively and objectively certain. Subjective certainty is the experience of believing that one's belief cannot be false. Objective certainty is the logical property that a proposition cannot be false. He found what he was looking for when he focused on his own thinking. In his thinking, he sees that he, the knowing-subject, is himself the object known. The thinker and the thinker's object are identical; so, his grasp of himself as a thinker is immediate. Since nothing mediates between the thinker and his object of thinking, there is no logical room for making a mistake. Descartes intuited himself in his thinking. An intuition is an immediate perception; nothing stands between the perceiver and what is perceived.

One might object that the interpretation presented here does not jibe with Descartes's most famous

---

sentence, "I think; therefore, I am." The presence of "therefore" makes it evident, the objection continues, that Descartes was arguing for his position. My reply begins with the observation that Descartes's "most famous sentence" does not occur in the *Meditations*, but in an earlier work, *Discourse on the Method of Rightly Conducting the Mind*. The omission of that sentence in the *Meditations* suggests that Descartes thought he could give a clearer expression of his position without it. The last sentence of Descartes's text above makes that clearer expression explicit, "I have determined that this proposition, *I am, I exist*, is true."

The Intuition Interpretation seems to have the same virtues as the Argument Interpretation, consistency, coherence, and palpability. In addition, it has another virtue as well, the virtue of *defensibility*. The Intuition Interpretation reports an objection that may be raised against it and then replies to that objection. By presenting and refuting the objection, the Intuition Interpretation shows its strength.

Exercise

1 Recall the outline of the structure of a philosophical essay in chapter 3, section 3.1. Where might the virtue of defensibility show itself in that outline? In our current discussion, defensibility relates to the substance or quality of an interpretation and particularly to the cogency of the argument. A person who reads an argument may become convinced that it is sound when he reads how the argument can answer objections.

2 The Argument Interpretation can be improved by answering the objection raised against it in the Intuition Interpretation or by raising an objection against the Intuition Interpretation. Expand "The Argument Interpretation" to make it philosophically better. (See chapter 4, section 4.5, on expanding an essay.) The objections or replies have to be good ones in order to display philosophical power. (Like most of the other virtues, some interpretations are more defensible than others.) See also www.wiley.com\go\Martinich.

11.6   Proportionality

I mentioned above that interpretations give different weights to their various *virtues*. An interpretation high in coherence will assign great weight to it. And an interpretation that explains almost the entire text will assign great weight to that virtue (see "completeness" in section 11.7). Interpretations also assign different weights to different parts of texts. The variation in assigned weights may be the cause of unresolvable disagreements about the best interpretation. The last paragraph of chapter 15 in Hobbes's *Leviathan* is an example of a text to which different weights have been assigned to different parts. In chapter 10, it was used to illustrate that networks of belief have gaps. Recall that "laws of nature" are laws about morality, not physics. (See chapter 2, section 2.2.)

> [1] These dictates of reason men use to call by the name of laws, but improperly; for they are but conclusions or theorems concerning what conduces to the conservation and defense of themselves; whereas law, properly, is the word of him that by right hath command over others. [2] But yet if we consider the same theorems as delivered in the word of God that by right commands all things, then are they properly called *laws*.

One interpretation, "The Not Literally Laws Interpretation," weighs sentence [1] highly and discounts [2]. The other interpretation, "The Literally God's Laws Interpretation" weighs sentence [2] heavily (but also explains [1] in relation to [2]). Here are the two interpetations:

HOBBES'S LAWS OF NATURE ARE NOT LITERALLY LAWS (NLL)

According to Hobbes, the laws of nature, as they function in philosophy, are those propositions deducible by reason that advise people about how to preserve their lives. As counsel or advice, they are not anyone's commands and consequently not literally laws. Hobbes makes this point by calling the laws "dictates of reason" and "theorems." The view just argued for is confirmed by the placement and length of [1]. The beginning of a paragraph is stylistically the most important, and this importance is underlined by its length. Why did Hobbes include [2]? If one goes outside of philosophy to religion, then one

---

may call the laws of nature *laws* if one believes that God commands them. But it is impossible to know by reason that God commanded them, and what cannot be known by reason is not part of philosophy (or science). Most likely, [2] is a sop to his Christian readers.

HOBBES'S LAWS OF NATURE ARE LITERALLY GOD'S LAWS (LGL)

According to Hobbes, the laws of nature are those propositions deducible by reason "by which a man is forbidden to do" what destroys his life (*Leviathan* chapter 14, paragraph 3). As being deducible, that is, as theorems, they are not laws. But if they are not commands they could not be *forbidden*. Hobbes explains how theorems can be the (propositional) contents of laws by identifying the authority who commands them, namely, God. He explains why they are laws in sentence [2]. In addition to [2], this interpretation is directly supported by two later passages in *Leviathan*: "reason ... [is] the undoubted word of God" and "the law of nature ... is undoubtedly God's law" (*Leviathan* chapter 32, paragraph 2, and chapter 26, paragraph 40, respectively). The end of a paragraph is as important as its beginning, so the placement of [2] is not an indication of a throw-away line.

Both essays may be equally good. Someone may think the Not Literally Laws (NLL) interpretation is better because of the virtue of *simplicity;* the laws of nature are only propositions. In contrast, someone may think "Literally God's Laws" (LGL) is simpler because God's command of the propositional part of the laws does not add any substantive complexity; it merely satisfies Hobbes's requirement that laws be commanded. (The proponent of LGL might claim that it is better than NLL with respect to completeness because it includes two passages from later chapters.) The proponent of NLL may object that he does take Hobbes's comment seriously. The seriousness is that the laws of nature in philosophy should not be confused with the use of the term "laws of nature" in religion.

Exercise

1 What does the disagreement about whether interpretation LGL or NLL is simpler say about the virtue of simplicity?

2 What does the disagreement about whether interpretation LGL or NLL is more complete say about the virtue of completeness?

3 Suppose the author of LGL went on to criticize NLL for not taking [2] seriously? How could the author of NLL respond? What objection could the author of NLL raise against LGL's response?

Both NLL and NGL can benefit by being expanded to include more about Hobbes's laws of nature. Here are expanded versions of each interpretation.

HOBBES'S LAWS OF NATURE ARE NOT LITERALLY
LAWS (NLL EXPANDED)

According to Hobbes, the laws of nature, as they function in philosophy, are those propositions deducible by reason that advise people about how to preserve their lives. As counsel or advice, they are not commands of anyone and consequently not literally laws. Hobbes makes this point by calling the laws "dictates of reason" and "theorems." This view is confirmed by the placement and length of [1]. The beginning of a paragraph is stylistically the most important place, and this importance is underlined by its length.

Why does Hobbes include [2]? If one goes outside of philosophy and appeals to religion, then one can call them *laws*. But since Hobbes is doing philosophy alone in the first thirty-one chapters of *Leviathan*, whatever activity may be attributed to God has no place in philosophy.

One may wonder why Hobbes said anything about God in *Leviathan* since he had explicitly excluded religion and theology from philosophy in both *The Anti-White* and *De corpore*. A plausible explanation for Hobbes's comments about God and the laws of nature is that *The Anti-White* was unpublished and read only by a handful of people, and *De corpore* would not be published until five years after *Leviathan*. So he could not expect his readers to know that he excluded God from philosophy. He also knew that almost all of his readers believed in God and that theologians regularly indicated that some of God's commandments, those "written into the hearts of man," were equivalent to the "laws of nature." Consequently, he needed to say something about the inappropriate use of the phrase by theologians. One should also notice where he places his concession that religious people incorrectly use "the laws of nature." It is in the last sentence of his discussion of the nature of the laws of nature. It is appropriately placed because it is the last and least thing to say about them.

I will end by replying to an objection that goes to the heart of my interpretation that the laws of nature are not actual laws. One might think that it is self-contradictory to use, "laws of nature," for things that are not laws but only theorems or precepts. However, Hobbes's use of the phrase "the laws of nature" is strictly correct. Semantically, "laws of nature" is a single semantic unit. Despite its appearance, "Laws of nature" does not consist of three words that compositionally refer to laws. Rather, it is what W. V. Quine called "a fused expression," better thought of as "lawsofnature" or "laws-of-nature." In other words, the word "law" does not appear in "lawofnature." Semantically, "laws of nature" means precepts. It is similar to idioms like "Kick the bucket" (die), which semantically does not refer to either kicking or a bucket, and like "left in the lurch," which involves no lurch. To paraphrase Hobbes, men used to call the precepts by the name "laws," but improperly; they are theorems of reason.

HOBBES'S LAWS OF NATURE ARE LITERALLY GOD'S LAWS (LGL EXPANDED)

According to Hobbes, the laws of nature are those propositions deducible by reason "by which a man is forbidden to do" what destroys his life (*Leviathan* chapter 14, paragraph 3). As deducible, that is, as theorems, they are not laws. But if they are not commands, they could not be *forbidden*, contrary to his definition. Hobbes explains how theorems can be the (propositional) contents of laws by identifying the authority who commands them, namely, God. He explains why they are laws in sentence [2].

Hobbes had committed himself to speaking literally when he was speaking scientifically or philosophically. So by calling the laws of nature laws, he committed himself to their being *laws*. He explains why they are laws in the last sentence of the text above: God, who everyone knows is Lord, uses reason to convey his commands to human beings. The end of a paragraph is as important as its beginning, so the placement of [2] is no indication of a throw-away line.

His placement of the explanation of how the laws of nature are commands at the end of his discussion of the nature of the laws of nature was appropriate because one of the controlling principles of Hobbes's philosophy was that philosophical truths must be deduced from definitions solely by reason. His proofs of the laws of nature from his definition of a law of nature wonderfully illustrate that principle. If one objects that his comment about God and the laws of nature should not be given much weight, a proper reply is that it is a long-standing maxim of rhetoric that the beginning and the end of a paragraph, chapter, or treatise are the two strongest positions. So Hobbes's last sentence should be given substantial weight.

There is more evidence for the interpretation that Hobbes thought that the laws of nature, as considered in philosophy, were commands of God. In chapter 32 of *Leviathan*, Hobbes wrote in the second paragraph that reason is "the undoubted word of God." Since he held that the method of philosophy is to use reason deductively, he shows how reason connects with the word of God. And in chapter 26, he wrote, "the law of nature ... is undoubtedly God's law."

One might object that Hobbes asserts that reason is the word of God, but he does not prove it. My reply is that the objection is correct but toothless. Although Hobbes provides no demonstration that reason is the word of God, no demonstration is necessary because his audience took that proposition for granted. What this shows, as far as philosophy is concerned, is that Hobbes's political philosophy does not satisfy his own requirements of adequacy.

Exercises

1   The essay, "NLL expanded," discusses some philosophical matters that most student authors (and readers) would not know, such as Hobbes's book *Anti-White* and the idea of "fused expressions." Should the student author have provided more information about these matters, not included them at all, or something else?

2   Which interpretation do you judge to be better NLL or LGL? Now, evaluate them with respect to the virtues of simplicity, coherence, consistency, defensibility, and proportionality? Does your original judgment match what is indicated by their virtues? If it does not, why is there a mismatch?

3   A third interpretation of Hobbes's laws of nature stands midway between The Literally God's Laws Interpretation and The Not Properly Laws Interpretation. According to this third one, "Hobbes's Laws of Nature are Literally Reason's Laws," (LRL), the laws of nature are genuine laws because human beings are rational, and rationality requires "reciprocity" among people. This interpretation gives great weight to Hobbes's definition of *law of nature* near the beginning of chapter 14. It is plausible that in the definition, people are "forbidden" from endangering their own lives by reason. Compared to the first two interpretations, the third one gives little weight to the last paragraph of chapter 15 because Hobbes has already explained why the laws of nature are laws. Is it an advantage or disadvantage that the third interpretation does not weigh the last paragraph of 15 heavily?

   Write an essay in which you evaluate RLL in comparison with NLL or LL. (For the third interpretation, see S. A. Lloyd,

Morality in the Philosophy of Thomas Hobbes (Cambridge University Press, 2009) 97–120 and 263–94.) (See the online website for help on this essay topic.)

When an interpretation assigns appropriate weights to parts of a text, it has what I have called proportionality. I am ambivalent about calling it a virtue because an author-interpreter assigns a great weight to the part of the text that most favors her own interpretation. So, the author-interpreter of NLL may give great weight to sentence [1] because she prefers secular interpretations, and similarly for the author of LGL *mutatis mutandis.* The usual source of these preferences is the author-interpreters' webs of belief. But there are some guidelines for assigning weights independently of particular webs of belief. The most familiar one is that the beginning and end of a text are the most important parts. When a paragraph consists of two sentences, that guideline is unhelpful. Also, interpreters who look for secret messages claim that the middle of a text is the weightiest.

Many languages have the resources to signal greater and lesser weight: "My thesis is," "I will argue that," "My first premise is," "I add parenthetically," and "It is not important but." However, nothing prevents a "hermeneuticist of suspicion" from asserting that the author was pretending to use these phrases seriously in order to deceive the naïve reader. Knowing that every attempt to mean what one says can be frustrated by a suspicious mind, I nonetheless will mention one more guideline about weight. Published texts typically should be given more weight than unpublished ones because unpublished texts are a sign that the author was not satisfied with them. This does not rule out the use of early manuscripts, an author's marginal comments on published works, and letters. But for the most part texts published by the author have greater weight than others. Some decades ago, a scholar promoted a substantially new interpretation of Descartes on the basis of an unpublished letter. The interpretation did not gain broad acceptance to my knowledge. A new interpretation requires more and better evidence in order to change the opinion of a community of scholars.

11.7 Completeness

When an interpretation covers an entire text, it has the virtue of completeness. The author of LGL could criticize the interpretation of NLL in the preceding section as not considering the entire text or not considering it completely because NLL discounted sentence [2]. Can the author of NLL also be criticized for not discussing the two additional passages mentioned by the author of LGL, *Leviathan* chapter 26, paragraph 40, and chapter 32, paragraph 2? This is a difficult issue. Fortunately, students usually do not have to worry about selecting the precise text since their professors will assign it. Let's call the assigned text the primary text. There are usually secondary texts also. For example, LGL uses short texts from chapters 26 and 32 of *Leviathan* to support her case. I think LGL's use of these secondary texts is appropriate.

Using secondary texts can be abused. The principal abuse is quoting out of context. It is known as "proof texting" especially when it is used to interpret the Bible. An easy example comes from Eusebius of Caesarea, the first historian of the early Christian centuries. He claimed that the word *word* in the verse "He sent his word and healed them" refers to the Son of God because in the Gospel of John "word" is used to refer to the Son of God in the Greek Bible (Psalm 107: 20 and John 1:1; see Eusebius, p. 5). But the verse from Psalms is about thanking God for saving Israelites. Scholars who think that Hobbes was an atheist in effect accuse those who refer to various passages in which Hobbes refers to or otherwise appeals to God of proof texting.

Exercise

Does a scholar who thinks Hobbes was a theist have a good response to the accusation that they are proof texting? If so, what is it?

Two other virtues of good interpretations, conservatism, and frugality are closely connected with properties of networks discussed in chapter 10 and will be dealt with only briefly. In revising their networks, people try to keep as many of their current beliefs as is reasonable; put the other way round, people try to eliminate as few of their beliefs as is reasonable. An interpretation that requires giving up fewer beliefs than another is the better one. One interpretation is more conservative than another if it requires fewer beliefs to be given up than the other. When people begin with different beliefs relevant to interpreting a text, disagreement about their interpretations may be irreconcilable and sometimes neither interpreter understands the source of the disagreement.

The other virtue, frugality, is analogous to conservatism. An interpretation that does not require giving up tenacious or strongly held beliefs is preferable to one that does. One interpretation is more frugal than another if the total weight of the beliefs given up is less than the other. An author needs to consider the frugality of her audience's beliefs as much as her own.

Exercise

There are other properties of good interpretations, not discussed in this book. Describe one. Hint: consider competing interpretations that have been given to a text discussed in your class.

Appendix A:
"It's Sunday Night and I Have an Essay Due Monday Morning"

You have already promised God that if he gets you out of this mess, you will never wait to write your essay until the night before it is due. What do you do now?

The first thing to do is to think about your topic. The topic may have already been assigned, or you may be allowed to choose from several, such as

the nature of universals;
the nature of free will;
the concept of determinism;
the relationship between mind and body;
Plato's theory of the Good;
Anselm's ontological argument;
Descartes's use of *cogito, ergo sum*.

The next thing you should do is to make your topic more specific. The easiest way to do this is to transform your topic into a thesis. Notice that the topics listed above are formulated as noun phrases. They do not commit the author of an essay to any particular position. The topic, the problem of universals, does not require that the author argue either for or against the existence of universals. It is important for you to write a sentence that does commit you to some particular position, such as

There are no universals. (Only particulars exist.)
No humans have free will.
Determinism is true.
Mind and body are identical.

Philosophical Writing: An Introduction, Fifth Edition. A. P. Martinich.
© 2025 John Wiley & Sons, Inc. Published 2025 by John Wiley & Sons, Inc.
Companion website: www.wiley.com/go/Martinich5e

For our purposes, it is not important whether you argue that there are or are not universals. What is important is that you commit yourself to one position or the other. Your thesis, whatever it is, motivates everything that you write in your essay. It is what causes everything else to hang together in a logical way. To change the metaphor, your thesis gives you a perspective on the problem and helps shape what you will say and how you will say it.

The next thing to do is to think of reasons why a rational person should believe the position you have chosen to defend. Your professor is not interested in how you *feel* about the proposition but in how you view the world. He is interested in how well you can *argue* for your position. (See chapters 2 and 5.) Don't just think about these reasons; write them down. If possible, work them into a brief outline. Which reasons are the most important and which ones less? Which reasons are subordinate to which others?

One more thing before you begin writing; think about the qualities you want to aim at in your writing. I suggest these four: clarity, precision, orderliness, and simplicity.

Clarity is important because your first obligation is to communicate with your audience. If your professor does not understand what you are getting at, it is very likely that you will get a bad grade.

Precision is important because it makes your essay more informative. Vague, inexact, ambiguous, or otherwise imprecise language is less informative than precise language.

Orderliness contributes to clarity; it makes your argument easier to understand. Your reader ought to know at all times where your argument is taking him; how he is going to get there, and where he is at any particular point.

Finally, simplicity is important. Keep your syntax as simple as possible. This does not mean that your sentences need to be short or choppy. The syntax of your sentence should only be as complicated as the thought you want to express requires. Use subordinate clauses when one thought is genuinely subordinate to another. Students often try to write complicated sentences because they (think that they) were taught to do so in high school. What they should have been taught is how to write complicated sentences when such sentences were necessary but not to write them as a matter of course or to mimic profundity.

Now begin writing. But do not try to write your essay in one draft. Your first draft should be a short version of what you intend the completed essay to look like. That is, in 50–150 words, write a draft in which you put only the most important reasons for your thesis.

Once this is done, rewrite your original draft. Expand it by filling in some of the details you need in order to make your original draft more intelligible or persuasive. Your second draft should be somewhere between 50 and 100 percent longer than the first one – precisely how much longer depends upon how long the original is and how much more you can think of at the time.

Continue rewriting and expanding in this way until you are within the word limits that your professor set. (I am not being sarcastic. You have an obligation to work within the limits set by your professor, and word limits are a kind of limit. Professional writers are restricted to word limits all the time.)

This method of successive elaboration, which was discussed in chapter 4, does not increase the time it takes to write your essay if you are using a computer. You simply insert the additions at the appropriate place, and the word processing program makes the required adjustments.

One advantage of the method of successive elaboration is that you never lose sight of the basic structure of your essay. Whenever you add something, you know why that particular place needs further elaboration in order to contribute to the whole. Another advantage is that each part of the essay has the right proportion relative to all the other parts. If one part of the essay begins to overshadow the others, it can be brought back into line by expanding the other portions in successive drafts. However, you might alternatively find that if one part naturally grows while the others remain stunted, then the naturally growing part may be the one that should be nurtured and the others pruned in editing. If you add material to each part of the essay in each draft, then no part should be overdeveloped or underdeveloped.

Appendix B:
How to Study for a Test

Different professors have different attitudes about how to test a student's knowledge. The advice given below assumes that your professor asks essay questions and that the questions allow a student to demonstrate both general comprehension of the most important issues discussed in the course and specialized issues that demonstrate a student's exceptional achievement. (I think exclusively true/false and multiple-choice tests, for example, in a course on "Contemporary Moral Problems," are a scandal even if the questions are "really hard," because answering such tests does not allow a student to demonstrate the discursive skills that are essential to philosophizing.)

The advice here also assumes that you have been studying responsibly in the course and have allowed yourself sufficient time to study in the correct way. Now the advice.

(1) Reread your textbook. If there is too much material to reread all of it, then read those parts that you marked as the most important, either in the text or in the notes you made while reading it the first or second time through.
(2) Reread your class notes and handouts.
(3) Outline and organize the material to be tested, so that it forms some intelligible pattern.
(4) Write down specific questions that you think might plausibly be asked. Then actually write out answers to those questions. Write essays to answer essay questions. Do not merely think about answers. The best way to find out how much you know is to see how much

Philosophical Writing: An Introduction, Fifth Edition. A. P. Martinich.
© 2025 John Wiley & Sons, Inc. Published 2025 by John Wiley & Sons, Inc.
Companion website: www.wiley.com/go/Martinich5e

you can put down correctly and coherently on paper. You will be graded for what you put down on paper, not what is in your brain. (G. F. W. Hegel wrote that every young man has a great novel in his head. He was being sarcastic. What he meant is that such novels, not being produced, are worthless.) Actually writing out an essay will force you to organize the information.

(5) Revise your essay answers. Reorganize and supplement your essays with detailed information and examples. Aside from the structure of an essay, the single most important difference between an A and a C is the amount of orderly detail and argumentation that the student provides. Even if none of your essay questions is asked, it is very likely that parts of your prepared essays can be used in other essay questions.

A good essay answer has the same features as any good essay: a beginning, a middle, and an end. Be sure to state in general what your answer to the question is in the introduction; then support that answer with detailed information and argumentation in the middle of the essay and then very briefly summarize what you have done. For example, in answer to the essay question, "What is Plato's view about universals?," your answer might take this form:

> Plato believed that universals exist, separate from physical things. He believed this because.... I have just explained why Plato is a realist with regard to universals.

It is quite possible that you cannot follow all of the suggestions just given. Do what you can. Although the suggestions are presented in the order in which they should be done, they are also presented in inverse importance. That is, suggestion (5) is the most important and (1) the least. If you must begin your study with (5), then you will know what you must look for in taking the earlier suggestions.

Appendix C:
Research: Notes, Citations, and References

A research essay is one in which the professor expects you to present your informed and reflective view about some topic, in contrast to simply reporting the view of another philosopher. Reflecting on the topic may have begun when you read an assigned text, or in the classroom when the professor was explaining it or the philosophical issue it discussed, or when you read some text related to the class but not explicitly discussed in it. That is, your reflection may have begun in various ways. In addition to your own reflection, it is important for you to investigate what other authors have said about the problem or text that you are writing about. Even the best philosophers learn from others, because they may be smarter, have thought about the problem longer, or have a perspective different from your own. It is essential that you identify the sources of your information. Identifying these people falls within the category of scholarship.

"Scholarship" refers to the practice of letting your readers know (1) where they can find more information about your topic and (2) giving credit where credit is due to those people from whom you have learned and to those who first made the point that you are making. Point (1) is a matter of courtesy and cooperativeness. It is rare that an author can say everything that a reader may want to know about a topic. So giving references to other works shows consideration for the reader. Point (2) is a matter of honesty. Not to give credit where credit is due is a kind of theft.

Concerning scholarship, instead of the harsh word "theft," the word "plagiarism" is used. There are many ways to plagiarize. Using the substantive words of another person without quoting or crediting her is

Philosophical Writing: An Introduction, Fifth Edition. A. P. Martinich.
© 2025 John Wiley & Sons, Inc. Published 2025 by John Wiley & Sons, Inc.
Companion website: www.wiley.com/go/Martinich5e

plagiarism. Using the ideas of another person without crediting her, even if her exact words are not used, is plagiarism. Considering the idea of another person without crediting her, even if the idea is considered only to be refuted, is plagiarism. Give credit where credit is due.

Credit is given in two places: notes, either at the foot of the page or at the end of the body of the essay, and in the bibliography. Notes and bibliographical references can take many forms. Follow the style that your instructor or college requires. There are many style handbooks to help you if no specific form is prescribed. A good book is *A Pocket Style Manual,* by Diane Hacker and Nancy Sommers, 6th edn. (Boston: Bedford Books, 2012). Presented below is some basic information about the form in which notes and bibliographies should be presented. (You may notice that different books have different styles for notes and bibliographies. This is because most publishers have a "house style.")

Most of the great works of philosophy exist in many editions. So if you use a particular edition of a work, your professor may not have it or be familiar with it or have access to it. Fortunately, many of these works exist in a standard edition and other editions include the pagination. For example, almost all editions of Plato's works include Stephanus numbers, named after the 1578 edition of Estienne Stephanus. Almost all editions of Aristotle's works include Bekker numbers, named after the 1841 edition of Immanuel Bekker. All good, recent editions of Hobbes's *Leviathan* include the pages of the 1651 edition. Of course, you will also have to give full bibliographical information for the actual edition from which you quote, e.g. Plato, *Complete Works,* ed. John M. Cooper (Indianapolis: Hackett Publishing, 1997).

When a classic work is divided into parts, chapters, sections, or similar segments, good editions will provide that information and it is customary to use those divisions to identify the passage being used. Citations of Thomas Aquinas's *Summa Theologiae* are to Part, Question, Article, and then some subparts of the article. "*ST I–II.* Q. 37, art. 5, c" refers to *Summa Theologiae Prima Secundae, Questio 37, articulus 5, corpus* (the body of the article). It is not unusual for the numbers to be a mix of Roman numerals and Arabic numerals. Citations of Locke's *Two Treatises of Government* are to the number of the treatise – this will usually be the second treatise – and the section number. "*TT* II.237" refers to the second treatise, section 237. There are obvious variations on this kind of reference, such as "*Two Treatises* 2.237." David Hume's *A Treatise of Human Nature* consists of three books, each of which has several parts, and an Appendix. Citations may take the form *Treatise* II.2.7 (or *Treatise* 2.2.7). The introductions to editions of classic works usually indicate or explain the standard way to cite parts of the book.

The form of your notes and of your bibliography work together. If you are referring to only one or two works, you do not need a bibliography. In this case, give complete bibliographical information in the first note that makes reference to that item, and then refer to that work in some short form, either the author's name or the title of the work. Here are the note forms for a book, an article in a journal, and a chapter in a book with an editor:

> [1]Name of Author, *Name of Book*, nth edn., tr. Name of Translator, ed. Name of Editor (Place of publication: Name of Publisher, year of publication).
> [1]Name of Author, "The Name of the Article," *The Name of the Journal* volume-number (year-of-publication), page numbers.
> [1]Name of Author, "The Name of the Selection," in *Name of the Anthology*, ed. Name of Editor and Name of Other Editors (Place of publication: Name of Publisher, date of publication), page numbers.

An example of each of the above forms:

> [1]Robert Lingual, *The Philosophy of Language*, 3rd edn., tr. Benjamin Gavagai, ed. Alex Blupen (New York: Brilliant Publishing Co., 2020).
> [1]William Buffalo, "The Matter of Idealism," *The Philosophers' Review* 78 (2005), 48–61.
> [1]Hayden Cargo, "Materialism versus Idealism," in *Classic Essays in Metaphysics*, ed. Maury Putten (Whimsy, MI: Tintype Publishing Company, 1944), 78–90.

In these cases, the first name of the author, editor, or translator comes before the last name, e.g. "Thomas Hobbes." Suppose that you are referring to Hobbes's *Leviathan* and have given the bibliographical information in the first note. Subsequent references can be given in notes either by using his last name and a page reference –

[2]Hobbes, p. 32.

– or by giving the title and a page reference –

[2]*Leviathan*, p. 32.

A second way of giving references is to supply them inside the main body of the text and indicate the year of publication and the page reference.

For example, this fragment refers to page 59 of I. M. Smart's *The Problems of Philosophy Solved*, published in 2020:

> According to I. M. Smart, there is only one way to solve philosophical problems (Smart 2005: 59).

If you are referring to two works by an author published in the same year, use lowercase letters to distinguish them, e.g. (Smart 2005a: 59) and (Smart 2005b: 103).

In order to use this system of internal references, you need to give the complete bibliographical information somewhere. If you are using multiple works, then you need a bibliography. Extrapolate the correct form from these examples:

Bibliography

Adams, Margo, 2001. *The Ideal of Materialism*, 3rd edn., tr. Terence Humphrey. New York: Prestigious University Press.

Buffalo, William, 1964. "The Matter of Idealism," *The Philosophers' Review* 49: 28–39.

Cargo, Hayden, 1944. "Materialism versus Idealism," in *Classic Essays in Metaphysics*, ed. Maury Puttem. Whimsy, MI: Tintype Publishing Company, 78–90.

Notice in this bibliography the alphabetization of authors by last name, the placement of the date of publication immediately after the author's name, omission of the year of publication after the place of publication, the absence of a "p." or "pp." to refer to pages, and the way the entries are punctuated.

If you are using only one source or predominantly one source, then give the full bibliographical information – in the *note style*, not the bibliographical style – in a note, and add the comment: "References to this work are embedded in the text." In this case, you do not need to mention the author or year in the internal reference, e.g.:

> According to I. M. Smart, there is only one way to solve philosophical problems (59).

Alternatively:

> According to I. M. Smart, there is only one way to solve philosophical problems (p. 59).

Appendix C

The bibliographical note for this essay is the following:

[1] I. M. Smart, *The Problems of Philosophy Solved* (Brilliant, NY: The Philosophers' Press, 2005). References to this work are embedded in the text.

This note may be placed early in the text, say, at the end of the first sentence, or at the first reference in the text, e.g. immediately after "(59)."

Here is an example of an essay fragment that contains footnotes. The essay fragment is followed by some explanatory comments.

Types of Ethical Theories

Two kinds of ethical theories are commonly distinguished today. The first kind is teleological theories, according to which ethics prescribes how a person is to achieve a certain moral end, for example, happiness, even if doing so contravenes one's duty.[1] The second kind is deontological theories,[2] according to which ethics prescribes what a person's moral duty is, regardless of the consequences in particular cases.[3] In other words, teleological theories focus on what is good and deontological theories focus on what is right.[4]

Aristotle thought that happiness was the chief end of man.[5] Kant thought that "Nothing in the world ... [is] good without qualification except a good will."[6]

Notice in the above example that when a reference is repeated, e.g. to Aristotle's work in footnote 5 and Kant's work in 6, an abbreviated form is advisable. Aristotle's name is used in footnote 5 because only one work of his was referenced earlier; the relevant book by Kant is used in footnote 6 because two of his books were referenced earlier. Abbreviations of Latin words, "ibid.," "op. cit.," and "loc. cit.," which once were standardly used, are rarely used today.

---

[1] Aristotle, *Nicomachean Ethics*, tr. J. A. K. Thomson, rev. Hugh Tredennick (London: Penguin Books, 2004).

[2] Robert Goodin, "Utility and the Good," in *A Companion to Ethics*, ed. Peter Singer (Malden, MA: Blackwell, 1991), pp. 241–8.

[3] Immanuel Kant, *Critique of Practical Reason*, tr. Lewis White Beck (Indianapolis: Bobbs-Merrill Company, Inc., 1956), and Immanuel Kant, *Foundations of the Metaphysics of Morals*, tr. Lewis White Beck (Indianapolis: Bobbs-Merrill Company, Inc., 1959).

[4] John Rawls, *A Theory of Justice*, revised edition (Cambridge, MA: Belknap Press, 1999), pp. 392–6.

[5] Aristotle, pp. 14–15.

[6] Kant, *Foundations of the Metaphysics of Morals*, p. 9.

Here is the same essay, except that internal references are used, and the requisite list of works cited appears at the end:

Types of Ethical Theories

Two kinds of ethical theories are commonly distinguished today. The first kind is teleological theories, according to which ethics prescribes how a person is to achieve a certain moral end, for example, happiness, even if doing so contravenes one's duty (Aristotle: 2004). The second kind is deontological theories (Goodin 1991: 241–8), according to which ethics prescribes what a person's moral duty is, regardless of the consequences in particular cases (Kant 1959). In other words, teleological theories focus on what is good and deontological theories focus on what is right (Rawls 1999: 392–6).

Aristotle thought that happiness was the chief end of man (Aristotle 2004: 14–15). Kant thought that "Nothing in the world ... [is] good without qualification except a good will" (Kant 1959: 9).

References

Aristotle, 2004. *Nicomachean Ethics*, tr. J. A. K. Thomson, rev. Hugh Tredennick. London: Penguin Books.

Goodin, Robert, 1991. "Utility and the Good," in *A Companion to Ethics*, ed. Peter Singer. Malden, MA: Blackwell Publishers, 241–8.

Kant, Immanuel, 1956. *Critique of Practical Reason*, tr. Lewis White Beck. Indianapolis: Bobbs-Merrill Company, Inc.

Kant, Immanuel, 1959. *Foundations of the Metaphysics of Morals*. Indianapolis: Bobbs-Merrill Company, Inc.

Rawls, John, 1999. *A Theory of Justice*, revised edition. Cambridge, MA: Belknap Press.

Appendix D: On Grading

Students often wonder how it is possible to grade philosophical essays. They think that philosophy is just a matter of opinion, and, as long as they honestly express their opinion, everything they write must be true; so every honest student deserves an A+.

In fact, philosophy is not just a matter of opinion. Although few philosophers agree with most of what any of the great philosophers wrote, there is a great convergence of opinion about who the great philosophers are: Plato, Aristotle, Augustine, Aquinas, Descartes, Locke, Hume, Kant, Russell, and Wittgenstein. What these philosophers share is an ability to say something important about the most basic and important aspects of reality that has not been said before and to convey those thoughts in a way that seems rationally compelling.

No teacher expects a student to say anything great. What the teacher expects or hopes for is a certain competence in form and content. Concerning content, the student should be able to give either a plausibly argued position of her own or an accurate rendering of the position of some philosopher, plus some moderate criticism or improvement of that position. Concerning form, the student's essay should be clearly written and have an easily identifiable structure. The structure makes clear how the argument develops.

Many students think that there is an inverse relation between the number of comments a grader makes on an essay and the quality of it. In fact, there is not. There is not a high correlation between the quality of an essay and the number of comments on it. A perfect essay and a perfectly awful essay may both contain no comments, the first needing no criticism and the second

Philosophical Writing: An Introduction, Fifth Edition. A. P. Martinich.
© 2025 John Wiley & Sons, Inc. Published 2025 by John Wiley & Sons, Inc.
Companion website: www.wiley.com/go/Martinich5e

being beneath criticism. A good essay and a bad one may have equally many comments. A very good essay may be improved by many small changes, or perhaps one or two things that need substantial explanation need to be provided. A very bad essay may have many flaws that are correctable. In between these extremes, there is great variation as to how many comments are appropriate. Here is a grading scheme, with explanatory notes:

Summa cum laude (trans: with highest honors) (A+) This essay is so perfect that it needs no changes, except perhaps for the addition or deletion of a comma, or a long sentence broken into two shorter ones. On this and other essays, a check mark or double check mark in the margin indicates strong approval.

Magna cum laude (A/A−) Clear, well-structured, and substantive. These essays often invite a fair number of comments about minor points of style, organization, and substance.

Cum laude (B+/B) These essays often require many comments, which, if incorporated, could raise the grade to an A/A−. There is probably at least one major flaw in content or form, but not more than two.

Bene probatus (trans: good try) (B−/C+) These essays are often similar to the group above, except that the content may be not as good or the form is more defective and hence weaker overall.

Probatus (trans: you tried) (C/D−) These essays always require a substantial reworking of either the structure or the content. Concerning form, they may be marred by ungrammatical sentences and improper word choice. Concerning content, they may contain major errors of fact or interpretation. Alternatively, the content may be too trivial to be philosophically worthwhile. In some cases, the problems are so severe that few suggestions can be made for improvement.

Non probatus (trans: you didn't try) (F) These essays do not deserve any comments, and in fact it may be difficult to say anything that would improve them.

In putting comments on your essay, your professor may use abbreviations or signs that are conventionally used by proofreaders or by graders that are suggestive of the full idea. Here is a list of some abbreviations and signs that your professor may use:

≡   Capitalize this letter. Example: "jones" should be "Jones"

ante   The antecedent of this pronoun is not clear.

→‖	Indent the text (usually applied to a block quotation or a displayed sentence).
frag	This piece of text is a fragment of a sentence, not a complete sentence.
‖←	Move the text to the left margin.
Arg	You need an argument for this proposition.
Evid	You need to provide evidence for this proposition.
l.c.	Make this letter lowercase.
PW	See the discussion in *Philosophical Writing*.
reason	You need to give a reason for this assertion.
ref.	You need to cite your source for this idea or quotation.
rep	You are repeating something you said earlier in the essay.
RS	Running start. You do not need this introductory sentence or paragraph.
stet	(Latin: let it stand.) I, the grader, made a mistake. Your text is correct.
taut	Your sentence is a tautology and adds nothing to your argument.
trans:	You need a transitional word, phrase, or sentence to go from the preceding topic to the next one.
w.c.	There is something wrong with your word choice. You may be using the wrong word or using a word with the wrong connotation.

Appendix E:
Essay Checklist

(1)   Are all the pages numbered in the appropriate place?

(2)   Does the essay have a title?

(3)   Have you placed your name where your instructor specified?

(4)   Is the entire essay double-spaced?

(5)   Is the essay in a standard font and size, such as Times New Roman, Calibri, or Cambria, 12 points?

(6)   Are the right- and left-hand margins wide enough for the professor to write comments, such as 1.5 inch left margins and 1.0 right margin?

(7)   Have you provided references for all the ideas and quotations that you have taken from other documents?

Philosophical Writing: An Introduction, Fifth Edition. A. P. Martinich.
© 2025 John Wiley & Sons, Inc. Published 2025 by John Wiley & Sons, Inc.
Companion website: www.wiley.com/go/Martinich5e

Appendix F:
Glossary of
Philosophical Terms

This glossary is selective. It consists of both philosophical and stylistic terms. If a term is not included in the glossary, check the index for a possible discussion of it in the body of the text.

act/object ambiguity   Some words are ambiguous between meaning some activity and meaning the result of that activity, for example, the word "building." Building is both a process (events) and a product (object). Philosophers have been concerned about the ambiguity of such terms as "action" (it may refer to an intentional event or the result of one); "reference" (it may mean the activity of referring or the object referred to (the referent)); and "statement" (it may refer to the activity of stating or its result).

ad hoc (literally: to this thing)   Something invented or devised for one specific thing, typically to save a theory on the brink of refutation, and not independently motivated or justified by some general or theoretical principle.

ad hominem (literally: against the man)   (1) It is usually used to designate the fallacy of inferring that what someone said is false because of his personal characteristics (such as physical appearance and religious or political affiliation) or his circumstances (such as his financial condition or his social relationships). However, it is not a fallacy to consider a person's personal characteristics or circumstances as part of the evidence for evaluating whether what he says is true or false, reliable or not. (2) It is sometimes used

Philosophical Writing: An Introduction, Fifth Edition. A. P. Martinich.
© 2025 John Wiley & Sons, Inc. Published 2025 by John Wiley & Sons, Inc.
Companion website: www.wiley.com/go/Martinich5e

to refer to the valid argument tactic of showing that your opponent's principles commit him to a position that he does not approve of.

ad infinitum (literally: to infinity)   The phrase is often used in discussions of infinite regress. If everything in motion must be put in motion by something else that is in motion, then this process must go on without any end, that is, *ad infinitum*.

a fortiori (literally: by something stronger)   Example: If one vague or ambiguous sentence is difficult to understand, then a series of vague or ambiguous sentences is *a fortiori* difficult to understand.

a priori/a posteriori (literally: from the prior/from the later)   The first term is typically used to refer to what is epistemologically prior to or independent of sense experience, such as knowing mathematical truths "(2 + 2 = 4)" or tautologies ("A white horse is white"). The second term is typically used to refer to what epistemologically comes from or is the result of sense experience, such as knowing what colors, smells, and sounds are. These epistemological terms should not be confused with the logical or metaphysical terms necessity/contingency.

argument   A series of propositions that are intended to give an audience reasons for believing something. The propositions expressing the reasons are called "premises"; the proposition expressing what is to be believed is called "the conclusion." In the example below, the first two propositions are premises and the last is the conclusion:

All humans are mortal.

Socrates is human.

Socrates is mortal.

(See also syllogism.)

assertion   A proposition (something that is true or false) expressed by someone without giving any evidence or argument for it. There may or may not be evidence that could be given for an assertion if it were demanded (cf. ARGUMENT).

begging the question   In philosophy, it means inferring a conclusion from premises that already contain or presuppose the conclusion. In recent decades, common usage invented a new meaning. A speaker's saying something that invites information that has not been given is said to be begging the question. Saying "The American troops in Afghanistan conducted themselves in an honorable way and cannot be criticized" begs the question of "why the troops were sent to Afghanistan at all."

ceteris paribus (literally: other things being equal)   In actual use, the phrase means, "under normal circumstances." The difference is important. All other things being equal, a human being is better able to kill a lion when each is in his own protective cage and each is given a loaded high-powered rifle. But since these circumstances are not considered normal, a person should not claim that a human being is better able to kill a lion, *ceteris paribus*. If a lion and a human are being evaluated for the ability to kill the other, it is normal for each to be about 15 feet apart, not in cages, and without weapons. In this kill or be killed situation, one can say the lion is better able to kill the human *ceteris paribus*.

compatibilism   see DETERMINISM.

counterexample   An example that goes counter to something; that is, an example that shows some proposition to be false or some argument to be invalid. "A counterexample to the proposition that no nonhuman animals have facial expressions is the fact that chimpanzees do."

de dicto/de re (literally: concerning what is said/concerning the thing)   Often used with respect to necessity. All bachelors are necessarily (*de dicto*) unmarried, because of the meaning of the words "bachelor" and "unmarried" and not because of something inherent in the people who are bachelors. Humans are necessarily (*de re*) rational because of their inherent nature and not because of the meaning of the words "human" and "rational." The meaning of the word simply reflects the fact about the thing itself. The distinction is also applied to cognitive states such as belief. If Adam believes that murderers are criminals, then his belief is probably *de dicto*: Adam believes the sentence "Murderers are criminals." If Adam believes that Beth is a murderer (because he saw her do the crime), then Adam's belief is *de re*: Adam has a belief about Beth, and what he believes is that she is a murderer.

de facto/de jure (literally: concerning a fact/concerning what is right)   If an unjust rebellion succeeds, then the rebel leader is the *de facto* ruler though he may not be the *de jure* one.

determinism   The doctrine that every event has a cause and only events are causes. Determinism is often understood to exclude the possibility of free will, when free will is understood as a faculty or ability to choose or act in ways that are not determined or constrained by prior causal events. However, according to the doctrine of compatibilism, free will and determinism are compatible or mutually possible. Being free, according to some versions of compatibilism, means that the causes of one's choices are one's desires.

eo ipso (literally: by that very thing)   SEE IPSO FACTO.

epistemology/metaphysics   Epistemology is the study of what can be known and how it is possible. Metaphysics is the study of the most general features of reality.

equivalent   Propositions are materially equivalent if they have the same truth-value: "Snow is white" and "Grass is green" are materially equivalent. Propositions are logically equivalent if they have the same truth-value in every possible situation, for example, "Beth is rich and happy" and "It is not the case that Beth is either not rich or not happy."

equivocation   To equivocate is to use a word with one meaning in one place and with a different meaning in another place, as if it had the same meaning in both places, for example, "Since Mary was determined to go to the party, and every action that is determined is not freely chosen, Mary did not freely choose to go to the party." The word "determined" in the first occurrence means "firmly resolved" but "was caused by non-voluntary causes" in the second.

ex nihilo (literally: out of nothing)   God supposedly made the world *ex nihilo*.

false dichotomy   Used in two senses: (1) It applies to a dichotomy that does not exhaust the alternatives and hence is not true, for example, "The US must either use nuclear weapons against Haiti or not go to war at all." A third alternative, not mentioned in the example, is using conventional weapons against Haiti. (2) It applies to a choice that is forced between two alternatives that are compatible with each other: "You must either go to the football game or be with your child." Both are possible if one can take the child to the game.

fine-grained   Usually used comparatively about distinctions. The distinction between self-propelled vehicles and non-self-propelled vehicles is not as fine-grained as one that makes that distinction and then goes on to distinguish among self-propelled vehicles between those with internal combustion engines and those without, and then among those that are self-propelled, those that use internal combustion engines exclusively, and those that do not. Refining the grain can go on at some length. So those that use internal combustion engines exclusively may be divided into gasoline and diesel fueled.

flesh out   To explain in greater detail: "Jones needs to flesh out the skeleton of his argument." (Sometimes mistakenly thought to be "flush out.")

form and content   Philosophers have used these two words in multiple ways. Both can be used to express something substantive in contrast with something trivial. In Aristotelian philosophy, form contrasts with matter. Form makes matter to be the kind of thing it is. Some stuff that is carbon, water, calcium, and some other things is a human being if it has the form of a human being; it is that form that enables a human being to be rational and to laugh at jokes. Logic studies logical form, so it is interested in linguistic patterns – see chapter 2, Logic – such as *not-p*, (*p* or *q*), and (*p* and *q*). These examples are not sentences because *p* and *q* are not sentences. They are symbols that help indicate the forms that sentences can have: "Snow is not white," "Show is white or black," and "Snow is white and cold." If we use the word "content" to contrast with "form," then "Snow is white" is the content of the sentences indicated. In logic, "form" is approbative. But in other contexts, it is pejorative: "Lee presented the form of an explanation, but it lacked content." "Content" is never pejorative. Let's now shift to a different form. Reports of what a person believes often have the form, "Lee believes that *p*." That form does not say what the content of Lee's belief is. The sentence, "Lee believes that snow is white and cold," does.

free will   see DETERMINISM.

ignoratio elenchi   (literally: ignorance of the question)   This fallacy is committed when a person proves one thing when something else is required. Suppose that a person needs to prove that *it is wrong to kill any innocent, nonthreatening human being* but instead proves that *all societies have made laws against anyone's killing an innocent nonthreatening human being.*

inference to the best explanation   creating a proposition that provides the best account of some phenomenon because of the way it fits into other beliefs of a person's network.

in se   see PER SE.

intuition   (1) The judgment a person makes before he thinks about the issue seriously; it is the commonsense view. The adverbial form is often used ("Intuitively, human beings have free will and are not constrained by earlier causal chains"). Intuitions can either be proven wrong by presenting theoretically well-established principles that conflict with them, or they can be supported by theoretically well-established principles. Intuitions are starting points for philosophical reflection.

(2) A nonsensible, nondiscursive faculty or method of knowing the truth about profound or difficult issues. Neoplatonist and idealist philosophers often appeal to intuition and appeal to its great value.

(3) In Kant's philosophy, nonconceptualized, perceptual experience.

intuition pump   Any example that effectively illustrates or strengthens an intuition (in sense (1) above).

ipse dixit (literally: he himself has said it)   This means that the pronouncement is authoritative. The phrase is often used disparagingly against a person who does not argue for his position, because in philosophy a position needs to be grounded in reasons or argument, not in the authority of a person.

ipso facto (literally: by that very fact)   Example: Being the president of the United States is *ipso facto* being the commander-in-chief of the armed forces.

limiting case   If you think of things that belong to a certain type as spread out on a spectrum from most to least, then the things at each extreme are the limiting cases. If Socrates is the wisest of humans and Simple Simon is the most foolish, then Socrates and Simon are limiting cases of wisdom.

materialism   The doctrine that only material objects and their relations exist. It denies that mental objects exist or are anything other than material objects or manifestations of the functioning of material objects.

metaphysics   SEE EPISTEMOLOGY.

modal fallacy Because the location of a modal word, such as "possibly," "necessarily," and "must," is important to the sense of a sentence, fallacies are sometimes committed by mistaking what the modal word modifies. It is fallacious to go from "If John was a murderer, then he must have been a killer" and "John was a murderer" to "John must have been (necessarily was) a killer."

mutatis mutandis (literally: changing what needs to be changed) "It is people, not proper names, that primarily refer to things; the same holds for predicates, *mutatis mutandis.*" (That is, it is people, not predicates, that primarily predicate properties.)

necessity/contingency What is necessary is what must be true, what cannot be other than it is; it is what is true in every possible world. What is contingent is what happens to be true but need not have been; it could have been different, and it is true in some but not all possible worlds. See also, DE DICTO/DE RE.

network of belief All the beliefs of a normal person; these beliefs have such properties as unity, connectedness, multiplicity, and degrees of generality, of certainty, and of tenacity. Beliefs are often added or subtracted from the network in light of additional evidence or lack of use.

non sequitur (literally: it does not follow) Any fallacy that involves going from a premise or premises to a conclusion that is not validly derived. The lawyer's fallacy is a *non sequitur*: "Since someone needs to defend the accused person, I need to defend him." This fallacy is usually committed only when a lot of money can be made from taking the case. Another example (inspired by an irate email message from a criminal lawyer): "Since the previous example makes fun of some lawyers, the author of it must have disdain for all lawyers." The first example is just a joke; in any case, the word "usually" indicates that it does not apply to all lawyers, not even all the criminal lawyers.

obtain Conditions are said to obtain when they are fulfilled or satisfied: "If x has injured y, then one of the preparatory conditions for y's forgiveness of x obtains."

overgeneralization This is the fallacy of inferring that some general proposition is true from evidence that supports only the truth of a logically weaker proposition. For example, it is fallacious to infer from the fact that some (or many or most) members of a group G have some characteristic C to the conclusion that most (or all) members of G have C. For example, it is fallacious to infer from the fact that some criminal lawyers are avaricious and unprincipled that most or all criminal lawyers are avaricious and unprincipled.

per se*/*in se (literally: through itself/in itself)   Essentially: "Happiness is good *per se* or *in se*."

possible worlds   Ways in which the world might have been. The actual world is one possible world. Many philosophers think of possible worlds as something like consistent sets of propositions that describe every possibility ("maximal consistent sets of propositions") and that they are useful fictions. In contrast, David Lewis thinks that each possible world is really real for the people in it and that our favoritism toward the (our) actual world is parochial.

prima facie (literally: on first appearance or at first sight)   When this phrase is used, it usually is a signal that the author will show that what appears to be true is in fact not true. The phrases "*prima facie* rights" and "*prima facie* obligations" have been used in two very different senses: (1) things that look like rights but in fact are not; (2) genuine rights that can be superseded by other more important rights.

properties   Often used interchangeably with "qualities," "characteristics," and "universals." Properties are typically anything that is expressed by the predicate of a sentence. For example, redness, tallness, and squareness are properties because "is red," "is tall," and "is square" are predicates. Two exceptions are existence and truth. Many philosophers do not think that "exists" and "is true" express properties.

quantifier shift fallacy   Because the order in which quantifier words occur in a sentence is very important, a fallacy often results from interchanging them. It is fallacious from "Everything begins to exist at some time" to infer "At some time everything begins to exist." And it is fallacious from "Everyone loves someone" to infer "Someone loves everyone."

realism   Has many senses; e.g. in general metaphysics, a realist believes that the physical world exists independently of human minds. With respect to universals, a realist believes that they exist independently of other minds. In ethics, a realist believes that ethical propositions are made true by some kind of fact (usually nonnatural facts).

realized A mental phenomenon is realized in a brain state when the brain state is the physical basis or foundation for the mental phenomenon. It is possible that the same mental phenomenon could be realized in different physical states.

received view The standard view, the conventional wisdom, or the opinion typically held by experts. The term is often used disparagingly.

reductio ad absurdum A method of argument that begins with the opposite of the proposition that is to be proved. From that opposite, one shows that absurd consequences follow. Since the opposite is absurd, the proposition to be proved must be true.

sine qua non (literally: without which not) A necessary condition. Intelligence is a *sine qua non* for knowledge.

special pleading The fallacy of judging certain members of a group according to one standard and other members of the same group according to a different standard. For example, suppose that Jones is given a job as a scientist because he has a PhD from Harvard but Smith is denied the same kind of job because she is a member of religion X or political party Y.

strawman When an author supposedly describes the argument or position of an author in an unfair way, specifically a way that makes it easy to refute (as easy as knocking down a genuine strawman) the author has constructed a metaphorical strawman. Fairness to your opponents as well as the cogency of your own position requires that you not construct a strawman version of their arguments.

strong/weak As applied to arguments and ideas, what is stronger has more content and excludes more things than what is weaker. "Strong" and "weak" are value-neutral. Sometimes it is better to use a weaker sense of some word, to use a weaker argument, or to espouse a weaker proposition than to use a stronger one. It depends on the context. ("There are two senses of punishment. In the weaker sense, punishment is any suffering inflicted by an authority for a real or imagined crime. In the stronger sense, punishment is only that suffering inflicted by an authority for a crime actually committed by the person who suffers.")

sui generis (literally: of its own kind) The phrase means that something is unique. It is the only object that belongs to some category.

summum bonum (literally: the highest good) Traditionally either God or happiness has been considered the highest good by philosophers. Recently, tenure.

Syllogism Any argument that has exactly two premises.

tabula rasa (literally: a clean slate) Empiricists think that the mind is a *tabula rasa* when a human is born. All ideas come from sensation and in effect write on that slate of the mind.

tendentious Language is tendentious when it is colored to promote a cause without argumentation; it often tends to beg the question. Group names are often tendentious, for example, the names of the opposed groups, "Pro-life" and "Pro-choice." Someone who is "pro-life" may support the death penalty and preemptive attacks on other nations, and someone who is "pro-choice" may not support allowing people the choice of marrying a sibling or owning a handgun.

thought experiment A made-up or imagined situation that is supposed to show something, usually something about the limits of a concept. For example, a famous thought experiment that is designed to show that computers do not genuinely understand begins, "Suppose that a person is inside a room into which pieces of paper covered with Chinese writing are given to him. His job is to look up those characters and then ...."

tu quoque (literally: you too) The name of a fallacy, which responds to a charge of wrongdoing by arguing that the objector has done the very same thing. It is a fallacy because if the wrongdoing of Jones is the focus, then the wrongdoing of Smith is irrelevant. Roughly, two wrongs do not make a right.

universal/particular These are contrasting terms, which must be understood together. A universal is what is general or common to many particular things. A particular is what has or instantiates a universal. Fido, Bowser, and Spuds are particular things that instantiate the universal *dog*. Caesar, Elizabeth I, and Napoleon are things that instantiate the universal *human being*. Roughly, subjects express or refer to particulars and predicates express or refer to universals. E.g. in the sentence, "Fido is a dog," Fido is one particular dog but being a dog is common to many things.

unpack (an argument or idea) To analyze or explain.

weight A value assigned to something taking into account its importance relative to other things. Being the lawgiver of the Hebrews has more weight than being saved from the bulrushes as an infant, when we are concerned with establishing the identity of, say, Moses. *A weighted most* is the thing that scores the highest points taking weights into account. Suppose that Jones can choose one and only one prize: either one house, which she rates at 100 units of satisfaction, or two automobiles, each of which she rates at 30 units of satisfaction, or 8 dresses, each of which she rates at 10 units of satisfaction. Then the house is the weighted most satisfying object (100 units, determined by multiplying 100 by 1). The dresses are the second most desirable (80 units), and the automobiles are the least most (60 units). Or, to return to Moses, think of some descriptions that are believed to apply to Moses:

saved from bulrushes as a child: 1
brother of Aaron: 2
Hebrew prophet: 5
greatest lawgiver of the Hebrew people: 20
lived before 1,000 BCE: 10

Some of these descriptions are more and some less important to the identity of Moses, as indicated by the numbers. Moses is the object described by the weighted most of these descriptions.

Index

Philosophical Writing: An Introduction, Fifth Edition. A. P. Martinich.
© 2025 John Wiley & Sons, Inc. Published 2025 by John Wiley & Sons, Inc.
Companion website: www.wiley.com/go/Martinich5e

Index

form and content 266
free will and responsibility 82–4,
    113, 149
free writing, *see* conceptual note
    taking
French, Peter 171

Gaunilo 142
Geach, Peter 141
gender and pronouns 6–7
generality 216
genus and species 115–16
Gettier, Edmund 146
Gilson, Etienne 163
God 32, 33, 35–6, 51, 54, 77, 114,
    134–5, 142, 148
  existence of 37, 54, 142–3
  justice of 51, 114
grading 258–9
grammar 2–4
Great Fear and Ignorance Argument
    72–5
Grice, H. P. 153–4, 188–90

hedging 153
Hegel, G. F. W. 152–3, 156
Heidegger, Martin 2, 170
Hirsch, Eli 96–7
Hobbes, Thomas 3, 31, 65–75, 80–1,
    113–15, 162, 168, 202, 209–10,
    224–6
honesty 252
Hume, David 133, 253

incoherence, *see* coherence
inconsistency 47–9
  see also contradiction
indeterminateness 175–6
inference to the best explanation 203,
    266–7
insight 202–3
Internet Encyclopedia of
    Philosophy 92
interpretation 206–12

and coherence 231–2
and completeness 245–6
and consistency 232–3
and defensibility 234–8
good and correct 227–8
and proportionality 238–45
and simplicity 229–30
understanding 206–12
introductions, problems with
  running start, the 190–5
  slip sliding away 184–8
  tail wagging the dog 188–90
intuition 18, 21, 22, 267
intuition pump 267

justice 116, 120–1

Kant, Immanuel 91, 100–11,
    125, 180
Kierkegaard, Søren 119, 202
knowledge 3, 117, 124

Landesman, Charles 169
language and gender 6–7
logic 18–56
  and conversation 188–90
  formal 27–32
  material 26
Lucifer 230

Machiavelli, Niccolò 168, 192
Mad Hatter, the 140–1
Marcuse, Herbert 171
meaning 198–200
metaphysics 265, 269
method, philosophical 15–17
Milton, John 203
mirabilis consequentia 150
Montaigne, Michel de 168
Moore, G. E. 169, 181–2, 218
modus ponens 29–33
modus tollens 29–32
moral, why be 154–7
mutatis mutandis 268

272

Printed and bound by CPI Group (UK) Ltd, Croydon, CR0 4YY

10/06/2025

14686702-0001